THE DEAF DOCTOR

THE DEAF DOCTOR

HIS LIFE AND TIMES and HIS DAUGHTER'S MEMOIR OF A 1950s CHILDHOOD ON A COTSWOLD HILL FARM

Marian Eason

The Book Guild Ltd

Published in Great Britain in 2024 by
The Book Guild Ltd
Unit E2 Airfield Business Park,
Harrison Road, Market Harborough,
Leicestershire. LE16 7UL
Tel: 0116 2792299
www.bookguild.co.uk
Email: info@bookguild.co.uk
Twitter: @bookguild

Copyright © 2024 Marian Eason

The right of Marian Eason to be identified as the author of this
work has been asserted by them in accordance with the
Copyright, Design and Patents Act 1988.

First published in Great Britain by Ryelands/Halsgrove in 2009

All rights reserved. No part of this publication may be
reproduced, transmitted, or stored in a retrieval system, in any form or by any means,
without permission in writing from the publisher, nor be otherwise circulated in
any form of binding or cover other than that in which it is published and without
a similar condition being imposed on the subsequent purchaser.

*Every effort has been made to trace any copyright holders. In the case of omission
the author apologises and would welcome any information that would enable the
oversight to be corrected in subsequent editions.*

Typeset in 11pt Minion Pro

Printed on FSC accredited paper
Printed and bound in Great Britain by 4edge Limited

ISBN 978 1916668 898

British Library Cataloguing in Publication Data.
A catalogue record for this book is available from the British Library.

*Left cover image: Ted swath-turning with the Little Grey Fergie (Ferguson TE34) on
the Home Ground, Bourton Far Hill, July 1955.*
Central cover image: Nigel Lovett painting 'Rhythm' at Bourton Far Hill 1955.
*Right cover image: Ted resting by Honister pass, Hause Gill, Borrowdale, Lake
District, May 1952*
Main cover image/background: Ted doing a 'roll' over a gate, Newmarket c1936

To my parents, whose lives have provided the inspiration for this book.

To my son, William, without whose initial enthusiasm it would never have been written.

To my husband, Simon, whose unfailing patience, support and good guidance ensured its completion, together with some sound advice on matters both military and sporting, and whose incredible skills on the word processor I have now acquired, at least in part.

And to all its readers, without which no book would ever exist.

Marian Eason

CONTENTS

	ACKNOWLEDGEMENTS	ix
	PROLOGUE	xi
	FOREWORD	xv
	INTRODUCTION	xix
1	Before The War	1
2	The Deaf Doctor's War	28
3	A Marriage	60
4	The Farm Takes Root	77
5	The Staff	126
6	Farming Matters	141
7	Spring Hill	155
8	The Hunt	177
9	Animal Farm	206
10	Gin And French	223
11	"The Little Girl With A Kirby Grip"	237
12	Of Myriapoda And Medicine	273
	Appendix I	286
	Glossary	293
	Appendix II	294
	Index	296

ACKNOWLEDGEMENTS

The characters who populate this book are pearls beyond price, all of them, but those still living and those no longer with us must be thanked for their memories and knowledge going back before my time. These include our good friends, John Taylor of Baldwyns Farm at Pebworth and John Redfern of Hill Farm between Pebworth and Dorsington, who farmed as tenants on what remains of the Pebworth Estate in Warwickshire which belonged, as it still does, to my late mother's family.

John Robbins, whose family has farmed for generations in the Pebworth/Evesham Vales, and whose memories are uniquely valuable.

Allan Ward, a former Joint Master of the North Cotswold Hounds, whose knowledge and experience of hunting in the West Country provided me with inspiration, and whose recollection of the same was unrivalled.

Glenda Weil (née Hannay), whose incomparable generosity has allowed me recollections of life at Spring Hill in the days of our childhood, which otherwise I might have missed, and whose advice regarding publication of this book has been invaluable.

Christopher Bourne at Snowshill Hill, generous with both his time and his knowledge, which extended a little further back than mine; a treasury of information, especially in the matter of our fathers' relationship, which was patchy, unlike our own.

Professor Wilhelm Engström, the keenest of Swedish foxhunters, of Uppsäla University, without whose help and advice my father's specimens and notes would not have found the expert and caring home in Oxford University's Natural Museum, where they now reside.

My cousin Caroline Haynes, our family archivist, who helped me with the detail of family relationships and origins.

Maeve Horsfall, who helped us with horses, and everything really, during our early years at Bourton Far Hill – a great friend of my mother's and of us all, and who reminded me of incidents, amusing and otherwise, during her time with us. Many of the farm photographs were taken by her and show off her considerable talents as a photographer, which even rivalled my mother's.

Chris Hickman, who came to farm at Kineton near Guiting Power in 1951 – the same year that we went to the farm, and whose memories nudged my own.

Duncan MacLeod, whose grandfather was a partner with Walter Hannay (who appears in this book) in the business of cotton, and who gave me essential detail relating also to our family's involvement in the trade, just in time for inclusion!

Xandra Bingley, author of *Bertie, May and Mrs Fish*, who mentioned in an interview that very little had been written about farming in the '50s – so I thought, *why not...*

PROLOGUE

A recent encounter with Jeremy Nabarro, a friend from later years at Bourton Far Hill when we were both in our late teens or early twenties, reminds me of the importance that Ted, my father and the subject of this book, attached to the farm water supply without which the farm would not have been a viable farm at all.

By the 1970s we no longer employed direct labour; contractors came to do much of the necessary and Ted entered into various share-farming arrangements, the most important of which was with Robert Wharton, my contemporary and a near neighbour some three farms away – the other side of Bourton Hill and Hinchwick – at Luckley, on the way to Stow-on-the-Wold. He and Jeremy were close friends, their group being completed by Richard Clifford and Colin Studd. As we no longer had any farm staff, employing only general help housed in one lodge, the other was let to likely tenants – in this instance Jeremy, who shared it with Richard.

They assumed something of the character of the Wild Bunch, the four of them not quite the terror of the highways, but bordering on the anarchic. I always remember one night lying in bed, almost asleep, when a crashing sound came from the road running past the end of the drive a quarter-of-a-mile away. I returned to my slumbers with one thought: *I bet that's* Rob and Richard. In the morning an inspection of our boundary wall separating the Snowshill Field from the road revealed a large dent and all the toppers (vertical stones placed atop a dry stone wall) cast to the ground. Later that day my suspicions were confirmed as I viewed their jointly owned Land Rover the worse for wear with damage in all the tell-tale places. Luckily there was no stock in the field to make an escape and the damage was quickly repaired, probably by Ted who was a dab-hand at walling.

In view of the 'water situation', as Ted always liked to call it – a satisfactory phrase with a sufficiently urgent ring about it – the springs never actually ran dry, even with two hundred head of sheep, fifty of cattle, seven horses, and sundry humans on the place. The only emergencies occurred when the mechanism of the ram, or later the electrified pump, broke down – both lodges were fitted with hand pumps with wooden handles such as may still very occasionally be seen on old petrol pumps. These meant hard work as two hundred returns of the handle were needed for a bath, and twenty even for a flush of the lavatory. The use of water was most satisfactorily limited thereby.

"He must have known that we couldn't [wouldn't?] cope with anything like that," Jeremy laughed all these years on. By 'we' I rather think that he meant 'I' – Jeremy has all the quick wit and brains of his late father Gerald, he of the handlebar moustache and MP for South Worcestershire at that time – and he was most certainly a stranger to any unnecessary physical labour, finding a way round all things not to his taste. Richard (Clifford) was enlisted to perform the actual task, crime even, of electrifying the offending pump, and for some months their water-supply flowed in large quantities without arousing any suspicion.

Then came the day when Ted needed to get into the lodge for some reason, or perhaps he wanted to carry out an inspection.

No notice was given, he simply let himself in with a key during the day while they were both out. The question of water being always uppermost in his mind, the alteration to the pump was immediately apparent. His fury knew no bounds, but as was usually the case Vivian (my mother) was the more vocal of the two. Jeremy, as the tenant so thus bearing the responsibility, was summoned up the drive.

"What the hell do you think you're doing, bypassing our regulation?" she shouted. "It's in your agreement that the water supply is limited to what you can pump by hand. You know that."

Jeremy was a charmer: "But Mrs Eason, we didn't think you'd mind. And Richard has done a good job; it's more modern, isn't it?"

This was as a red rag to a bull. Vivian's fury mounted, as she was unfairly left to defend the right – deaf people are often angry, but can find it hard to express in an encounter: "Modern be damned!" she exclaimed. "You know the demands on the water here. Dismantle the pump immediately."

Jeremy waxed furious at this; I can remember as I was there. To be thwarted in such an excellent scheme to make life easier was more than he could bear. The clash of wills was vivid as they swore at one another. But curiously, by the next day we were already entering calmer waters. Ted's sense of humour got the better of him and I think he secretly admired Jeremy's *chutzpah*. They were allowed to keep the pump for the duration of the tenancy, returning to manual only for Jeremy's successor. My mother understandably felt rather betrayed, declaring that she would not front for Ted again.

At one point during this tenure a mutual friend of ours, Malcolm Green, came to stay temporarily in the lodge with his Irish fiancée, Veryan. The story got out that Jeremy had tied bells onto the springs of their bed, but how could anyone be angry, when even Malcolm and Veryan joined in the laughter? Jeremy was, and still is, quite purely and simply, irresistibly funny, and life will never get the better of him.

The anxiety over the water supply at around this time temporarily poisoned our good relations with John Bourne, who farmed at Snowshill Hill, just across the road from Bourton Far Hill. He was a big dairy farmer and dairy-farming uses a great deal of water – my father was convinced that this was having an adverse effect on the level of the local water-table and managed to lock horns with John in no uncertain terms. They were both stubborn men and it took several months for the dispute to simmer down, my father in the end having to admit that the water-table was unaffected. Interestingly, the water-table is higher now than it was then, forty years ago.

Now, some twenty-five years since Ted's death, Bourton Far Hill has taken something of a hit – the old house and cottage, and indeed all the buildings save for the two stone barns, and the (superbly modernised) lodges at the end of the drive, were demolished to make way for a much grander dwelling, while the barns were turned into state-of-the-art accommodation for Tim Holland-Martin's high-class bloodstock enterprise. He has since turned to livestock farming. Hounds and followers may still cross the land but with much restricted access, quite different from the free-for-all that existed in my father's day, a more spacious and easier time for us all. He was of the old school and believed somewhat excessively in *noblesse oblige*, sharing one's good fortune with others; though there were already three rights of way across the farm, he was planning a fourth just before he died.

What would he say now? I think I know. It would be short, and to the point: *Well I'm damned!*

FOREWORD

May, 2006 – against the noisy, cobbled backdrop of a Neapolitan street, I begin. Perhaps it is the incessant hustle and hubbub of this chaotic maritime southern city which provides the spur. The smooth sheet of existence is more insistently punctured by memory, triggered by smell, taste and sound here than anywhere else in my experience. The narrow alleys, just wide enough for a car, adorned with external wiring, washing, birdcages, and rubbish (contained and otherwise) lead me down their sightless ways to some necessary destination.

Ah, time, you say? I haven't the time. There is always something else to do. One day I'll do it, but not now. And so on and on. Anyway, who would read it? A book about a time too close to be counted historic but too far to be counted in any way relevant to contemporary mores, a time belonging to the childhood of the boring old-aged, and to quite a small section of the old-aged at that. And what is this book about anyway? Farming, you say? Ah well, there might be something in that I suppose. It is in the news a good deal, and young people too are concerned with the way things have gone and are going in agriculture and food production, and might be interested to read of how such things were ordered more than sixty years ago. Such matters might be counted political too, as you can't get much more political than when considering how food is produced and how much the social life of the rural populace has changed in a half-century.

I was an only child, born into what I suppose you would call an upper-middle-class family almost exactly halfway through the twentieth century. The after-effects of war were very evident and now that we are seventy-five years distant from that decade it is even clearer how true this was, and what a very transformed world we live in today. The whole of life was still bound by rigid convention – dinner-party guests were lucky to be asked back again if they made no return invitation; wedding presents were never gift-wrapped, contenting themselves with brown paper and a formal calling card attached, embellished with a suitable handwritten greeting; women, unless relatives of the deceased, did not attend funerals, that duty being undertaken by the man, in morning dress, complete with a rolled umbrella and a silk (top) hat. If someone who should have known better transgressed, particularly if he was not from quite the same social class, he was often described as not being able to carry his corn, an equine metaphor for forgetting himself, or even worse, as hairy-heeled, a perverse homage to the draught horse who is in fact one of the noblest of creatures. Rationing was still in force, and would be again come 1956 and the Suez Crisis.

As a farmer, my father was plagued by the WarAg, the War Agricultural Board, not disbanded until the late '50s, telling him what he should or should not grow, how much land he should plough each year, and how much livestock he should carry on our 230 acres. *Plus ça change,* we might say today, as an ignorant government, devoid of all rural or agricultural knowledge, attempts to dictate food policy. 'Ah, but it's the EU,' they used to say, by way of excuse for all their wrongdoing. But that fig-leaf has been removed; our withdrawal from the EU has if anything made matters worse as the British penchant for rule-making as an end itself makes itself fully evident. Our farmers are clients of the state, their hands held out for subsidy, which until 2007 paid them at times to grow nothing, though it is true that wild places are thereby conserved. There must be a median way to be found, accommodating food-producers and conservationists – give-and-take is all it takes, together with just a few sensible rules. Opinion and policy are rapidly moving at last to the support of locally produced food, much safer in a dangerous world, and a far cry from the stated opinion of one Labour minister that the countryside should be turned over entirely to tourism, while the rest be concreted over for more building. Are we ruled by madmen? And who maintains the countryside anyway? Farmers, that's who.

Farming in the '50s: what a welter of emotion, what a myriad of memories that phrase conjures up. Haytime and harvest saw conical stooks erected after cutting, although we ran a modern farm and quite quickly bought a baler. This produced the small bales which are now a sought after and specially produced rarity used by the two or three-horse owner only. Billy cans of tea and 'doorstep' sandwiches would be brought out to the field by my mother, and we would sit in the shade of a newly made stook with the recently harvested stalks of hay or straw sticking though our clothes in the heat, gratefully consuming the sugar-laced tea and the jam-laden bread which had been brought. Although only some six or seven years old at the time I felt that I had fully earned my repast merely by taking my young legs up to the field.

Haymaking time was generally a more urgent endeavour as the onset of rain could be quick and unexpected, and usually happened just as the grass had been cut and was lying at its most vulnerable upon the ground. The Wyatt brothers from Temple Guiting, Geoff and Keith, were our necessary allies in this weather-spotting game when later on we used them as contractors. My father would get on the 'blower', something of an ordeal for him because of his deafness: "Everything alright for tomorrow, Geoff/Keith?" he'd ask.

"I'd say so Doc. Looks set fair for the next four days anyway. Should give us enough time for the Thin Field."

The Thin Field, so called after a previous owner, not because it was thin. What fine, dependable people they were, these workers on the land, never on holiday at the crucial moment but available immediately when the time was right.

INTRODUCTION

My father, Edward Holt (his mother's maiden name) Eason (1915–1999), always known as Ted ('Teddy-boy' when my mother was feeling affectionate, or 'Huntoo', the Malay word – learned in her Oriental childhood – for haunted spirit, when he seemed anxious) was born at the end of 1915 at Holmes Chapel in Cheshire. His father had inherited a Manchester cotton-broking business from his father before him, formed from an alliance with a Scotsman named Ritchie and a Syrian immigrant named Hashim. Thus was born the business of Ritchie and Eason, which weathered the economic storms and the crash in the cotton market of the 1930s with equanimity. This was due to the sharp management and diversification into the revolutionary rayon yarn initiated by my great-grandfather Edward Adolph, and the subsequent soundness of my grandfather Wilf, finally to be sold for a handsome sum to Glazebrook Steel in the mid-1960s, my father having no interest in the business – "I'd've lost the lot," he would later say to me. They must have formed an odd trio, Ritchie, Eason and Hashim, but the business prospered. My great-grandfather's sister-in-law married Hashim, and my grandfather, being very deaf, continued the business through the Great War 1914–1918, partly because it was important for the war effort and partly because his disability debarred him from military service.

My paternal grandmother's family, impoverished and genteel and proud of it, relied heavily upon my grandfather's considerable generosity in providing them with houses and general wherewithal, at the same time sneering at him and his origins behind his back (there had been some question of the illegitimacy of my great-grandfather, though my father could never quite get to the bottom of it) and his preoccupation with money and the making of it.

His descent from one of the seventeen Lancashire Witches of Pendle Forest, wrongly convicted in 1634 on the evidence of an impostor who was fortunately discovered to be such before the sentence was carried out, counted for nothing with them, as they were entirely uninterested in history or anything not connected with the narrowest of social considerations. My paternal great-grandfather's struggle to prosper against all the protests of his (likewise) genteel family that he was nothing better than a 'counter-jumper' (tradesman) if he went into business was evidence of a similar mindset. Business and its practitioners, though they provide our lifeblood, are similarly despised now by a different class, the socialists who supposedly wish for our betterment and prosperity.

In common with many northern industrial entrepreneurs and industrialists, my great-grandfather entertained strong liberal leanings, believing that all should have an education sufficient for the coalman to converse with the aristocrat. Idealistic perhaps, and a far cry from the ineptitudes, infelicities and class obsessions of twenty-first century educational mores. He supported many up-and-coming artists in all media, and left (somewhat to his children's regret) a large and fine collection of Pilkingtonware (a glazed pottery of distinctive design and vivid colours) to the Manchester City Art Gallery – some pieces of it are always on show, as the gift of Edward Adolph Eason.

My grandfather and his brother Arthur were both educated first at home by a governess – as was often the case in the late nineteenth century amongst children of their circumstances – and then in Switzerland in the expectation that as they were both to go into business they would need languages as a useful tool.

Nonetheless, my grandmother's common complaint against my grandfather was: "Wilf, he thinks of nothing but money."

She seemed to have not a care in the world as she annoyingly sang her way around the house, though I am sure that living with someone as deaf as Wilf took its toll.

Various disreputable relatives of my grandmother's hung around for greater or lesser lengths of time, including once-handsome Uncle Percy who had long ago returned from India after perilous adventures into commerce and an affair with Lady Willingdon, the Viceroy's wife. He drank prodigiously, and was one day found dead in a ditch having been decanted from his motor during a collision.

Auntie Katie, my grandmother's unmarried sister, was a health fanatic who espoused the teachings of one Doctor Severn whose magazine *Radiant Health* was said to be the source of all wellbeing. No one ever knew how much of Grandpa's money – for he supported Katie and even bought her a house at Remenham, near Henley-on-Thames – was spent on Dr Severn's proprietary remedies. She managed to infect Granny too with the bacillus of *Radiant Health*, and as grandchildren my cousins Margaret and Wendy and I dreaded our stays with Granny. This was desperately unfair as she was a wonderful grandmother, and I now realise was doing her level best to make up for the difficulties that were already becoming evident in my life at home, where strictness was regarded by my mother as all-important and an essential component of upbringing for a satisfactory later life.

But when I stayed on my own at the grandparents I found the enforced games of Pelmanism in Granny's snug completely unnerving. My memory, normally rather good, would fade to a blank and Granny uncharacteristically would often emerge victorious as I ended up with perhaps two or three pairs of cards. She obviously felt that my mind needed improving and I endured one theatre outing, aged about seven, to Stratford where we saw *Troilus and Cressida*. I don't think either of us understood much of the play but the voice of Peter O'Toole as Thersites has stuck with me to this day. The outing was treasured for that reason alone.

Every morning the question arose as to our bowel movements. "Have you been to the lavatory yet?" she would ask.

"No, Granny," we invariably replied, as we separately strained away on the lavatory bowl – I think that we were all in different lavatories, at least I hope so.

"Then you'll just have to keep trying."

In the end we became so desperate to get on with the important business of the day – riding, chasing each other around the garden, making Mrs Mainwaring's life a misery and plaguing Brown the groom with endless questions about horses (his duties were by now quite light, having only the grey Friar and the liver chestnut Pedlar in his care, who spent their summers in the ridge-and-furrow paddock next to the garden) – that we raided the kitchen cupboard for currants and dropped them into the lavatory after a credible interval each morning.

Granny was entirely deceived by this performance, or perhaps she was just relieved that she no longer had to nag us. Either way, we were mightily grateful that we no longer had to undergo regular dosage with Dr Severn's Innaclean, a foul concoction of dried herbs taken with a glass of water.

Currants played a part in my father's childhood too. He had early become aware that Syrians ate a good deal of dried fruit. One lunchtime when Scan and Ran (members of the aforementioned Hashim family) were present, my father, being a keeper of rabbits, presented each of them with a plate of rabbit droppings. Closely resembling currants, they were broached with relish. Some sort of punishment must have followed, but the grandparents were poor disciplinarians. Ted was an inveterate practical joker when young and retained a dry humour to the end of his life, though Granny said that unsurprisingly his personality underwent a big change when he became deaf.

Childhood was something of an idyll for my father. Probably partly as a result of having bad ears, which eventually necessitated a series of major operations for infected mastoids and which chequered his boyhood, he was spoilt rotten by my grandmother. I know that it was a source of great annoyance to Wilf. Insensitive and very deaf as he was, he callously told Ted in later years that he was never expected to live beyond thirty. This makes him sound a beast, but he was no more than a product of the age and was actually possessed of wonderful humour and great generosity.

Until my father was twenty the family lived in a rented house (as many in all walks of life did in those days, and as many would like to be able to do again) known as Oak Brow at Styal just outside Manchester, close to the present-day airport. My father and his elder sister Joan were little subject to discipline and led a life free of most constraints, spending their time in dangerous games of roof-climbing with the Jordans who lived next door (Ann Jordan married Ted Oates – Oates of the Antarctic's nephew and heir who inherited all his of his uncle's estate, Titus having been unmarried and childless) and later on, beagling and hunting.

Other neighbours included the Greggs, whose ancestors had been one of the first socially aware manufacturers, owning the cotton-mill at Styal which is today a tourist destination and educational facility, and Ken Hay whose Swiss uncle had invented a dyeing process – the details of which elude me but which is used to this day. Ken's father was a prosperous tradesman who spoke with an 'accent', something which was anathema to Granny (Mabel) who couldn't bear to have anyone in the house who was not 'educated'. Consequently, Ted did a fantastic Lancashire accent.

Ken however was allowed in the house, accentless, as he had been one of the founder pupils at the then newly-opened Stowe School in Buckinghamshire, attended more recently by such luminaries as Peregrine Worsthorne and Richard Branson.

Granny was in fact a crashing snob but with a firm belief in her own social superiority, unlike many of that ilk.

"Oh, Wilf," I can hear her saying. "We can't possibly have those people here. They're simply not *comme il faut.*" In other words, not 'out of the same drawer'.

And when my father became engaged to my mother, whose own mother was German, she could not bear that either. Foreigners of any sort were not to be admitted because she thought that they tended to be on the 'dark' side; my mother had a wonderful creamy complexion but with suspiciously black hair.

All this was notwithstanding my mother Vivian's direct descent on her father's side, in two lines, from Alfred the Great and Charles II – at least one was legitimate, the other being through a minor mistress of Charles', Jane Roberts, who died in childbirth sadly bequeathing no more than a coat-of-arms. Angry letters addressed to the king from her father, a Worcestershire clergyman, can be found in the Worcester County Archive. Quite apart from this the family had been large landowners in Worcestershire and Warwickshire, though much reduced by the end of the war in 1945.

"I always used to wonder why Granny drew her skirts in when I came to sit next to her on the sofa," my mother said to me when I was a little older.

"Why do you think it was?" I asked.

"Oh, she didn't like my black hair, and being (half) foreign didn't help either, like a red rag to a bull I should think. I don't think the German bit helped, the war and all that you know."

Vivian's ability to paint and draw and to play the piano and the cello also furnished good grounds for suspicion. Her first intention on leaving school was to play the cello professionally but her parents, just retired from Malaya (as it was called then), attempted to dictate who her tutors might be, and she not unnaturally resented this after so many years of making her own decisions, and turned to horses instead. Her abilities and her lack of money lay uneasily beside the pragmatic materialism of a northern liberal atheistic family, where reading anything but the most conventional of books was a cause for worry.

We'd laugh at this; I am afraid that we both held Granny in slight contempt for her half-baked views on many things, but she was a good person who wouldn't have hurt a fly, loved her dogs, Cora her Border Terrier being the one I remember best, and her garden, and was a devoted wife to Grandpa and a devoted mother and grandmother too.

It has to be said that my mother too was no slouch when it came to snobbery. Besides her descent from Charles II and Alfred the Great, she was well-connected through kinships with such Yorkshire families as the Worsleys, the Cayleys and the Illingworths, as well as having the landed Shekells of Pebworth as her direct forebears. Thus, when disputes blew up with my father, she was not above resorting to class warfare: "Of course, the trouble is that you're not really a gentleman. I've married beneath myself. No two ways about it." No doubt to her annoyance, he would just laugh.

In 1936 the grandparents moved from Cheshire to Warwickshire, accompanied by the incomparable Mainwarings (who provided a seamless comfort to their lives), to live at Radway in what my father always described as "that jerry-built little house" – a 1920s villa-ish dwelling labelled, rather ingloriously, Hemp Close; an Indian echo there perhaps.

As Ted would say to me, "I loved Cheshire and all my friends, so I never much enjoyed coming back to Warwickshire at weekends. The hunting in those days was very good though, much better than Cheshire." This had been one of the main reasons for their move. So Mainwaring would pilot Grandpa, in a very large Rover car, to Banbury station so that he could spend three days a week in Manchester, staying at his club. He would describe these in after-years as his 'free' days; there was more to Grandpa than met the eye, though it was never discussed.

When I was about five I can remember thinking to myself, *why can't they have a Bentley, like our other richer friends?* Only children can be snobbish too.

1

BEFORE THE WAR

'His strongest tastes were negative. He abhorred plastics, Picasso, sunbathing and jazz – everything in fact that had happened in his lifetime.'
– From *The Ordeal of Gilbert Pinfold* by Evelyn Waugh
(1903–66)

Plastics, or at least viscose (a plant derivative used in textile manufacture), did of course play their part in the Eason fortunes as already mentioned, but although my forebears were quite ready to adopt the conveniences of modernisation – my great-grandfather was one of the first owners of a motor car in Manchester, using it often despite its slowness and unreliability – they abhorred anything which could remotely be described as 'trendy'. 'Long-haired', a 'fringe type' – these were epithets used to describe and distrust anything remotely *avant-garde* and which frequently came up in my childhood, much to the irritation of my mother.

Ted often used to say, when more recent economic difficulties came into view, "I never really remember any problems connected with the Depression although I was in my teens by the time it began. Life just seemed to go on as before."

Of course he was from a privileged background, but perhaps the difficulties have been exaggerated with hindsight as we all now know that people did not hurl themselves from windows when the Crash came in New York – one man did, for a reason not directly connected with the economic collapse – and that most people survived, with the help of charity, government help and sufficient mobility to find a job in another part of the country. Times were hard, as they are and will be, again, and stupidity and greed exacted their price from the innocent and the not-so-innocent too. But life goes on with all the determination of more prosperous times. And in the long run we're all dead, as John Maynard Keynes said. My father was a great pragmatist and roundly subscribed to this view. In those days disaster was not talked up as it is now, and there was little general instant communication which must have helped people to keep a sound mind.

The likelihood of deafness was always present in his life, and his boyhood, so circumscribed by frequent ear operations, bore witness to this in interrupted attendance at school and the frequent absence of Granny from home as she journeyed to wherever he was at school in times of illness. At the age of twelve he underwent a double mastoid operation and almost died, at the same time being diagnosed as suffering from acute nephritis (inflammation of the kidneys). It was thought unlikely that he would live beyond the age of thirty. Nevertheless, he grew up tough and fit, a good athlete (successful in the Ledbury Run at Malvern and winning the mile there also, then running for his college at Cambridge, only narrowly missing a half-blue), and a good horseman too. His time at Cambridge was marred only by an enforced absence for two months early in 1936 due to a serious bout of *psoriasis universalis*. He was a martyr to eczema for the rest of his life as it came and went entirely of its own accord.

His childhood was a happy one; the younger brother of Joan by three years he was close to her and they shared many of the same outdoor interests. Oak Brow, built in brick with beam-and-plasterboard intervening, a typical, fairly modest, recently built Cheshire house provided a jolly background to their young lives. Earliest schooldays were spent at Tanarchy, a small pre-prep school in Derbyshire, at the age of six. Ted hated it, the headmaster was something of a Mr Squeers and he ran away during his first term, never to return. Granny restored him to the tender mercies of the governess Annie Barnett, from whom he probably should not have been parted at such an early age. Annie had led an adventurous life, having been with a Russian princely family at the time of the Revolution. She was lucky to escape with her life though little else, through the port of Vladivostock: the princely family were all massacred. Our family was a port in the storm, and she stayed with them until Ted left for a more successful time at St Anselm's, a prep school at Bakewell, also in Derbyshire. From there he spent two years at Bilton Grange on the outskirts of Rugby, which is still a feeder school for Rugby School itself.

One day, we were discussing illness, he and I, probably in relation to his deafness as it so marked his schooldays, and mine to a lesser extent. I was recovering from measles which could, even in the '50s, result in permanent deafness. I had had it fairly badly but luckily my hearing remained unimpaired. We had girls at school who sometimes had a whole term away because of illness.

Taking things a stage further, I asked him, "Dad, did any boys die at school?"

It seemed too dramatic to contemplate, but he replied, "Oh yes, from scarlet fever rather than anything else. There was a boy in my year at Bilton who died from that; it was more of a 'killer' than any of the other childish diseases. I think that there was a younger boy who died from measles during my time there too."

"What about other illnesses?" I asked, warming to my theme.

"Well, diphtheria was probably the one that I can remember most. A boy caught it at St Anselm's and didn't survive. There were drugs by then of course to deal with these things, but they weren't as well synthesised as they are now." This in the '50s; how even luckier we are now.

"And then there was Dick, can't remember his surname now."

"What about him?" I asked breathlessly.

"He was my best friend at Bilton. We did all our prep together and played games and did gym to pretty much the same standard; we were together a lot. His parents lived quite near to Rugby. They were big landowners I think. I used to go there when we were allowed out for lunch because it was near enough and it made a change from just going into town. They were very kind to me, and I even got the odd ride on one of their ponies. I wasn't that keen on riding then, though."

"Why not?" I asked. Someone who was not keen on riding as a child must have been a little mad, mustn't they?

"I was rather nervous of horses. I only got keen when I saw Joan and a lot of my friends going hunting a bit later on."

He paused and I thought how sad he looked as his memory turned to those days of fatal illness, then clearing his throat, as he often did when he was upset about something, he went on. "One afternoon after school, as we went onto the pitch for rugger practice, Dick said to me that he felt really ill. He had gone terribly red, it all happened so quickly. He was sent to the sick room. I wasn't allowed in there to see him. The doctor came; I saw him go in through the door as I had been allowed off games so that I could keep in touch with what was happening. After a while, Matron came out looking really worried. "He's not well dear, not well at all." I wanted to know what was wrong with him, but she wouldn't tell me except to say that he had a very high temperature."

"How high?" I asked, being keen on detail and hoping to hear of the establishment of a record.

"105°," he said briefly.

"Gosh!" I exclaimed, and then put my hand on his arm as I saw his sadness – a tightly buttoned exterior hid often high emotion.

"I was told that I should go down to hall for supper; I seemed to have missed prep. Didn't feel like eating much I can tell you. Then it went on all night. I was sent to bed of course but I couldn't sleep, and crept along the corridor to the sick room. Matron was up all night with him. He couldn't breathe very well by that time and I could hear him through the door, fighting for breath."

"By the morning he was dead. I wanted to go in and say goodbye, but they said it was too dangerous. The whole school was put into quarantine for diphtheria but no one else got it, luckily. It was impossible to say how he'd caught it though I did hear later that one of the boys at the stables – Dick managed to keep a pony at school – had become very ill. We didn't hear what it was he had and he recovered anyway. Dear old Dick, what a good chap he was. I think he might have been something great if he'd lived."

We were quiet together for a few moments.

I could not help thinking how kind everyone had been in the story, and I could see why Ted always said how happy he was at school – after Tanarchy, of course. Somehow, people seemed to be more 'messed up' by the Second World War than the first, though it is quite hard to see why when we read of the terrible experiences of so many servicemen fighting the first truly industrial war of 1914-18. All I knew was that it was hard to imagine most of the staff at my prep school behaving with half the humanity of those in the story which I had just heard.

I thought of the few of my friends who I knew had been seriously ill, mostly by virtue (hardly the right word) of the polio outbreak in the early part of the decade. Not one, as far as I can remember, died, though I had a great friend Michael Boone who had had calipers on his legs since the age of five; it didn't stop him from hunting though, using a specially adapted saddle.

These friends had somehow slipped through the net of the vaccination programme which was in force at that time. I remember even now the dreaded attendance at Moreton-in-Marsh Hospital on no less than three occasions so that I could complete the immunisation programme.

I would yell at my mother as she dragged me by the hand. "Oh please Mummy, it hurts so. I don't want it. I don't want it."

Heart-rending no doubt, but on this occasion how right she was to ignore my pleas. A sore arm for a few days was a small price to pay for spoiling polio's crippling chances. It took no less than three nurses to hold me down and administer the vaccination, one for either side and one to do the deed.

Despite bouts of illness throughout his childhood and adolescence, Ted especially enjoyed Malvern – Marlborough was the original choice but it was thought that Malvern offered a more salubrious climate for one who had ear problems. This did not stop him from excelling on the athletics field nor from being a keen member of the OTC (Officers' Training Corps, now re-named CCF – Combined Cadet Force). His was a straightforward time there, no hints of homosexuality nor much trouble of any other kind marred a happy five years which were greatly enhanced by his housemaster Mr Robinson and his wife, who acted as mother to all the boys in the house.

In those days there was a policy generally employed by all public schools that housemasters should be married as it made their job easier and helped to guard against unsuitable relationships. So highly did my father regard Mr and Mrs Robinson that he made a point of visiting them at least once each year, as they continued to live in Malvern until the end of their lives.

Boys will be boys though: one Smith Major showed considerable initiative towards the end of his time at school.

"Smith Major was lucky enough one day," my father told me with something approaching glee, "to discover one of the masters, Gleeson I think his name was, in bed with one of the maids. Gleeson was a bit of a weak character, and Smith Major knew it. He had his eye to the main chance and said to him that he would keep quiet as long as he, Gleeson, kept him in whisky and cigars for the remainder of his time at Malvern. This must have been an expensive business for Gleeson as the school year had only just begun. We had a marvellous time, all those of Smith's friends in his final year. His study was the busiest place in the school."

"I suppose you all knew why he had so much in the way of cigars and drink?" I asked.

"Of course we did. Couldn't stop laughing about it. Poor old Gleeson. Nothing he could do about it."

It put my own school escapades fairly in the shade.

My father went up to Pembroke College Cambridge in the autumn of 1934 to read Medicine. His enthusiasms were scientific and military in the main; he had a lab at home in Styal (in those days all the necessary ingredients for medical experiments could be bought at the local chemist) where explosions were not unknown, and his interest in entomology was to become an abiding and lifelong passion, of which more later. His preferred subject was Zoology but Grandpa, prosaic as ever, insisted that any scientific bent should also be put to a more practical use, so he read both subjects. Despite his father's telling him that he really did not need to work as it took the money out of a needier person's mouth (a common enough idea then) Ted was to be well-equipped for later challenges. Mr Robinson's estimation of him at Malvern as 'a quiet, sensible boy who would work hard' at Cambridge was to be well-proven.

"Do you know," he once told me, "I never discovered where the college chapel was in the three years that I was there. Atheism was quite the thing in those days, it's nothing new. Now, I'm not sure how good an idea it is."

"Well, you must have known people like Burgess and McLean then?" I wondered.

"Oh no, or if I did, only vaguely, and certainly I'd've had no idea what they were up to. People like that were completely beyond the pale as far as people I knew were concerned. If we had known what was going on, politically and in every other way, [Ted was not an advocate of homosexuality] we'd've debagged them and thrown them in the fountain or the Cam or something."

Beagling, hunting and racing were his chief pastimes, together with frequent rides with the Cavalry (Yeomanry). Cambridge being close to Newmarket was an ideal base for a racing *habitué*. Aunt Joan (Ma), Ted's sister, was a brave point-to-point rider although she tended to pull up before the finish as she felt sorry for the horse as he tired. Frenchie Nicholson, father to the late 'The Duke' David Nicholson, trained there before coming to Prestbury by Cheltenham Racecourse.

In September 1935 Joan and Ted went on a trip to Scotland, which included a stay with friends or relations, I am not sure which, at Torrisdale Castle near Tarbert on the Scottish west coast. On the morning of the 16 September Ted rose at 4.30 and went for a run.

> Joan and I started at 5.45. We went through Warrington, Newton-le-Willows, Wigan, Preston, Lancaster and got to Kendal at 9.00 where we breakfasted at the Kendal Hotel. Continued at 9.45 with me driving through Shap, Penrith and Carlisle (11.00) when we purchased some fruit, etc. At Lockerbie we filled up with gasoline. Stopped after Lockerbie to eat fruit, then Joan drove. Went on through Brattock, Crawford, Strathaven and Paisley. Crossed the Clyde by Erskine ferry and continued through Dumbarton, Helensburg [sic] and Anochar, where we had tea at 4.30 at the Ross's Hotel. I drove the rest of the way... Rained nearly all day.

The following day:
> We went through Lochgilphead, Tarbert and then we filled up with petrol and oil. Continued on the Campbelltown [sic] road and six miles outside Tarbert we turned to the left towards Skipness and started looking for pubs... then went on to Campbelltown and up again on the west side of Kintyre where it is exposed to the open sea... exposed and very black. We continued up through Glenbar [sic] where it becomes protected by Islay and Jura and therefore wooded again... I got a room at the pub we noticed this morning, the Claoraig Inn (temperance) [a possible reference to the West Coast Wee Free Church prohibition of alcohol consumption, very prevalent then and still with some force today]... the pub is primitive and rather dirty [not a Wee Free characteristic], but just the thing I want. I changed and went for a walk to Skipness two-and-a-half miles away and back. Had a meal (bacon and eggs) in a room downstairs with a fire. Retired at

9.00. The pub looks over toward Arran and is surrounded by lowish hills.

Joan meanwhile went on to Torrisdale on her own, while Ted had a couple of days to devote to walking and natural history.

> The next day, at 10.30 I went out for a walk… towards Tarbert and after about three miles struck off the road to the right and followed a stream up to its source in the hills. Scaled a tor, the highest mountain for some way around. Saw grouse, hares and one duck. Also remarkable numbers of caterpillars and bumble bees [oh, happy days], some seatophaga (?) and some moths. Apart from the grouse the fauna strongly resembles that of Dartmoor. Got back at 3.30… Joan came over with Pixy [the dog] in the car and I arranged to quit here tomorrow. Had chops for my supper – the butter has become somewhat rancid. Retired at 9.00. The woman who does most of the serving, presumably the daughter of Mrs Campbell, the proprietress, is most extraordinary with a violent stammer. [Later on] Major McAllister Hall tells me that Peter Campbell, the proprietor, cut his throat a short time ago.

The next afternoon, Ted:

> Took the bus to Canadails (?)… dropping me at the gates of Torresdail [sic]Castle. I got there at 5.00. The family consists of the father, a very decent old fellow, with two daughters, ? and Rosemary, and two sons, Peter and Donald, two younger sons being away. Also staying there are Beryl ? and another girl called Daphne Barclay – a cousin, who is training to be a nurse in a hospital in Glasgow and seems to spend most of her time strangling babies. [I'm not sure what he is referring to here – it was not unknown in those days for babies with

serious disabilities to be euthanised at birth.] Pixy has made herself very much at home – they have two spaniels.

The next day, he:
Caught several insects – one Diptera, one Colroptera, one Homoptera, two Hermiptera, one Enoptera (?) and one I am not sure of, probably a longicorn beetle. Rosemary showed me some amazing mummies, two heads and a cat, her father got in Africa. After lunch we tested Pixy with a little cannon, to see how she would behave with a gun. I walked up the glen again and caught sundry other insects including Hermiptera, Diptera and Hymenoptera. The number of Hermiptera (Homoptera and Hetroptera) around here is remarkable. I arrived back at the Castle at 4.30 to find everyone had gone to Campbelltown, taking both cars; apparently they had been looking for me all over the place. The butler explained all this and I took the 5.15 bus to Campbelltown and after wandering about the town for a bit, met them and we went to a film – rather poor but quite funny in parts. We got back soon after 9.00, Joan, Rosemary, Donald and I in our car, the rest in theirs. After eating a cold meal we talked and tried getting a glass to answer questions by laying our fingers on it and arranging letters all round it; of course it didn't work but some of them seemed to think it did.

The next morning:
They all saw us off in various stages of [un]dress. Saw a seal on a rock near Tarbert, also numerous herons, curlew and hawks. We came home the same way as we went… Started to rain when we got into England… It got dark outside Preston and the rain got worse, we had an awful time getting on to the Wigan road as a policeman had stopped us using the usual road. Got to Warrington by 9.00 and home by 9.30. 360 miles in under

thirteen-and-a-half hours, including stops – not bad, we'd have been home by 9.00 if we hadn't been held up in Preston. Retired after an enema! [There was an acute concern over bowel movements in those days, so this was nothing unusual].

A few days later, the driving test having just been made compulsory:
We all three went into town in Kenneth's car… Kenneth and I met a very decent woman who gave Kenneth his driving test. First she asked him questions on the highway code then we went all over Rusholm backing into gateways, turning in the road and obeying traffic signals – very entertaining. Needless to say he passed… We finished up in Jim's digs where we stayed till 11.15. Kenneth took Dalton and me home.

On 27 September:
A remarkable number of some species of Hymenoptera Parasitica, probably Proctotrypidea, have settled on the lavatory ceiling, caught a few with spirit.

One of my childhood memories is of my bedroom wall literally covered with various insects, particularly in hot weather. Such a spectacle is unknown today.

The next few days saw such activities as:
Exercising myself on my bars in the morning [Ted was a fine gymnast, able to do press-ups well into his sixties], going to the Dirt Track, I very unwillingly! I reckon it is a bloody silly sport. They also had Midget car racing and a framed up crash which relieved the monotony, going to Charlie Cook to be measured for some riding breeches, discussing alternative medicine with Mrs Hay, Kenneth's mother – "osteopathy is coming into its own now I will say!" and climbing out of my bedroom window by the rope I have in case of fire.

In the afternoon of 6 October, a Sunday, wintertime started [much earlier than now]... Joan and I departed for Cambridge. We went by Congleton, Stoke, Lichfield, Nuneaton, Lutterworth and stayed the night with the Spillers at Husbands Bosworth. Mrs Spiller is deaf so that one has to use a trumpet, only one daughter, Toni (?) is at the moment in residence, and Colonel Spiller is a very decent little fellow who can talk about horses for hours. The house is in a pretty bad way as they are almost broke, but they are remarkably decent and easy to get on with.

The Spillers papered all the ground floor walls of their house with pages from *The Sporting Life* for warmth as well as decoration, as the Wordsworths at Dove Cottage had done before them – the Newspaper Room is still there. On 7 October Joan and Ted:

Got to Cambridge at 1.00. Joan departed, leaving me at Pember (Pembroke)... I got my bike from the garage and went to the bank to see how things stand.'

In those days, a white fiver (they went out of use in the early '50s) would buy you a full night out – dinner, drinks and a show.

The entry for 16 October describes a supervision:

After hall I went to Broadby in Station Road for a super. The first thing he said was that he had come down on the Cesarewich. We talked racing for a bit then he talked about bull-fighting, butterflys [sic] and his holiday in Pompei [sic] and Sicily and I talked about my Finnish trip [Ted had accompanied Grandpa on a business trip that summer, which took in Estonia and Sweden as well. Estonia, independent for two decades between the wars, was enjoying something of a boom, and was the site of the largest cotton-spinning mill in Europe, Kraenholm Mills, run by the German firm of Knoop and Co. It enjoyed a large investment from the Fleming banking family, of which more later...] we also did a little zoo(ology). Quite refreshing to come across a Cambridge scientist who talks a little sense (comparatively) after these narrow-minded, dull, uneducated fellows one usually meets among demonstrators, supervisors and lecturers. Worked till 11.30 on returning.

Here is a typical entry from the previous day, showing the varied and busy life of a reasonably average undergraduate in those days:

Letter and shoes from Mummy [she seemed to send him a lot of cakes too!] Dissected for an hour after phys (iology?) lecture, then came home and made some anatomy notes. Phys practical 2-4. Chaudhuri and I met Frank in the ? and we had tea at the Waffel. Met Shunter on the way back. Did some work before hall. After hall Smith and I went to a Cavalry meeting. Cohen showed a flick [film] he had made of dummy-thrusting [a military exercise where the mounted rider at full gallop must impale with a sword a stuffed figure placed at a suitable height – this exercise has recently been forbidden by the mounted police as being élitist]. Michael, Kenneth Watt, Donald? were there. Smith and I had a drink in the Still before returning. Worked till 11.00.

Another entry, for a Monday morning, reads:
Rose at 6.00. I rode with the Cavalry.

This would have been a squadron of the local Yeomanry, or Volunteer Cavalry which was first formed in the late eighteenth century. They ran the horsed part of the Cambridge University OTC. Commissions then were vested in the hands of the Monarch's county representative the Lord Lieutenant, who was often either the commander himself or deputed to a member of his family. It was a good countryside club with a purpose. The officers were from the ranks of the foxhunting gentry while the majority of the troopers came from the tenant farming community on their estates. They provided their own horses, and found in this a useful opportunity for showing off young horses which they had bred to the officers in the hope of effecting the sale of a hunter. In 1908, with the formation of the Territorial Army, the Yeomanry transferred to this force having previously provided elements of the Imperial Yeomanry in the South African War. Many Yeomanry Regiments served in the First World War in the Cavalry Division in France or Palestine, as they did in Palestine in the Second, Ken Hay being one of the members of the Cheshire (Earl of Chester's) Yeomanry in this theatre, fighting the Vichy French in Syria, and to which my father also belonged. The entry continues:

> We paraded at Quay Side. I rode Canham's 'Nigger'. Williams is Troop Officer. Michael Johnson, Eric Bates, Bill Rae-Smith, ? and many other people I knew were out. Had a very good ride. Had no breakfast. Working all morning. After lunch I went to Fenners and ran three miles. At 3.30 I went to ? and dissected till 4.45. Chaudhuri came to tea. Smith came in after hall. Ate very little all day – trying to start a strict diet. Retired early.

One Yeomanry story that Ted told me might amuse, and gives some idea of the still feudal powers still sometimes exercised then:

> A young soldier by the name of Boon was up on a charge for the third time, and having been brought before his kindly local landowner commanding officer, was stood at ease by him, much to the disgust of the escorting Sergeant-Major. The two witnesses were dismissed and the Colonel issued an admonishment: "Now look here young man [a rather

informal mode of address], this can't go on, and if it does I shall have to have a word with Mrs Boon and see about you being put out of your cottage." [He was his landlord as well as his commanding officer.] Well, do you know that did the trick. There was no more trouble from Boon, and he became a boon to the Regiment, rising to the rank of Lance-Corporal in short order.

Well, several comments spring to mind after reading the last diary entry – that Ted 'took the biscuit' for industry, on this day at least; that the industry was varied; that he was always spare of frame (the diet might possibly have been thought helpful in preventing recurring bouts of psoriasis); and that, even after such a well-filled day, he found time to write his journal. That shows discipline; journals and diaries today are becoming rare, as the word processor and e-mails take over from handwriting, and it is noticeable that handwriting is not up to previous standards as the pen now lies uneasily in the hands of many young people. This journal was the fourteenth volume, each one covering between three and four months.

An entry earlier in October, just before the start of term, paints a picture of walking and riding and of daily social contact with friends:

Kenneth [Hay] came round at 9.15 and we went and caught Friar and saddled him on the spot. I rode and Kenneth motored to Miss Clements' where he got a horse and we rode round by Morley and Mobberly and over Soss Moss. Very enjoyable. Unsaddled Friar and turned him loose into the field and came back in Kenneth's car. Kenneth stayed for a drink. Letter from Mac [Cope] and my cert A from Cambridge [presumably the mail for the day]. Ambrose rang up ref booking parts for dissection. I sent him a P.C. to Cambridge. Rained most of the afternoon. Did some Embryology notes after tea.

And the next day:
> Mummy and Joan went into town [Manchester]. Philip [Gething] came round and we went to Wincle in his car and lunched at The Ship with the intention of doing some walking. All we did was to walk one-and-a-half miles up a lane and back, three miles in all. We then went on through Rudyard and retraced our steps to Macclesfield, coming back home for tea. Joan went to the Smalleys for the night [the family of her future husband]. Abyssinia and Italy are at war.

That last simple sentence brings us back to the wider world of the time, where many refused to see 'the fog of war' approaching. The Easons were not among them, and Ted knew that when war came he would have to fight, if only to make up for Grandpa's non-combatance in the First War.

In common with his contemporaries, and because it was one of the main entertainments available, the cinema was much frequented; my father remained a keen movie-goer into old age. Here is the entry for 25 October 1935:
> Went round to see Smith after hall and we went to a flick at the Central, Clark Gable in *After Office Hours*, not bad much as I dislike the look of the man.

A further cinema trip is recorded on 23 December:
> Went with the Hays into town to see *The Prisoner of Zenda* at the Repertory Theatre... not a bad show.

This, one of Errol Flynn's great successes and now a movie classic of all time, was made eighty-seven years ago.
Christmas Eve must have been celebrated in fine style:
> ...started having 'normal' food [no doubt in anticipation of Christmas, though we are not told whether there was any improvement in his psoriasis, which could go as quickly as it

came]. Jimmy brought Daddy back from shooting fairly early and Daddy and I went for a walk before tea. Uncle Arthur [Midget, Grandpa's brother, of whom more later] arrived for tea. At 11.00 Dot, Donald and Michael [relations I think] came round. We nearly made Donald ill with some foul concoction of Mummy's meant-to-be punch.

Christmas Day passed uneventfully:
...after lunch I went for a walk over the aerodrome site (bloody business) and down by the river, over the cow-bridge and back by the mill where I met Daddy and Uncle Arthur with Jill. Had an excellent dinner and felt quite comfortable inside for the first time in three weeks. [Poor Ted.] Retired fairly early.

'Bloody business' must refer to the beginnings of the construction which eventually developed into Manchester Airport. Many familiar landmarks, such as those described, would disappear under concrete soon enough, as many more did all over the country when war came and airfields became a military necessity.

On Boxing Day Daddy and Uncle Arthur went shooting – Joan and I went beagling with the Cheshire – met at Broxton. Raining to start with, but cleared later, turning into a swell afternoon. We stayed to the end. Pearsons, Chris [Joan's future husband], Peter and Anne, Colin Oddling and sundry other people were out. We stopped at Nantwich to see Brown about tomorrow and had tea (Joan, Chris and I) at The Lamb. I motored the Humber back [he had just managed to get a driving licence before the compulsory test was made law] and Joan went in Chris's car. I smoked some of Chris's twist, which made me come over all queer on the way back – but it passed off. After dinner the Worthingtons and Mrs Havers came round with her daughter and we played a most complex card game of Mrs Worthington's. They stayed till 12.30. Chris went home.

The following day:

Went hunting. Met the horses at Burleydam. I rode a new horse this season of Brown's, which went very well all things considered. Very heavy going indeed. We waited around for ages, then got an excellent run broken up by narrow bridges, etc. Two-to-three mile point [the distance in a straight line from where the fox was found to where the run finished] I reckon, but seemed much longer owing to the heavy going. Killed twice [i.e. two foxes]. Got home by 4.30... Ate at 6.15 and went into town afterwards. Mummy, Daddy and Auntie Katie [Granny's sister] in the Humber, and Joan, Dan [Chris's sister], Monica Havers and me in the Wolseley. Met Chris at the Opera House. The show, *Follow the Sun* – a Cochrane review – was very moderate. Saw Gethings, Dicks, Pen, Wilsons, Chick and others among the audience. Katie slept in my room and Chris and I in the spare room as Dan slept in a bachelor's room.

The next day:

I went into town in the evening and met Guy at 6.30 at the Café Royal. We ate then saw *Scrooge* (Seymour Hicks) at the Paramount, one of the best flicks from books I have ever seen. Took Guy home and got home myself at 12.00.

On New Year's Eve:

Went hunting – meet at Brindley Lee. I rode the same horse. In the middle of the first run my horse refused a very easy hedge and swerved off to an iron gate which she thought was a gap, couldn't pull up, tried to jump it and got her off-hind thoroughly entangled in the twisted cross-bars of the gate, coming down on the other side – why she didn't break her leg beats me. With the help of several other folk we got her clear after much pushing and twisting. I started to lead her home, thinking she would only just be able to walk – if at all – but funnily enough, after a bit, she didn't even show signs of lameness so I got on and walked back to Nantwich (2.30). Talked to Brown until Joan and Daddy arrived. Went home via Wilmslow where Daddy got some sand shoes for beagling. Got home at 4.15. Bathed and changed before dinner. After dinner we all went round to the Worthingtons… We played vingt-et-un until close on 12.00 then refreshed ourselves in the dining room. Daddy was the New Year and went out a few seconds before 12.00, coming in again carrying a piece of coal in one hand, a sandwich in the other, and wearing a nose and a moustache. We drank a very good burgundy cup then went on playing until after 1.00. Here endeth 1935. Since there are only two more pages in this book I am going to start 1936 in another book.

Quotations from Ted's diary must end here, as the journal for 1935 is the only one to survive.

The move away from his beloved Cheshire to Radway in Warwickshire came soon after the end of the year; his diary records several trips that Granny made to Radway in preparation for the move, driven by the faithful Barnshaw who did not go to live in Warwickshire with them – though I am fairly sure that the Brown mentioned as the keeper of a livery yard in the diary entries is the selfsame Brown employed as their groom after the move. Ted would make periodic trips to Cheshire even much later on during my early years, to catch up with him and other members of our extended family.

Many friendships, both in Cheshire and later in Warwickshire, centred upon the hunting field. Hunting here refers specifically to foxhunting, although I know that my father used also to go out with the High Peak Harriers as well as the local pack of beagles, both of which hunted the hare. Hunting in this context never refers to shooting, unlike in America.

I am lucky enough to possess a wonderful book of drawings by Hard Hide with pithy captions by Tough Skin (real names unknown) entitled *Cheshire Cats and Cheshire Cheeses*. These celebrate the talents and reputations of prominent hunting folk in Cheshire between the Wars, Ted's great friend Rosemary Tulloch, being described rather inelegantly as 'Bunty the nagsman', included as one of the 'Kittenish Kittens – sometimes they scratch and sometimes they purr'. I remember her well in her later years as more on the scratchy side. 'Nagsman', someone who schools or nags young horses actually described her whole persona rather well, a woman of determination with the utmost conviction that she would succeed at anything she tried. Her flinty exterior decked always with a forbidding pair of glasses in the end proved too much for her more phlegmatic husband Ander, who left her after many years for someone younger and more easy-going. Their daughter, Alison, continued in flinty style by riding round Badminton (Horse Trials) successfully on a horse called Samba.

Others more famous include Oswald Mosley, portrayed in attendance at a cock-fight: 'A great sportsman. Hunting, shooting, polo and cockfighting are among his recreations.' His son Max, with his now-revealed lifelong preoccupation with sado-masochism, caps his father's more orthodox sporting predilections. Lord Daresbury is described as 'one of the most generous and beloved of all sportsmen. Hounds are always welcome on his estate, and not a strand of wire! [This refers to the fences, making them safer to jump.] This year [?] he had the

Point-to-Point at Owls Nest. His kindness is untold. One of his greatest achievements is the Royal Show [no longer the annual event it used to be at Stoneleigh in Warwickshire, it now holds more specialised events for different aspects of agriculture]. Its success is largely due to all the work he has done in the past.'

Toby Greenall, the second Lord Daresbury, joint-master of the Belvoir for thirteen years followed by thirty years as master of the County Limerick Foxhounds in Ireland, was another whose descendants are doughty defenders of the latter-day rights of such sportsmen: 'Joint Master of the Belvoir, and a wonderful good sportsman. Knows no fear, and we are glad to say that he has not entirely deserted us for the Belvoir, as he always comes out when hounds meet on the Walton estate and provides us with great sport.' His wife, the former Joyce Laycock, was champion lady point-to-point rider three times, in 1934, 1935 and 1938. They went very fast in those days as not all ladies could hold their horses. Grandson Johnny Greenall was Master and amateur huntsman of the Meynell and South Staffs Foxhounds, one of the largest hunting 'countries' (with the biggest fences) in Britain, while the great-grandsons Thomas, Oliver, Toby and Jake have all had various and successful raceriding careers, Oliver winning the Cheltenham Foxhunters (the blue riband of amateur steeplechases) on Amicelli in 2008. The 2022/3 season was the last for the Meynell as they have had to disband and the hounds will be drafted (given) to other kennels.

Mrs Billy Clegg – 'away lipsticks, powder and other things vain – she's off full split to Groby [a well-known fox covert] again' – was one of the Clegg family who made a fortune building gas engines. As the quote would have us believe, she was definitely not one for frippery, being a foxhunter of the grittiest sort.

The Tarporley Hunt Club was a popular outlet for sporting exuberance and was the social hub of the hunting world in

Cheshire. It still exists though now only as a dining club. Peter Sayce, a great friend of my father's and later on Secretary to the Cheshire Hunt, was a keen habitué. Grandpa, though no great horseman, was a brave rider out hunting and was an enthusiast of the more nocturnal functions of the Club. His riding deteriorated with age and great was the consternation, I remember, when the Warwickshire Hunt eventually asked him not to come out any more as he constituted too much of a hazard to other followers (never 'huntsmen', as hunt followers are invariably termed in the uninformed press).

My father graduated with a 2:1 from Cambridge in 1937, taking his BA by proxy that summer. He gradually grew out of ill health and although his ears would always be delicate his hearing was so far unaffected, and he looked forward to a career in medicine and a lifelong passion for entomology together with the indulgence of all the enthusiasms already described. In possession of his degree he now went to train at University College Hospital in London's Gower Street, part of London University. Amusing characters included one professor of anatomy, whose sage advice when it came to remedying sleeplessness was to "read *Old Mortality*", this delivered in a broad Scotch accent for good measure – a most unjust slur on one of Scott's most splendid stories, who enjoys a better press now than he did then. He also made one of his greatest, and most entertaining, friends there, Ronald Canney, later an eminent surgeon who had an unsurpassable career at Canterbury Hospital.

Ronald made a habit of coming to stay when we had our annual Pony Club dance, and even at the age of eight or so I was keenly aware of the honour done to me when he asked me to dance with him. He rather played on this, as he was more than a little debonair and a touch on the arrogant side, but he took the pressure off my father whose strongest suit was definitely not dancing, and any boys that I knew at that stage in life were as leaves blown on the wind or else too uncivilised to be considered human.

Ted's 'digs' were two rooms in Chepstow Villas (shared with a great friend from Cambridge, Patrick Pringle) which was then in one of the distinctly unsalubrious areas of West London. The 1930s were intensely violent years, 'razor gangs' roamed the streets and violent crime in the cities was as commonplace as breathing. London was no exception, gang warfare (culminating in the Kray Brothers' rule of the East End in the '50s and their consequent lionisation by London's Beau Monde) was rife. Vice was rampant too, and the rooms in Chepstow Villas were sandwiched between two flats used as brothels.

"The ladies of the night could be heard pursuing their professional ends with the greatest vigour!" These were my father's very words, related to me in later life of course.

"Sometimes our nights were pretty sleepless, especially with the noise from above, and the comings and goings on the stairs. But the police left them alone most of the time. After all, prostitution isn't illegal, only soliciting, and they would have been doing that on the street or somewhere other than where they lived. The rooms were cheap though, so we couldn't really complain."

Other details of a sexual nature came to light when I was a little older, too. Part of a doctor's training must include the recognition of venereal disease: "We used to visit the women's prison at Holloway, where all the prisoners had to have a regular examination to make sure they were 'clean'. It was one of our most unpleasant duties. Personal hygiene wasn't high on the agenda for most of them."

"Were people very poor then?"

"Well, it depends what you mean by poor. The working-class areas of London certainly had enough to eat but families didn't have many pairs of shoes between them. There was Social Security, that had come in before the First World War, so basic medicine was provided, but there wasn't anything left over for entertainment or any luxuries for families if they were unemployed, which happened to a good many of them during the slump in the '30s. Nothing like as bad as in America, though."

"Did people actually go barefoot?" I asked incredulously, having seen this only in pictures or on holiday.

"Oh yes, the children mostly. Usually because the fathers spent too much on drink, but then you could hardly blame them. It was nothing like as bad as in the nineteenth century though. I always remember going to deliver a baby somewhere in the East End; the house had newspaper on the floor rather than any sort of carpet. Hygienic though. Perhaps that's why it's used for fish and chips. The baby was delivered on the kitchen table, perfectly usual then, but you had to watch out for complications. Well, this baby was a thumping ten pounds, far bigger than you normally found in those areas. The delivery took a long time, six or seven hours I should think."

"Was anyone else there to help?"

"Oh yes, the midwife, of course, and members of the family. A doctor wouldn't normally have been there, but it was part of our training to do some midwifery."

"Was everything alright in the end?"

"Well, everyone was a bit exhausted. It was a forceps delivery, as I remember, so the poor baby, a boy, had a bit of a swollen head at first, but that soon wears off. The family was so pleased, they even gave me some sort of present – can't remember what it was now. Another mouth for them to feed though, and they already had five children. I do remember that."

"What were the patients like in the hospital?"

Ted laughed at a recollection suddenly returned. "Well, outpatients was always interesting. One day a chap came in with very sore feet. His socks were stuck to them as he hadn't had a change of clothing for God knows how long. When we peeled them off, and it took two people to do it, we found that his toenails had got so long they had curved round to the point of impaction, and grown back into his feet."

I was aghast at this – Mum was fanatical about nail-cutting. "But he must have known you have to cut your nails?"

"Not necessarily. Not all parents, especially those less fortunate, tell their children these things. Poor man, he was actually terribly grateful. I think we had to admit him for a day into the hospital, so that we could get the nails cut. It was quite a difficult job, you can imagine."

Actually, I found it hard. The gaps between social classes in the '30s, and in the '50s too, were still very large; they still are today despite (or more likely because of) desperate government attempts (especially in the field of education) to bring everyone down to the same level, but such ignorance of the most basic physical routines was a real eye-opener, and for the first time I was glad of regular nail-cutting.

War was on its way by now, and at its declaration in September 1939 Ted was an officer in the Cheshire Yeomanry, well groomed for such through his cavalry pursuits at Cambridge with the OTC Cavalry Squadron. He qualified as a doctor in 1940 and transferred to the Royal Army Medical Corps. Training on Dartmoor with the Field Ambulance gave him the opportunity to hunt with Mr Spooner's Harriers, a privately owned pack, and with the South Tetcott Foxhounds whose hereditary masters were the Kings. Calls for 'Doctor, Doctor' during the heat of the chase were thought by Ted to refer to him as a newly qualified medic. "What a fool I felt when I realised that they were calling for Doctor King, who was Master then as well as being a doctor," he once said.

My father became an MA by proxy in 1941, having gained his first MB in 1934/5. By this time he was on his way to the Far East – Japan was beginning her fateful advance down the body of South-East Asia: a letter from him to Joan dated 7 December, 1941 and giving his address as c/o Lloyds Bank, Rangoon, Burma, contains a PS: 'There are rumours that the Japs have declared war, so there should be some action soon.'

2

THE DEAF DOCTOR'S WAR

'...the war in Burma is not just a magnificent story, it is a whole host of magnificent stories. Fantastic individuals are their heroes and, at times, their narrators... The Japanese say Java was their happiest station in Asia, Burma their worst; and the latter verdict might well be shared by the British soldiers who fought there. Farthest away from home, often for years at a stretch, at the end of a long and often rickety supply-line, they remained largely unnoticed by a public in the United Kingdom for whom the war was, by its very nature, remote from everyday experience... the mutual views of British and Japanese have been one of my constant intellectual preoccupations ever since.'
– From the Preface to *The Longest War* by Louis Allen – one of the very best, and best written, books on the subject, by one who was there, serving as an intelligence officer throughout, from 1941 to 1945.

The 'phoney war', so-called because there was no actual combat with the enemy, lasted some seven months, from September 1939 until April 1940, when Britain made an unsuccessful attempt to invade occupied Norway and had to evacuate the British Expeditionary Force from Dunkirk. The Battle of Britain followed in late summer, breaking the terrible tension which had attended the nation from the outset. The courage, on both sides, shown by the fighter pilots and their crews, is next to impossible to imagine, but against all the seeming odds (actually, the Germans did not have the superior numbers that we were led to believe – largely because Goering, though a brave pilot in the First World War, was incompetent when it came to administering the Luftwaffe, his main strength lying more in the area of personal display. Indeed, he and Goebbels had a mutual loathing – Goebbels disliking and distrusting ostentation, and having campaigned ceaselessly and unsuccessfully for another leader of the Lutftwaffe. As he wrote in his diary in 1945: 'Bemedalled idiots and vain perfumed coxcombs have no place in our war leadership… strut[ting] around in a silver-grey uniform) Britain survived those hot and terrifying weeks in the summer of 1940.

'We were all frightened, we were alone in the world, and Germany's invasion of most of Europe had been so rapid. How could we possibly prevail?' These were the almost universal sentiments expressed initially by those who lived through that time.

Aunt Joan married Chris Smalley early in the war. Besides being a beagler and a keen hunting man, he was also much involved with racing; his brother Dick was a Jockey Club starter for many years. Ted and he got on splendidly, and all looked set for a happy enlargement of the family. But this marriage, like so many others, was to suffer the fatal intervention of the war, and moreover the burden of Grandpa's lack of active service was to be placed squarely on my father's shoulders, as he had always felt that his own lack of military experience was something slightly disgraceful. As a doctor, Ted was to serve in the Far Eastern theatre, and then later on as a civilian doctor on the home front.

Chris's war was of a more vividly heroic hue. He was a fit man with a considerable turn of speed, and of more than average intelligence – he became one of the roughly 1,500 commandos to take part in the ill-fated raid on the harbour of St Nazaire in 1941. Of the 3,000 or so men who took part in the operation, only about a third would return, as the wooden boats sent to bring them home were mostly set on fire by the Germans. Just two men would make it back via neutral Spain and Portugal. The rest were either killed or spent the remainder of the war as prisoners of the Germans.

Chris, a member of No. 5 Commando and very quiet on the boat going over, as Chant Sempill recalled in his book, *St Nazaire Commando*, actually made it on to one of the escaping motor launches with one of his team, Robert Burtenshaw, but it was shelled in the water, as Chant actually remembered seeing. He had been one of four men under the command of the same Chant, a stockbroker in civilian life, who broke into the main pumping station and blew it up, making a successful escape through the complicated walkways just ahead of the explosion whose fuses they had laid.

Ma (Joan), in her 90s, talked of it thus: "What a marvellous way to go. I heard afterwards from one of his friends who saw him elated and rejoicing at the success of the raid just before he made his way to the boats. Mission accomplished." I could see, even so many years later, how proud she was of him. A lump in the throat was all I had to offer.

Such raids were far too costly in terms of lives and material, although they went far in boosting morale – at least, *something* was being done – and after a similar attack on Dieppe in 1942 they were discontinued. But they gave vital experience for the eventual Normandy Landings.

Sometimes very old people are surprising in their views; they can be entirely outspoken and controversial without fear of contradiction or reprimand: "Of course, they were terrorists" Ma had said, speaking of the Commandos, "at least from a German viewpoint, and they, after all, were in the driving seat." But if the raiders were classed as such they were still accorded the treatment due to prisoners-of-war: the injured were sent to hospital, and some were even congratulated by the enemy for their daring and courage, one German officer even going so far as to recommend that a boat commander should receive a Victoria Cross. Some, of course, were shot... on Hitler's orders.

It seems sad now, in view of this mutual respect, that a number of Germans met their end when *The Campbeltown* – the vessel used to ram the St Nazaire harbour gates – blew up as planned a few hours later with a number of German curiosity seekers aboard. War is no game, even at times when it seems that it might be.

A while after the National Arboretum opened in 2001, I, Ma's daughter (my cousin Margaret) and our respective husbands paid a visit and sought out Chris's memorial. Although I never knew him, and neither did my cousins of course, they have always shown a great sense of respect and affection for his memory. For my part I am so pleased that I have a corner cupboard which Chris had made and given to my father.

My father's war, the Deaf Doctor's war, began in earnest with a defective operation on his ears: "My (y)ears [it always sounded thus when he spoke of them] were very bad, and I had these openings behind them where they had operated several times for infected mastoids." The bone had healed, but the openings had to be closed to guard against infection if he was to fight an active war.

The army was desperately short of doctors, and as he qualified in 1940 he found that he was in demand as long as this operation was performed, that is. Then the unthinkable happened: though the mechanics of the operation were completed, the surgeon's knife must have 'slipped'. My father's hearing was now not just vulnerable but actually seriously damaged in that one ear, his left, which was rendered stone deaf while his right had only around half its normal hearing capacity. His state of mind after the operation can only be imagined. Having undergone a serious operation to such a sensitive organ, and no doubt having dreaded it in the first place, his reasons for dread were now fully borne out.

There was no question, in those days, of suing the surgeon, the hospital or the army for negligence (the surgery having been performed at the military hospital then at Colchester) or of refusing to go on active service, although he would legally have been entitled to do so. No, it was his duty not to complain and to cope as best he could.

The worst of all possible theatres was his destination: Burma and the jungle, with all its attendant hazards of disease, lack of all but the most basic amenities, and (most frightening of all) the Japanese. In after years, Ted told me that he saw only one Japanese taken alive, as it was the utmost dishonour for them to become prisoners – one of the reasons why allied prisoners were so shockingly maltreated; the Japanese and Korean soldiery were systematically brutalised also. One Chinese soldier in his care – the Chinese were our rather piecemeal allies, their country being riven by internal conflict between the end of Empire in 1912 and the coming of Communism in 1947 – survived despite having half his head shot away. The tolerance of pain and suffering shown by the Chinese, Koreans and Japanese made them formidable enemies or valuable allies.

The troopship left Liverpool in September 1941, bound for Calcutta and Ted's secondment from the Royal Army Medical

Corps to the Indian Army Field Ambulance (part of the 17th Indian Division). The tedium of the journey was ameliorated only by games, cards and reading. The food was poor, only to be exceeded in its mediocrity by that on the ship coming home two years later, by which time food was in very short supply, the Atlantic War against German U-Boats having yet to be won.

"We stopped in Cape Town for a couple of days," he told me. "The Suez Canal was obviously not open for business at this point, things being somewhat 'tricky' in the Mediterranean and North Africa. I stayed with some very nice English people, most hospitable. We were all billeted on families there. I didn't enjoy the rest of my stay though, apart from going up Table Mountain. The blacks were treated horribly; I saw the dockside labourers being beaten and sworn at as if they were less than animals."

An early letter written to Joan from the Officers' Mess, Royal Army Medical Corps, Rawalpindi, the Punjab, dated 26 October 1941 tells her:

I have just been posted overseas which means Malaya or the Middle East… I shall be commanding a small unit and I will be the only British officer and probably the only white man in it. I used to be rather keen on the idea of seeing the world but it looks as though I shall have had more than enough before I'm finished. Since I've been here I am supposed to have picked up the rudiments of Urdu. [The military *lingua franca* of India imposed by the Mogul emperor, Aurungzebe – the third son of Shah Jehan of Taj Mahal fame, and the last to reign before the Moguls began their decline in the face of Hindu opposition – in the seventeenth century, as an aid to efficient government, and latterly used by the British to communicate with non-English-speaking Indians. Urdu is a form of Hindi but with a strong admixture of Persian and Arabic words.] but the only word I know is *chota-peg* (whisky-and-soda) so how

I am to command a unit consisting almost entirely of chaps who don't speak English I don't know.

I had arranged to look after someone's English Thoroughbred during the hunting season [with the Rawalpindi Jackal Hounds] but now I am about to go I have had to call it off. There are, however, quite a lot of mounted units here, including one of the field ambulance, so I can usually get a horse to ride although nothing nearly as good as the one I would have had…

The beautiful Indian Countrybred, known as the Maswari horse, was entirely ignored by the British who imported Thoroughbreds and Australian Walers (so called because they came from New South Wales). The survival of the Maswari has lain in the balance since the British left India, although there are now successful campaigns to revive and strengthen the breed. They are characterised by wonderful curly ears and a most intelligent expression, as well as being ideally suited to a harsh terrain.

…Michael Johnson [from Cambridge days, who was killed later in the War] has just been staying with me, he is in the 14th/20th Hussars, Mechanised Cavalry, and seems fairly contented with his lot. I must say I do envy him being in a British regiment with white people. It was great fun seeing him after such a long time, one morning we went for a ride and his seat [his position as he sits on the horse] has improved slightly [!] as he has played a lot of polo and ridden almost every day since he has been in India.

Hunting starts next week and I hope to get a few days before leaving. They got onto a jackal while out exercising the other morning and had quite a good hunt… normally they hunt a drag [a trail] and only an occasional jackal – the foxes are all little things like rabbits and run into a hole if you start hunting them…

Indeed, I was the delighted recipient of a tale recounting the pursuit of a jackal through the hospital wing of the camp, straight through a ward to the great joy of the patients, who were much cheered, and cheering with many a *View Holloa,* thus aided in their recovery by the spectacle.

> …The post from England here is quite hopeless and I haven't received any letters posted since I left England yet.
> I wonder if there is any chance of my seeing Chris in the Middle East, but as he is meant for guerrilla warfare I expect they will keep him in England… One of the most irritating features of this place is the fact that one uses jerrys [sic] and commodes the whole time as there is no drainage system laid on, I am simply longing to sit on a decent lavatory again and have a plug to pull – that may seem odd but it is amazing how one notices little things like that.
>
> Much love, Ted.
> PS – Happy Christmas but I expect you won't get this till about February.

Some of the forebodings expressed in this letter were to be abundantly fulfilled, but the next one, written from Rawalpindi on 11 November, takes on a lighter feel as he had got his hands on some horses:

Dear Joan,
> I have been intending to write to you for ages but have been very busy recently. I am going abroad (ex-India) in a very few days in a mounted field ambulance – I managed to get in on the strength of my knowledge of horses as some of

the other officers [don't] know one end of a horse from the other so they are left entirely to me [his short Cavalry course at Weedon was standing him in good stead] – 13 horses and 30 mules. It is just like the Yeomanry all over again, the main difference being that the grooms can't talk English, so most of my instructions as to watering, feeding, grooming, etc fall on deaf ears unless I happen to have an interpreter with me. [Mr Robinson at Malvern commented to the authorities at Cambridge on Dad's weakness in languages, a difficult circumstance here.] There are only two other white men in the unit, both of whom are good fellows – one of the Indian officers is a good chap but the rest are awful – they eat with their hands, spit the bits they don't like out onto the floor, retch and belch after eating two to three mouthfuls and altogether behave in a most ungentlemanly manner. The extraordinary thing is that I'm starting to do the same things myself – after the war I shall be quite unfit to appear in polite society! When I'm eating with these chaps I try not to watch them but they fascinate me rather like a snake does a rabbit and I can't help looking at them.

I have had two days hunting with the Pindi' Drag but shan't have time for any more. They gallop flat out for one hour with one or two checks, over fairly flat country with no fly-jumping with lots of banks, nullas (dry river-beds) and terraces – the latter are not too bad when one is going up a step but rather terrifying going down as one doesn't see what the drop is like until almost on top of them – it is quite common to go up or down a sheer drop of six feet and it is pretty hard as it seldom rains. The dust is terrific and if one gets behind another horse it is like riding in a thick fog.

I have been hunting two of my troop horses which I have picked out as the best – I must say one is simply superb and with more food and exercise would be first class, five others would make good hunters, three are not *too* bad and the remaining four are awful, so I have quite a good bunch considering field ambulance usually get given rather dud horses.

Last time I heard from Mummy [the post was obviously at last coming through] Chris was at Falmouth – I wonder where he is now.

I am going to the Far East in case the Japs start, it will be very hot but quite amusing I'm told – much better than the Middle East which is very depressing. [A few years before he died I asked him if he would come with me to India to show me some of the places where he had been – "I can't think why anyone would want to go on holiday to India," he said.]

I am cabelling [sic] Mummy my address when I know it and will write you again when I get to my destination.

I am not looking forward to looking after the horses on board ship if the sea gets rough but they can't be much worse than the men [!]

Much love, Ted.

As well as an active equestrian life, his doctoring credentials had been greatly enhanced soon after his arrival in India when one day, his Commanding Officer's wife having a small son who was feeling seriously unwell, she worriedly consulted him. Ted duly examined the boy but was not much the wiser at the end of it. To be on the safe side he prescribed crushed apple, to be eaten in small quantities. Within twenty-four hours the child was right as rain and the new young doctor's reputation was in the making. Apple must be a universally recognised panacea, as its efficacy is realised in a similar way in Vassily Grossmann's Tolstoyan autobiographical novel of the Second World War, *Life and Fate*.

His next letter to Joan was written on 7 December, reverting to Lloyds Bank in Rangoon as his *poste restante*: he had been "moved to a place you'll have heard of mentioned repeatedly in one of Peter Dawson's songs". (In other words, he was no longer at liberty to say where he was stationed.) His anxiety about the lack of postal communication was clear:

I haven't yet received any letters from you since I left England – I probably shan't get any now for ages as all letters sent to Rawalpindi will have to be re-directed and I may never get them at all… I am staying here to bring the horses and mules on as they arrive by a later boat – how much longer I'll have to stay here I don't know but it is rather boring being in a large town with no one to talk to – much worse than being in the country. I met an officer I had known slightly from my Division in England last night, he is stationed about ten miles away, it is amazing how one appreciates meeting someone one has known, however slightly, in England as one can discuss people one has known at home.

… There is no hunting here as the country is too much like jungle. Although quite close to India this place [Burma] is completely different, the people are typically Eastern with slit-eyes and they all wear long skirts, not loin-cloths like the Indians. The architecture is just like the willow-pattern plate and there are lots of rickshaws everywhere. There are not many service people here like there were in 'Pindi, the Europeans are mostly civilians of rather a bourgeois type and lots of half-breeds – white, Indian and Burmese blood all mixed up.

Funnily enough I've been pretty fit since I've been out East in spite of a most unhealthy climate, unsuitable food (according to [Auntie] Katie's system) and lots of fever. I am pretty sure to get something soon as over 90 per cent of Europeans get something during their first six months and everyone who

I have heard of who came out with me has either had fever or dysentery by now. The weather here is unpleasantly hot, even at night, although it is nearly midwinter, but I'm told it is usually quite cool and should get better soon. The weather in 'Pindi when I left was just right, warmish at midday and cold enough for a fire at night.

The most pathetic thing has just happened – I am sitting writing this in my room with the door to the compound open and a tiny puppy has just hobbled in, covered with mange, lame and terribly undernourished – that is the one thing I hate about the East, they are foul to their animals. I shall keep it here tonight and take it to the S.P.C.A. tomorrow when I expect they'll put it down. Most of the towns with a large British population have things called S.P.C.A.'s run by the local gentry, nothing to do with the R.S.P.C.A. in England.

As long as the Japs continue to temporise I expect we will hang about here without much to do, but if they come in there should be a bit of action. They are more war-minded here than they are in India, they have a blackout and one sees a few tin-hats and gas-masks, which were unheard of in India.

Send me a little 'Air Mail' to the above address – I keep Lloyds informed of my whereabouts so that as long as I'm in Burma that address still holds.

Love to Chris.

Much love, Ted.

By March, 1942, Ted was writing from District Laboratory, c/o Base Postal Depot, Burma, a censored address:

The last letter I had from you was written on 12 September last so I can't remember whether I answered it or not, but even if I did I don't expect you will get the letter any more than you are likely to get this one as postal facilities here, both for sending and receiving letters, are none too good; even cabelling [sic] is no longer possible but they have started an arrangement for sending them Air Mail via India, so I am writing to everyone I can think of while the going is good because I expect that will fall through soon. It was awfully good of you to send me an Xmas present but I didn't get it as parcels aren't being delivered here [how different from the present-day war zones] – I may get it sometime after the war!!

I can't tell you any details about what's been happening to me as one has to consider this censoring, and although officers censor their own letters it isn't fair to take advantage of that and put down all sorts of stuff that one would have to censor in anyone else's letter.

I got your letter just before we moved up the line, so to speak, and although I had been recommended for laboratory work because of my deafness I spent several uncomfortable weeks scuttling about in the jungle [the worst possible environment for a deaf person] but fortunately came to no harm. At last my posting to the Laboratory came through and I was thankful to get out of it all, although I was very sad at leaving my charger [horse] who was still undamaged. Actually, with a British unit I would have managed quite well but with an Indian unit even the people who speak English speak so queerly that I can't hear what they say; of course I learned a little Urdu but only enough to tell the men a few simple things, not enough to understand them. Messing about in the jungle when one is deaf is not much cop as the visibility is so limited.

The job I'm on now is quite interesting and I was recommended for it before I left India, both because I was deaf and because I am keen on insects and worms, etc. At the moment I am learning and in about a month I will be sent somewhere else to take charge of a laboratory – the knowledge I will pick up will be invaluable to me after the war as I will be able to say that I have specialised in bacteriology.

This place is very restful with lovely scenery and a nice cool climate. In peacetime I believe it is quite gay but now it is deadly dull, but one can't expect anything else. In England when one gets a lot of soldiers stationed in a place they usually manage to get up quite amusing parties, even when there are no women, just drinking and singing songs, but here that sort of thing never seems to be done and I must say I rather miss it.

Another depressing thing is lack of letters. I've had none for weeks now and I'm afraid they have all been lost. When you write send Air Mail as ordinary mail, even when it is delivered, is taking round about five months. It is rather a grim thought that when I get back to England (if ever!) we will be getting quite old – almost middle aged I expect [of course middle age came sooner then, and no one was to know how long the war would last], and Mop and Pop will be really old. It's pretty sickening having to spend one's youth doing this sort of thing but I suppose I'm really damned lucky to be alive. I thought my hair was going gray the other day but it turned out to be merely bleached by the sun; it also started coming out in handfuls and I expected to be bald in no time but it's getting a bit thicker now, although alot [sic] comes out when I comb it. I'm also starting to loose [sic] my teeth, I had one out on the troop-ship coming over and now it looks as if another one will have to go. What with my deafness and trouble with my hair and my teeth I feel my youth slipping away. I should really like to get married before I get too old but of course I don't know anyone to marry and here one doesn't see any white women. By the time I get back to England with all my hair and teeth gone I'll have a job to get anyone to marry me!

I'm sorry to be so depressing but when one can't say much it's best just to put down what happens to be in one's head.

How's old Chris? He is lucky being in a Commando [?] although they get some pretty nasty jobs to do.

There is one bright spot on my horizon and that is that my psoriasis isn't troubling me now – I always thought that it might be better in a hot climate.

I'm wondering where this farm is that you're working on and whether you are still working on it or whether you are back at Combs. Are the old Wilsons still going, if they are give them my love, I expect Clifford is still as stupid as ever. How is Madeline Bisson – did she ever get to India? Also the Welches, I expect John has had another of those attacks by now. Also remember me to the Astells and Booths.

Now I've written such a lot I wish I'd used both sides of the paper but the writing shows through rather. Using another piece will make the letter rather bulky and I haven't enough to say to cover it completely so will finish off on the back of this.

Hoping all the animals are behaving themselves.

Give my love to Chris when you see him.

Much love, Ted.

PS – Write to the above address as it is the best I can give and when I move I'll try and get them to forward my mail.

This letter must have been written while he was at Mandalay, before going up to the front at Moulmein. By now the Japanese invasion of South-East Asia was in full swing, and the necessary retreat, which involved traversing the Irrawaddy, Salween, Ye, Chindwin and Bilin Rivers, sometimes with the horses and mules on rafts and sometimes swimming – Ted had made sure that they could swim in the moat which surrounded the fort at Mandalay – was hazardous in the extreme and sometimes conducted so close to the Japanese that even he could hear them shouting *Tommy! Tommy! Where* [are] *you Tommy!* He accidentally shot himself in the foot during the journey and had to be carried on a litter by helpful Naga hill tribesmen for the better part of three days, unaccompanied by any of his countrymen. Despite his fears that he might somehow suffer further harm at their hands – they spoke no English, of course – they proved staunch allies and delivered him safely at the other end.

The British promised the Nagas independence at the end of the war, which remained undelivered and does so to this day, as they continue their fight against the Burmese government. Nevertheless, they are, unbelievably, pro-British and still somehow revere us for the part that we played in the war against the Japanese.

The retreat through the jungle was accompanied by terrible hunger, so bad that at times another man's rations would be covetable even at the contemplated expense of his life – it never actually quite came to that, but rice and melon were the staple foods, and not much of those unless they came across a friendly village. So great was Ted's consequent aversion to melon that I never remember our eating it at home.

Lower Burma, and Maymyo in particular, provided a temporary safe haven, where he was put in charge of the No. 2 Burma Field Laboratory, diagnosing malaria, dysentery and other tropical diseases. During this period he made what he described as a number of important natural history observations. 'Notes on the Hunting Wasp, the Dung Beetle and the Tree Ant' were published in 1975 in *The Proceedings of the Cotteswold Naturalists' Field Club*.

In an account written for the Burma Star Association in its magazine, *Dekho* (see appendix) Ted explained how he and his men 'dug trenches to dive into when enemy planes were overhead. Normally an officer would give the order to go into the trenches. I couldn't hear the planes until it might have been too late, so one of my sergeants acted as my ears. When any of my men wanted a break from whatever they were doing the sergeant would shout "Aeroplane, Sahib!" whether there was an aeroplane overhead or not.' Thus was born the soubriquet, 'Deaf Doctor'.

By the end of June he was back in India as a patient in a British Military Hospital in the United Provinces, having at last had a bad bout of cerebral malaria, especially serious as his hearing was put at further risk by the fact that quinine, which has an adverse effect on the auditory nerve, was the only available treatment.

His letter to Joan, dated the 27 June, reads thus:
I was most terribly worried to hear that Chris was missing – I expect by the time you get this you'll know the worst; it is impossible for me to express on paper how sorry I am for you.

I've had none too pleasant a time and I'm afraid a number of my friends have been killed. I arrived in India with nothing but what I was wearing and a small pack after the most ghastly march through the jungle and over the hills from Burma. I started carrying quite a lot but got so exhausted that I had to throw nearly everything away except food and water. We were on very short commons, a small handful of rice per day and tea without milk or sugar; so that when I got back to India I was so thin that I had a job keeping my trousers up. At the moment it's a case of 'I've been very poorly but now I feel prime', as soon after arrival in India I got malaria pretty badly, that took off another couple of stone so now I am a mere wraith but feeling quite fit. In two days I go up to the hills for a month's leave so should get pretty fit again. After that I've no idea where I shall be sent and hope it will be somewhere fairly congenial. My address for the present had better be c/o Lloyds Bank, Rawalpindi, but I don't expect ever to go back there and don't particularly want to. I rather think I'm going to Poona but am not sure. This hospital is very comfortable and it is wonderful having baths and clean sheets after weeks of sleeping and hardly ever washing.

I've been out today for the very first time and managed to walk a few hundred yards, even though my legs are so thin they look quite ridiculous.

It was an experience seeing the 'seamy side' of war but I can't say I'm itching to be involved in another campaign yet awhile.

When I get out of here I'll send one of those aerograph letters which are all the rage just now, I believe they only take a fortnight.

It is maddening losing all one's stuff, I'm starting over again from scratch and gradually accumulating a wardrobe, but losing all my books really gets me down. I've lost nearly all my 21st birthday presents, a watch given to me by Scan [one of our Syrian relations from the formation of the business in Manchester], field-glasses by Edith and a flask by Freda, really sickening, but as I was fortunate to get away with my skin I shouldn't complain.

The whole way I wore those boots I bought to wear with leggings for my first day's hunting in Cheshire, just about ten years ago now. By the time I'd finished they were dropping to bits so I've thrown them away.

The heat of an Indian summer on the plains is inconceivable, how white men exist at all I can't think; it was like that here when I first arrived but now the monsoon has started and it is cooler.

It simply beats me how anyone can choose to spend their lives out East, but there are lots of tea and rubber planters, Indian Civil Service and Indian Army people who do it for preference – it really seems quite incredible to me; when there is a war on one puts up with it, but lots of these people live here in peacetime (like old Percy), [he of Lady Willingdon fame]; I certainly think they are awful fools.

I haven't yet got accustomed to Indians, they still give me the creeps and I'm afraid always will do, although I've met one or two admirable ones, but they are few and far between...

Colonel Sir Ransiji Kursiji, a Parsee (a high caste of Persian origin from the time of the Mughal invasions) was one, and I remember as a small child going with him and my parents to watch the polo at Cirencester. He would have been a King's Commissioned Indian Officer (KCIO), Sandhurst trained as part of the 'Indianisation' programme which was begun in the early twentieth century. These officers were distinct from the Indian Commissioned Officers (ICOs), Dehra Dun trained, who again were distinct from the Viceroy Commissioned Officers (VCOs), who were equivalent to the British Army Warrant Officer, and who directly officered the companies and squadrons of Indian Army regiments.

> I must make a superhuman effort and learn Hindustani properly so that I can shout at the beastly fellows. My vocabulary at the moment is extremely limited, 'come, go, bring me a glass of beer' and 'be quick' are about the only things I can say, apart from alot [sic] of horse jargon which I'm quite good at. I can't ask a chap where the pain is or anything to do with doctoring so that when I have to doctor these chaps they get rather a raw deal! It's really very like being a vet, just a matter of pummelling [sic] them all over until they let out a howl of pain.
> It was really rather comic when I was at the front and had to deal with Burmese casualties, I had to work through

a whole string of interpreters, one to translate Burmese to Hindustani and another to translate Hindustani to English as there were no people who spoke Burmese and English. There was a poor chap with a broken back and I wanted to know when he'd last passed water; I got my string of interpreters going and after a good half-hour's palaver they came to the conclusion that the question was too complicated so I never found out when he last passed water.

If I start another page it will cost the hell of a lot to send Air Mail owing to excess weight so I will send an airograph letter soon.

Much love, Ted.
PS – Tell Daddy I haven't forgotten today is his birthday.

Some two weeks later, while on leave, he wrote from the Royal Hotel at Naini Tal up in the hills:

I'm writing a whole spate of letters while on leave and I suppose it really is a waste of money as they will probably all arrive together and might as well have been sent in the same envelope, but eight annas here or there is a mere drop in the ocean when contrasted with the amount of cash I am getting through at this place; spent on clothes, etc, as well as drink, etc. Actually I am never going to have as many clothes as I had before going to Burma, as I shall probably only loose [sic] them again – alot [sic] of people here have lost their stuff three or four times since the war started, but each time they've become wiser and had less to loose [sic].

The similarity of my case to the man in that old gramophone record is rather extraordinary. [Not sure which song he is referring to here.] I met a chap last night who was on our draft coming out and who I had not seen since disembarkation. He looked at me hard, and before even saying 'hello' he said 'Christ, you must have lost at least three stone.' It didn't make me feel cast down as I know I look pretty ghastly but I'm rapidly getting normal again.

I can't remember whether I mentioned it in my last letter, but while in hospital I had some clothes made as I had to have something to wear; probably I forgot to have them made loose so that now I am regaining my normal dimensions they are getting too tight and soon will be unwearable unless I have them altered. I keep a check on the size of my legs by a pair of riding-breeches I managed to rescue from Burma – they have lace-up extensions and I know exactly how far they will lace up really tight, under normal conditions the bottom part won't quite meet. When they get to this stage I shall know that it is safe to be measured for a pair of jodhpurs.

There are lots of hirelings [horses for hire] here, but most of them are pretty good wrecks with about every fault one can think of and just about as unsound as they could be. I have ridden once or twice with another chap who is keen, on carefully selected horses which show least defects, but even they are pretty poor and we usually feel so sorry for them that we get off and walk at all the hills (up and down) and as this country is mostly hills I'm beginning to think it is hardly worth going out at all!

When I get to a fairly permanent job I shall buy a horse as I am likely to remain in India for the rest of the war for two reasons, first owing to the situation – defence of India and all that, second because I am 'Home Service' now because of my ears, and India counts as home for that purpose.

I sent Mop [Granny or possibly Old Auntie Edith] an airograph letter about a week ago just before I came here. I was about nine days at a very dull but very pleasant hill station after leaving hospital, then came on here where it is more expensive but plenty of gaiety if one likes to indulge in it, also better food and drink; I shall probably stay here till the end of the month when my leave expires.

I am still hoping Chris may be alive and should naturally like to know one way or the other as soon as you know. You know how terribly sorry I am about the whole business for your sake, as well as being fond of Chris myself. However I won't indulge in a lot of sentimentality. [That's how people got through, although it could make them emotionally challenged and quite difficult to deal with.]

Much love Ted.

His next letter, dated some four weeks later, though written c/o Lloyds Bank, Rawalpindi, in fact found him still up in the hills at Naini Tal:

I was delighted to get your P.C. It is the first written communication I have had in answer to letters I have written since returning from Burma, a cabel [sic] came from Mum a few days before your card. It came [the P.C.] very well as I got it on the 8th and it had been forwarded from 'Pindi so it can only have taken just over three weeks to get to India. Air Mail letters I'm afraid take much longer but I like getting them and writing them as one can say so much more.

I have not been to 'Pindi as you suppose but merely use the Bank as an address as I have my account there. I am still up in the hills at Naini Tal, I should have gone back to work several days ago but I had a recurrence of malaria so I am not going for another two days…

My maternal grandfather, Colonial Secretary in the Federated Malay States in the 1930s, continued to contract bouts of malaria into his old age while living at Leamington Spa – something which never happens now as long as you take the appropriate drugs as directed.

...I go to Lucknow, which I'm told is quite a good place but terribly hot during September when the rains stop, and a little cooler in October and usually cold during the winter months. There is jackal-hunting there during the winter and all the usual amenities so it shouldn't be too bad, but of course I may not stay there long; but will be somewhere in India for some time now. In fact I shall be in India until the end of the war unless I get very fed up with it, in which case I shall tell the whole truth about my ears and get sent back to England. That would seem rather a cowardly thing to do but I reckon I've done enough considering all my ailments and shan't hesitate to get home if I get really fed up with it all.

I've had a very enjoyable time up here and met some very nice people, I must say I prefer the non-military families to the regular army ones; the latter, with a few exceptions, are pretty impossible and fancy themselves enormously, I get the greatest amusement out of playing up to their snobbishness and then telling them that I'm all for trade and the lower middle class!

There was one quite nice regular I met who suffered from the usual regular army snobbishness – he is in the Indian Medical Service and a nephew of Hugh Meynell, name of Walker. He knows the Meynell people [meaning members of the Meynell Hunt] very well and was most amusing about all the scandal and loose-living which goes on among them.

I'm sorry you've no news of Chris, but there is still hope that he may be all right.

I think it is a very good show on your part sticking to that farming job, it must be terribly hard work but I expect you will get some respite after harvest. I suppose poor old Pop stays at the Queen's [in Manchester], actually he's damned lucky to be able to get out to Radway and I wouldn't be surprised if they stopped his petrol allowance. [Grandpa was still working in Manchester during the week.]

Have the Bissons still got Valley House? I wonder if Henry and Bill Astell are still in the land of the living. This war really is awful and I have very little to complain of really, having survived one campaign with the prospect of a fairly peaceful job in the near future.

The rain here is rather depressing and has been exceptionally heavy this year. My bedroom roof leaks and as I write I am surrounded by jerries catching the drips; I have to move my bed about to avoid the drops as new leaks develope [sic].

I hope you can read this writing on both sides of thin paper, but one might as well make these Air Mail letters as light as light as possible.

There really is very little else to say, except to enquire about all the members of the family – Katie and Beryl [a first cousin] and Guy [her husband] and Midget [Uncle Arthur, Pop's brother], etc. As you don't know any of the people out here its [sic] not much good talking about them. [I'm not sure about this, but there is nothing more boring than a long conversation about who said what to whom when you've never met the people concerned.] The manager of this hotel and his wife are a charming couple and come from Bury of all places, he loves talking to me about Manchester! There are lots of people here from Lancs. [Lancashire] and most of them are pretty common I must say.

All this Congress business (Ghandi [sic] and all that) gets on my nerves, the papers are always full of it and it is so absolutely absurd as the Indians aren't even capable of controlling themselves, let alone ruling a difficult country like India. They really are horrible people and will never do anything unless there is money in it. I have several times seen Indians (mostly beggars) lying on pavements or railway platforms dying of some filthy disease and not one of their countrymen attempt to help them, as there would be no money in it; they merely walk past and even step over them and only bother to remove them after they have died; that sort of thing just about typifies the Indians' outlook on life – never bother to do a decent act unless there is money in it. If it weren't for the war it would be a good thing to let them rule their damned country and see what a mess they would make of it. I bet they would start murdering each other and bribing all the Government officials straightaway.

Well, you certainly can't accuse Ted of any attempt to understand the Indians and their fatalistic approach to matters of life and death, but of course, with the help of a disastrous Partition plan, hurried along by Attlee and put into operation by the opportunistic Mountbatten against all advice on the ground, much of what he said came about. In 1952 the first Indian general election saw one polling station visited only by hyenas and tigers.

When you next write send me some snapshots of yourself and the animals etc as I should love to have some. I asked Mum to do the same. Also write a good long letter.

Much love, Ted.

P.S. I address all your letters to Radway as I'm never certain whether you will still be at Millers Dale. Do you hear anything about St. Anselm's through Jo's child?

My initials aren't E.A. but E.H. – E.A. are Midget's initials.

The final extant letter to Joan was written at the beginning of November, 1942:

Dear Joan,

I think I last wrote to you from Assam about a month ago and since then have had a letter written in July and a P.C. in August. Soon after my last letter my ear went all wrong so I'm now back at the same hospital I was in last June; I damned nearly went to hospital at Lucknow where Betty is now night sister on the Officers' Ward, I'm rather glad I didn't as it would have been rather a strain for us being on strictly professional terms so to speak. This place (Bareilly) is only a few hours down the line from Lucknow so that letters only take one to two days, which is a bit better than when I was in Assam where they took anything up to three weeks. I don't think they'll send me back there as the ear specialist here took a pretty poor view of my ear and talked about invaliding me out altogether, which I would have almost agreed with a few months ago but I hope to God they don't do it now as it might be awkward getting Betty back to England, although she would automatically be sent back as my wife I suppose – not that we're married yet but we reckon to be pretty soon. No, I think I talked him out of that and I hope to get a job in the Punjab, which is dry as a bone and agrees with my ear – it is the intense damp in Assam which seems to affect it.

A letter from you has just arrived since I started this, dated Aug. 20, the day after you'd sent the P.C. Many thanks for it, I simply love getting your letters and I was damned lucky to get this one at all as you always put them in such flimsy envelopes, the envelope had come to bits and of course the snaps you mentioned had dropped out – I really was damned annoyed as I want snaps so much to show Betty. Do use better quality envelopes in future – I think you must feel sufficiently ticked off after all this. Actually Ma sent one you had taken of her and Pop on the way back from Norway – that one with Pop's face obliterated [!]

Yes, it's a shocking business about poor old Chris and as you say so awful not knowing what's happened to him and imagining that he's going through absolute hell. You have all my sympathy and I feel pretty bad about it myself as I always liked him so much and admired him too. However he may turn up yet. [They were obviously imagining that he may have been taken prisoner.]

I must say I rather envy you your present mode of existence [sic], working hard must help you to keep your mind off less pleasant things and as you say, its [sic] to see something for one's pains. I agree also about too much society being a bore, I got terribly lonely in Burma when I was surrounded by Indians and had hardly any white people to talk to, but the social life in the Indian stations is rather oppressive and I feel I want to escape from it all, but one can't escape here as even the hill stations are worse still. Betty has exactly the same attitude which is fortunate.

I was sorry to hear about Bob but quite see your point, the chap might sell him back to you if you wanted if things improve but things aren't likely to improve for a bit. [I think that they are talking about a horse here.]

Why the hell isn't Edwin in the army?

I can't quite agree with you about beagling and hunting, if the latter is stopped after the war I'm afraid I will feel there's a bit of a blank to fill...

Plus ça change – a ban was being discussed even then, and there was angry protest from hunting people outside Parliament in 1947, led by Leonard Bennett, father of Roger (a stalwart of the North Cotswold Hunt) and grandfather of Edward the actor who took over the part of Hamlet while understudying for David Tennant at the end of 2009, something of a *tour de force*. Leonard, as a keen hunting campaigner from Upton-on-Severn, founded the Piccadilly Hunt Club which was instrumental at this time in preventing a hunt ban.

…A good show Bill Astell getting a D.F.C. – congratulate Pat for me if you see him – is Henry still alive and kicking? Betty must be getting quite grown up now.

Your friends certainly seem to be reproducing themselves, of course I remember Mary Freston saying she'd breed like a rabbit! You never told me what happened about Pen Russel's offspring – she was 'carrying' as Bob Mainwaring would say, when I last saw her and there was some talk about twins.

What's Madeleine's fiance's name? You never know I might run into him – even India seems a very small place the way one keeps meeting people.

I'm glad you're not sending me a parcel as these things tend to get lost and I never got the one you sent me last Xmas. In any case we've got a damned sight more of everything out here than you have at home and it's really my place to send you something – I know Betty is sending things home but I'm afraid I'm too lazy.

Now the winter approaches it's getting beautifully cool here and it's cold enough to sleep under a blanket at night, we'll be having fires in the evenings soon. I must say it does make a difference, I'm afraid I don't take to the heat at all, it makes me feel quite faint and its [sic] bad enough sitting about and trying to sleep but when one has to work right through the heat of the day its [sic] absolute hell.

Mail is coming through pretty well now, although Air Mails are taking a little over two months and airographs a month. Apart from yours I've had stacks of letters from

Mummy, a very good one from Ronald, one from Mrs Baxter and airographs from Mummy, Mrs Hay, Katie and Edith [Dad's aunt and Pop's sister] – not bad. I've answered all except Ediths [sic] which only came this morning – it was rather extraordinary all about what they are going to do with Peggy – she seems to be rather a problem child and Edith seems to have it on her mind rather!

I'm longing for you and Betty to meet – you'll simply love her I know. We have pretty well the same tastes and ideas but she's not really like me apart from that she's a bit temperamental I think, but she's not been like that with me yet! Anyway we're ideally suited and I'm certain always will be. I must say I count myself damned lucky because as you know, I'm rather an extraordinary bird, and I can't really think that if I hadn't met her I'd ever have met anyone else I wanted to marry, or who wanted to marry me which is far more important, I can't really think why she does as I'm a bit of a wreck with my haggard appearance (I look at least 35 now after all this malaria – 3 attacks in last 4 months) and my deafness; but she most certainly does so thats [sic] that. She gets alot [sic] of amusement out of my stories of what we used to do when we were kids at Styal and I think she knows the family pretty well from my description by now, I know she'll love you and Mummy and I expect she'll get used to Pop – I suppose its [sic] rather a shame to talk about Pop like that because he really is a jolly good person. I've told her she mustn't paint her nails red when he's anywhere about…

When I was about eight or nine, I remember Grandpa quizzing me as to how much or little work I did as my hands had no callouses on them!

…I haven't met her brother yet as I missed him by a few days by having to be sent down here – he sounds quite a good chap and I think is more or less resigned to having cotton in the family!

Mummy mentioned the possibility of their living in Combs if Pop couldn't get gas for the car, but the latest scheme seems to be for him to cycle to Leamington and get a train there.

I suppose I ought to wish you a happy Xmas etc – I imagine you'll try and get to Radway though I quite understand you not wanting to stay there permanently. You might mention the happy Xmas business to Mop and Pop as I clean forgot about it when I wrote to both of them a few days ago and my next letter probably won't get [to] them till the new year.

Betty and I are getting married at the very first opportunity which may occur in a matter of days if I get sick-leave on quitting this place, and in any case I expect we'll be married by the time you get this. If I get a job in a civilised station in India which I feel I ought after all this hoo-hah about my ear, we'll be able to live together complete with horse and dog – she has a grand little fox-terrier. However I'm not banking on that as one can never tell what they're going to do with one in the army, one moment they talk of invaliding you out and the next they're sending you up to the N.E.F. [North-East Frontier] to argue with the Japs.

Do write to Betty and enclose it in one of mine and I'll hand it on like. [A bit of 'Lancashire' creeping in there!]

Much love, Ted.

Ted and Betty did not marry. It must have been only a matter of days after this last letter was written when she told him that his deafness, with no possibility of any alleviation, would be too much for her to cope with. The exact circumstances of the break-up are unknown, but it sealed Ted's fate as far as India was concerned. He had a minor breakdown, became ill again not just from malaria but heartbreak too, and was invalided home the following year. The boat stopped at Port Said as the Suez Canal was by then open again: "What a God-forsaken place," he told me. "Nothing really there but a port and a lot of undernourished people. And the food on-board the ship was by then really poor – a monotonous diet of tinned meat, nothing much fresh at all. The blockade by the Axis powers, not just Germany, saw to that."

His face tight with emotion, he told me of the return into Liverpool: "Never was I so glad to see a place, even one so dreary. We all hung over the ship's rail in silence, and I'm not ashamed to say it, with a sob or two." His homecoming to Radway consisted of a greeting from Pop – "Ah, good" – from behind a newspaper, not even lowered for the occasion.

Dreams of spending the rest of the war in relative comfort with a decent job (and a far better lifestyle than in wartime Britain) and in the arms of a loving wife, and in the company of a dog and a horse, had been shattered. Instead it was spent working in various hospitals in the north, and in Birmingham and Oxford, as an immunologist and later as a pathologist, easier as good hearing was not a requirement, but morbid in the extreme as post-mortems were a major part of the practice and refrigeration was far from the perfect thing that it is now.

Betty Swann remained in a little corner of his heart I know. She married a man called March by whom she had two sons, but the marriage did not last. I can remember her visiting Bourton Far Hill, much to my mother's almost undisguised fury, which was made all the more extreme when she discovered that my father had been helping Betty financially, she having been left badly off after her divorce. 'Cotton in the family' was not such a bad idea after all. But for all that, I don't blame her for either

her calling off of the engagement – she was honest after all – or for her requests for help, as Ted must have been complicit, and it is no fun at all to be broke with two children in tow. He could afford it, after all.

I met her several times when I was small, together with her two boys. Vivian's imagination fevered with the conviction that some *mésalliance* involving me and the younger of Betty's two boys, Michael, was being planned – a sort of seduction at second-hand. I was no more than ten years old and thought Michael a useless creature, as I did all boys then; she had no need to worry. Betty was small and pretty, without my mother's reflective beauty, but she and Ted might well have made for an easier pairing in different circumstances. When my father was an old man and my mother had died, he and Betty would meet for lunch. Then he became ill just before the end.

"Send him my *sala'ams*," she said. "He'll know what I mean."

I did, and he smiled. *Sala'am aleycum* was the greeting used by the Indian Moslem soldiery and by all Arabic speakers – meaning 'peace be unto you'.

3

A MARRIAGE

'If they be two, they are two so
As stiff twin compasses are two,
Thy soul the fixt foot, makes no show
To move, but doth, if the other do.'
– John Donne (1572–1631)

My parents met on the hunting field, a common enough meeting ground for prospective spouses of their time and background, although I have always regarded it as the ultimate cliché, having never met anyone remotely prospective out hunting until I met my husband during the thrill of the chase.

This was 1947; my mother was living in Chipping Campden, the most attractive of all the Cotswold wool towns, with her Aunt Violet, in fact an older cousin. Living with her parents at Pebworth on the way to Stratford-on-Avon, and later in Leamington Spa, had proved unsatisfactory. My maternal grandfather, Alwyn Sidney Haynes, was far from a generous father, refusing to buy her a longed-for horse so that she might go hunting. She had been used to riding up to seven horses in a day with the Pytchley before the war, when she had shown horses to prospective customers for the renowned horse dealer Cyril Darby at Hill Norton near Rugby. Those not sold in the hunting field would be ridden through the streets from London's King's Cross Station to the Tattersalls sale ring, then at Knightsbridge Green.

Grandpa, though not rich, had bought back the manor which had been sold out of the family some twenty years before, and led a comfortably self-important life as Chairman of the Warwickshire Bench, amongst other occupations which included composting. His pre-war retirement (he had first gone to Malaya in 1901) from the Colonial Secretaryship of the Federated Malay States (present-day Malaysia) had been a disappointment to him – he always maintained that it was only my grandmother's German background which had prevented him from getting the top job of Governor, which was filled by Sir Cecil Clementi. He and my grandmother had met when Grandpa had gone to Germany to learn the language, as so many people did in that time before the First World War when Britain and Germany enjoyed the closest of social and familial relationships.

Alma Maria Susanna Legler was born in Dresden, into a German/Polish family (it was often hard to tell which in those confused times of constant border changes). She was the daughter of Dr Hugo Legler (who had been the Assistant Librarian at Windsor Castle during the reign of Victoria) and Alma Minckwitz (whose noble family were prominent in the service of the Kings of Saxony). Granny's country of birth was such an adverse factor, as war had now been declared, that she had had to pretend to a Dutch rather than a German accent on the boat going out to Malaya. She probably suffered from depression for much of her life, and it is safe to say that the advent of Hitlerian power in 1933 was truly traumatic for her: "I can't believe it, I won't believe it, it must be the end," she would constantly reiterate, breaking into perspiration, as one of those ranting speeches blared from the wireless. Neither was she helped by the separation from her children necessitated by colonial life; Mum was 'exiled' from Malaya and Kuala Kangsar (where she was born) when she was five years old, never to return, so that she saw her parents only during their six months leave every three years. Her younger brother Henry and older sister Evelyn were a little more fortunate (Evelyn even returning to Malaya when a young woman, as a member of the 'fishing fleet' in an unsuccessful search for a suitable husband). Although many young people were in the same isolated situation and appeared to be little affected, my mother bore a lifetime's sadness because of it. In later years she would never see me off at the station; it reminded her too much of sad childhood farewells.

She would often tell me of her just remembered childhood in Malaya: of the much-loved servants who mysteriously spent hours 'preparing the rice', not the easy process that it is now; of Nadhi San, the dignified chauffeur who frequently took the children and their mother to shop in the markets or to visit friends, and who called my mother 'Missie Bibyans', of Grandpa playing polo on his beloved ponies, Kelantan and Lady Bruce; of the occasions when a Malay person or people went *latta,* a sort of frenzy with undisclosed causes, possibly drug-related. I think she had an unassuaged longing to see Malaya again, and stored up her memories as if they were treasures in a chest, to be brought out and shown only to a select few.

A revealing account in the 'London Letter' by Jimmy Glover in the *Sunday Tribune* (Malaya) of 12 December 1948 shows both how much Grandpa loved the Malaya which he had by now left, and how obsessed he was with his own persona. He did not even refer to Granny's death the previous year although the interview was being given so that he might talk of his daughter's marriage the week before. The interviewer received scant information on his own admission, save that my mother was born in Kuala Kangsar, instead being treated to a potted autobiography of Grandpa – his British Residency in Kelantan (he named one of his polo ponies after the place), his nickname of 'Snipe' (he had an exceptionally long nose), the disastrous floods of 1926 and the consequent building of the dam on the Perak River to provide electricity for that state. He was a strong proponent of 'Malaya for the Malays', decrying Attlee's postwar policy of allowing the immigrant Chinese to take over the reins of business (the Malays were indolent in comparison): "Dirty work, Mr Attlee, dirty work," he had admonished him. An admirable attitude towards the people he had loved and served so devotedly; how much he would probably have wanted, in an ideal world uninterrupted by war, to have remained there for the rest of his life.

In his personal life though, as with so many eminent men, I can safely say that Alwyn Sydney Haynes CMG, JP was as self-absorbed a person as one would be likely to meet in an entire lifetime. Without even a vestige of humour, he ground my poor grandmother into the dust despite his devotion to her (my mother always insisted that Granny died young because of his treatment of her) and then proceeded to do the same to Auntie Evelyn, who eventually looked after him, having failed to subjugate Vivian. Granny was beginning her descent into invalidity through multiple sclerosis and Vivian was expected to help look after her, thus saving money. "It was an event for me even to walk to the post-box a mile or so away, when we lived at Pebworth. I just had to get away. Poor Granny, I shouldn't have left her. She was so ill and she went downhill so fast. I think that the bombing of Dresden [in early 1945, her beloved home] really did for her." And so Vivian made her escape to ever-loving Aunt Violet, who lived as a spinster in one of the most enchanting houses imaginable, the last in Campden to be lit by gas.

The war had taken its toll: "I was very ill towards the end," my mother told me as a child. "Living in a dormitory [serving with the Field Ambulance Nursing Yeomanry] didn't suit me at all. I slept badly and became so depressed. One day I was driving Sir Ernest Swinton [the general credited with the invention of the tank in the First World War, and the ancestor of Tilda Swinton the renowned actress]. I remember he looked hard at me as we drove off and asked, 'What's the matter with you, my dear?' I must have looked terrible, I certainly felt it. I told him how badly I was sleeping, and then do you know, I just burst into tears, as we were driving along. No one had asked me anything about myself for so long that I think I was almost in a state of shock. He was so kind, even lent me his hankie so that I could dry my eyes. He told me, by way of consolation, that sleep was not the important thing, at least not so much as lying down and having your feet on a level with your heart. I've never forgotten that, whether it's true or not. He'd been through the Great War, the trenches and all that, so he must have had some idea I suppose." I pondered this, and have always tried to remember it myself when sleep is slow to come.

The sheer boredom and loneliness of much of service life hit Vivian very hard. Working with people who you would not choose to work with in normal circumstances may be character building, but the impossibility of escape or change must have been especially difficult for one without an easy temperament. A broken romance with a Free Polish airman probably did not help. Illness came as something of a blessing, and the payment of her War Gratuity at the war's end meant that she could at last afford a horse, whose name was Rhythm. A bay mare, almost Thoroughbred and standing just under 16hh, she had been ill treated in her youth and had a chronic dislike of men; she would not allow my father anywhere near her for a long time after they first met. But her bond with my mother was absolute, and they enjoyed some five seasons' hunting before a weak heart turned her towards maternal duties and the bearing of three foals.

She was stabled in the yard at the back of the Noel Arms in Campden's high street, under the care of Roger Leadley-Brown, a charming, impecunious ex-public school boy who preferred the care and the company of horses to any other way of life. He rented the yard and kept a livery stable, and he and my mother enjoyed each other's company and shared a love of horses. "We used to sit in the tack room and play cards with the chaps that hung around there," she told me. "There was no electricity so we used the old stable lanterns."

"Just like *Black Beauty*, it must have been," I said, recalling the lovely stable scenes at Birtwick Hall where John Manly and James Howard led the devoted lives of grooms, and always seemed, in my childish imagination, to have a stable lantern in hand.

"Yes, just like *Black Beauty* darling, agreed my mother. It was such fun, the whole thing." She was happy then, almost for the first time in her life I think. A brief wartime engagement to Brian Spurgin, a Wimbledon tennis player, had ended in his death in action. "Roger was a darling and so good-looking too. But poor as a church mouse. I don't really know how he managed at all." She looked wistful for a moment. I remembered him in later years, funny and still very good-looking, a chain-smoker with the best of them, and absolutely one of my favourite grown-ups; he worked as head groom for the Binneys at nearby Kiftsgate, the home of the Kiftsgate Rose.

Fun too was the bedrock of Elsa Marland's life. Elsa and her husband Sandy lived in a large house which he had recently built at the back end of Campden. They were rich, Elsa's family had made a fortune out of pharmaceuticals in Glasgow, and

Sandy was not short of a bob or two either. Dad would come and stay at weekends to go hunting, from Roger's yard. Meeting Vivian was thus inevitable.

Inevitable too was the Saturday night dinner party. "Who shall we ask?" demanded Elsa, keen always on as much festivity as she could muster.

"Vivian, why not?" must have come Sandy's reply. The rest followed as night follows day, as a hunting field encounter blossomed into full-blown romance.

Elsa was an enhancement to many people's lives and a perfect counter-balance to the dry Sandy. She laughed at life, even at the end while enduring agonising bone-cancer. I must have been about ten when we went to see her for the last time. She lay in bed, unable to move without help, but still strong of voice: "Darlings, how marvellous to see you. Here I am, at death's door, as you see."

Never one to mince words, and brave as they come. She laughed, and delighted in the gossip which was fed to her: "Joan Crotty, carrying all before her as usual, I trust." Joan was similar in shape to Humpty Dumpty – we couldn't help laughing. Elsa's practical joking was legendary; the staid folk of Chipping Campden were once much put about on the night of Hallowe'en by a wailing banshee with a sheet over its head and carrying a lantern – Elsa, of course.

The local doctor on another occasion was surprised to find that all his patients' urine samples had been replaced by cider, rather a plus you might think – Elsa, again. Her death was a real loss to so many people, as her life had been an example to them. Shortly afterwards, the family home, which she had made so vibrant, burnt down and Sandy and their five children moved away from Campden.

My father and mother were married on 6 November 1948 in the wonderful Perpendicular church at Chipping Campden, one of the most resplendent churches in the Cotswolds, built on the back of the wool trade. A reception followed at the Cotswold House Hotel, which still exists, and they honeymooned on Dartmoor, taking the irresistible opportunity for a few days' hunting before returning to the workaday world of London and a married life built around busy medical practice in a London hospital.

"I hated it really," my mother told me. "I was bored and lonely, I had never lived in London, and I knew very few people there. We lived in Spring Street, near Paddington Station, in a crumby little flat. At least it was close to the park [Hyde Park], so I spent a good deal of time walking and feeding the birds."

"Why didn't you get a job?" I asked. Even at my tender age I knew that women had at least some employment opportunities.

"I honestly don't know," she replied. "I could have done secretarial work I suppose, but it wasn't really the done thing, and not when you were married to a professional man. It might almost have reflected badly on him, as if his wife needed to work for the money. It was all very odd, when women had worked their socks off during the war, that we were supposed to go back to how we were before, in the '30s. I think I was just very tired too, and my back [my mother's spine had had curvatures since her girlhood] was sometimes very painful. I had to wear a brace a lot of the time."

"But you must have had some fun?" I was attempting to inject some hope into this rather dull conversation.

"Oh, of course we did," she said, suddenly brightening. That was the thing about my mother – her mood could change as fast as a shadow speeding across the grass. "I remember once we'd been out to some club or other, and Dad was frightfully tight [such a good word for drunk] and we were all in the kitchen at the flat – Uncle Patrick, Uncle Ken, Ronald [for some reason never an 'Uncle'], Dudley Ryder [later the Earl of

Harrowby, an indecisive suitor, who hung around a good deal seeking advice and blessings upon his romantic designs] can't remember who else – but anyway he started just cracking eggs all over the floor, quite on purpose, instead of putting them in the pan. We must all have been the worse for wear as we thought it completely hilarious, never thought about the mess until the next day."

I found this rather endearing, but a bit pointless to my childishly serious mind, and somehow hard to imagine, as my childhood was spent in the keen pursuit of tidiness which came quite naturally, and my father would no more have dreamed of breaking eggs upon the floor of the kitchen at Bourton Far Hill than flying to the moon. He would have been in trouble with Mrs Leathers the cook for one thing, and for another, such waste would have been regarded as intolerable. Sometimes, parents are just incomprehensible.

Mac Cope, a brilliantly clever friend of my father's from schooldays, would definitely not have found such doings amusing. He was distinctly lacking in humour, and seemed to me to be in a permanent state of anxiety; his main claim to fame in my eyes was that he was married to Hilka, a hugely glamorous Finn with bright golden hair worn up, and bright red nail varnish – unfamiliar and fascinating to me as my mother rarely used it. They formed an unlikely couple; I believe that they had met in the war as Mac had served in Norway doing something very brave. They lived just off London's King's Road in a sharply elegant house, and sometimes their daughter Anna came to stay with us once we had moved to Bourton Far Hill, and was press-ganged into riding Pompey, of whom there is more in a later chapter.

My mother was highly gifted both musically and artistically, yet she seemed even then, as if determined to make the worst of a bad job, failing utterly to take advantage of the facilities which even a battered post-war London had on offer: all those wonderful galleries and concerts which had done so much to maintain the morale of Londoners during the very worst periods of the war remained for the most part untasted by her. Older friends who had helped and advised her towards a sophistication so much desired on her part seemed to have made little impression on her social life. She lost touch with Lady Guillemard, who had helped her to dress well in the years after school.

Edith Thalmann, who lived in Campden as a German refugee with her husband Ernest, remembered her to me in later years as "Vivian, darling Vivian, so difficult, so charming, she made life so hard for herself." Edith was the epitome of sophistication, her hats designed by Simone Mirman who died only in 2008. She and Ernest had contrived to leave Germany early enough in the '30s for their considerable fortune to remain intact. She provided Vivian with dreams of style and sophistication which were unsatisfied in the company of a deaf and somewhat philistine husband, though she had a great sense of colour and line and could make even the most unlikely garment look stunning when worn. As a small child I remember well her weekly perusal of Vogue and her regular, almost weekly trips to Cheltenham in pursuit of some fashion item.

She was a poor cook, even an incapable one at this point, with little interest in food, and she had no intention of learning any but the most basic rudiments, a circumstance which was not improved by my father's aversion to particular types of food – anything which he perceived as 'glutinous' or not 'white man's food', or anything with garlic in it. She attempted to pass on this dislike to me so that I used to find it incomprehensible that some of my friends at primary school enjoyed spending time with their mothers making such marvels as jam tarts and jellies. Mrs Leathers was my only hope in this department, but she never encouraged or allowed me to take any active part in kitchen activities apart from my licking of the raw cake mixture from the bowl. My mother did however give me some useful hints as to the judging of quantities (she always knew precisely what liquids would fit into which containers), that nothing will dry if placed directly upside down onto a hard surface (many men especially never grasp this) and that the surface tension in liquids prevents them spreading too far when spilt.

Vivian's discontent with her early married life became so obvious that Aunt Joan eventually took her courage in both hands and wrote to her telling her to stop complaining and that many other people had a much harder lot to cope with. Like most letters of this sort it did little good and more than a little harm, leading to years of friction between them before a rapprochement somehow effected itself.

London life did not impose itself for long on my mother; the following year found my father working in Birmingham at the Selly Oak Hospital. They went to live at Heightingon, between Worcester and Tenbury Wells in a small house without electricity known as Chapel Lodge. Despite years of war service and the consequence that Dad was now in his mid-thirties, his father's undertaking that he would supplement a doctor's pay sufficiently to buy a marital home for my parents took only the stingiest form. Their suggestion of a charming period house near Droitwich, Elmbridge Court, much nearer to Birmingham, was laughed out of court. He would help with only the most basic accommodation.

Vivian felt that her indignation was fully justified: "We had had six of the best years of our lives taken by the war, we were tired, Dad's hearing was bad and his eczema at times was awful, made much worse by these anxieties over our living conditions." So bad was the eczema in fact, that he contracted an accompanying allergy to horses which lasted for several years – it didn't stop him from hunting though. Grandpa was determined that the not-so-young couple should not be spoiled and should have to come up the hard way. My mother's later treatment of me must have been conditioned by this; jealousy too is never far from the mother/daughter relationship. My grandmother's need to spoil her boy from his earliest years – and who would not be tempted when a child was so much afflicted – made Grandpa jealous too; I am certain that much of my parents' early difficulties were born of his concealed anger at the way in which he saw his son being 'made a fool of' by Granny, and that, in unfailing male fashion, he bitterly resented the diversion of all her attention from him and his husbandly needs to the needs of an ailing boy, later to be a deaf man. Grandpa was always hard on his son, never congratulating him on his successes and keen to 'keep him in order' until the end of his life. His determination that Ted should perform his war service regardless of deafness was a real factor in the latter's perception that he would have to serve, come what may. His generosity to his more distant relations and in-laws contrasted oddly with his meanness to his son, and also to Granny, kept short of money until their final more easeful years spent in the Cavendish Hotel in Eastbourne.

I was born on 9 January 1950 at Selly Oak Hospital at eight o'clock in the morning. I weighed around seven-and-a-half pounds and had unusually large feet.

"She'll be a policewoman when she grows up," exclaimed one of the nurses. My gender was a disappointment to my father, I am sure, especially later when he had no more children. His father put it more succinctly: "You're a very disappointing woman" were his first words to Mum when he and Granny visited the hospital. Granny's words of reproof did nothing to lessen the sting and the cruelty of what he had said, yet I don't think he meant to be unkind. He was just 'like that', supremely insensitive and as he saw it, truthful. Ted though was overjoyed, more than anything at having a child at all, as an attack of mumps as a young man had called into question his fertility.

My mother's delight at this point was unalloyed. She obediently stayed in bed for the required week after my delivery, a universal requirement in those days, but nonetheless insisted on going hunting with the Ludlow on her beloved Rhythm when I was only a fortnight old. My father was so angry at her intransigence that he refused to accompany her on their other horse Mary as it might in some way have condoned her behaviour. Nursie, the monthly nurse employed to care for me and my mother, was outraged; she left, in fury, declaring that she was 'not needed'. Horses and hunting would always be Mum's priority though, bad back notwithstanding. She received little sympathy upon her return that day, feeling faint and sick; she would learn that it was always best to keep equestrian mishaps concealed from Ted as sympathy for any injury so sustained was ever in short supply.

The job at Selly Oak was to be my father's last full-time medical appointment. The inevitable tensions of hospital practice, the necessity of accommodating colleagues in their differing views, the morbidity of pathology (the only branch of medicine which could realistically employ a deaf practitioner), his other physical ailments, my mother's loud complaints and the effect of poor housing on his morale, all militated against the continuation of his career. Intellectually he undoubtedly found medicine interesting, and continued to practise as a locum at Gloucester for several years after, but his days as a doctor were over by the middle of the year that I was born.

Country life was an enjoyable preoccupation for both my parents. Horses and hunting were a mutual pleasure, but agriculture? Many men, displaced and disorientated by the war, and with minimal means too, thought to turn their hands to farming. Many of them failed, and many of them lost every last brass farthing – my son's grandfather, a test pilot from 1942 to 1944 with Gloster Aircraft – was one of them. Things would have to be placed on a firm footing if Grandpa's aid in this undertaking was to be solicited. The idea that farming provided a peaceful retreat from real life could not have been further from actuality. Agriculture was still highly labour intensive in the 1950s, mixed farming was still the norm (with its attendant benefit of bio-diversity) and it required all the skills of man management, without the support of service discipline. Moreover, state interference was at its height, food production being essential, the market still much affected by the preceding years of conflict, and politicians, as ever, relishing every opportunity for interference be it ever so ignorant.

No, agriculture was no soft option and provided an infinity of snares for the unwary, but it was also a way of life and sociability for those in love with the country, and in glorious surroundings if the choice was right. Horses could easily be accommodated and fed from the forage produced, and it was a fine life for a child.

My father knew nothing of farming apart from the unavoidable gleanings picked up from being a field sports enthusiast. 'How was I to learn?' he would muse later.

Sandy Marland, besides living in Campden, farmed two farms high in the North Cotswolds, close to where we would ultimately farm ourselves, and was keen to provide the answer. Slade Farm, close to the small village of Cutsdean and a mile from the main road running from the A40 in Oxfordshire to Tewkesbury and Wales beyond, possessed a small wooden bungalow, which even now exists, though in a much modernised and enlarged form. Yet again, no electricity lit or powered its three rooms and kitchen – poor Vivian must have wondered when she would ever move away from the diurnal rhythms imposed by lamplight and keeping the coal (or wood) fires burning. Despite herself though, she grew fond of the bungalow for the four months of Dad's apprenticeship on the farm. Almost anything would have been better than Chapel Lodge, which they left 'for good', as she succinctly entered in her diary, on 19 September 1950.

"It had a lot of charm, everything just happened more slowly, that's all. Washing your nappies wasn't much fun though! Lucky I had Mrs Daves to come in and help. And we were much nearer to darling Violet and to most of our friends."

The fact that Ted was doing something he wanted to do, free from the stress and strain of a difficult workplace, must have helped them both too. And at last he had the excuse, once we came to Bourton Far Hill, of a physically tiring day on the farm to indulge in impossibly hot baths every evening, while my mother – once Mrs Leathers had left – toiled over an Aga-cooked dinner.

My mother was not given to mothering, even putting on my nappy was a difficulty: "One day you cried more loudly than usual as I was doing the fastening. And do you know what? I was sticking the safety pin straight into your bottom, you poor little darling." Doubtless, she was not the first mother to have made such a mistake, but somehow it summed up her whole reluctance over baby matters. She really came into her own as I grew old enough to have a pony, to appreciate music, to read books, to (in short) become an interesting person with whom she could fully communicate. We listened to music together; her introduction to me of Grieg's piano concerto in A minor was an entire revelation, opening the gates to a lifetime of pleasure taken in music; I never hear it now without thinking of her. This golden age, and it was golden, would last only until the troublesome time of my puberty and adolescence, the onset of which disturbed her deeply and so sadly turned us away from each other into a mutual incomprehension, antagonism, almost fear, which would last until she died when I was forty-five.

My father had no understanding of such things. His only retort to Vivian's discontents, often loudly expressed, was a quiet request: "Really darling, can't you try to be a bit more amiable?" Either that, or an unconscionable outburst of temper, beating the table with his fists and crying out, "I'm going to shoot myself!" as he railed against my mother's unkindness or unreason – we would wait, breathless, for the report of the gun as he fled into the yard, but of course it never came.

The injury to Vivian's feelings found her weeping one Christmas over her present drawer, from which all goodness flowed and which I was hoping to explore one December day when I must have been six or seven. I rushed to her encircling arms: "Mummy, oh Mummy, what's the matter?"

The sight of a parent weeping uncontrollably, in the knowledge that the marital relationship is somehow skewed, rocked my small world. I was left feeling empty and exposed, unready for such difficulty. I would often hear them arguing far into the night as I fell asleep, a frequent backdrop to childhood, and my one feeling: "Thank you, God, that it isn't me."

"Oh, darling," she gasped through her tears. "It's just that he hates me listening to Christmas things on the wireless. He heard the carols and shouted that I should turn the bloody thing off and that he hated Christmas anyway." She sobbed and then went on, "He wants to spoil everything, to make it all mean nothing. It's just so sad. I just wanted to be able to enjoy the loveliness."

This helpless longing was encased in a fatal perfectionism, a sort of paralysis from which there was little or no escape – nothing was good enough, either on her part or on those of others. The horses were her only way into an easier world, although they were 'in for it' if they failed to oblige. This feeling only intensified with age, so that later on in life she fell prey to constant depression and even once declared to me that her chief feeling was one of failure. What a waste.

The deafness and the nerviness of my poor father and the longings of my poor mother had jarred against each other in that one moment which echoed and foretold so many others. They were good people, both of them, with shared values which ranged across so many important matters but they had vastly differing temperaments – sometimes a strength, but not always – and vastly differing upbringings, and they were scarred in different ways by the six years of war, still so recent for both of them. Vivian had had a lonely childhood, spending school holidays with aunts, friends, even at school, guarded by Miss Townsend her heartless headmistress, who enjoyed setting her to work painting walls and performing useful tasks. Such a displaced childhood was a world away from the strong familial upbringing which Ted had enjoyed, and so it was that my mother, Vivian Illingworth Haynes, suffered her whole life long from a hot desire for love which was not to be requited, or not in the ways for which she was looking, and from an inability to love except in fits and starts, for if she loved it might turn round and bite her, and leave her all the more alone.

4

THE FARM TAKES ROOT

*'To my darling Ted, from Vivian, Christmas 1950.
I give you this book on the eve of our move into a
Cotswold farm and a new life.'*
– Inscription on the fly leaf of *Through the Valley* by Robert
Henriques, one of the finest novels of immediate post-war
country life standing comparison with those of John Moore,
high praise indeed.

Bourton Far Hill, just those three words, spell an infinity of memory, an idyll of childhood; the hard embrace of winter wind and snow; the bathing in the water tank in the inner fold-yard, so that we might save water during an impossibly hot and arid summer; my bedroom wall, plastered in the heat with every known insect large or small; the lowing of cows at milking time; the mischievous intransigence of bullocks refusing to be 'drawn' (separated from the herd); Tinker, my mother's beautiful Border Terrier with whom I did so much of my growing up; sheep with their endless needs, and their lambs sometimes lodging in the coolest oven of the Aga after a difficult birth; Ted during lambing, a fortnight's sleeplessness showing in red eyes and stubble grown almost to a beard; impossible quantities of laundry somehow fitted upon the airer above the Aga, drying to perfection; the horses, so many of them, some of them good and some of them not so good, but always beautiful in my eyes; the rushing wind in the beech trees behind the house, which sounded outside my bedroom window like the call of the sea; my old grey pony Shadow, watched from that same window as he cleverly undid the knot securing him to the hitching rail – this trick repeated countless times for my, and his, entertainment; the urgency of trimmed lamps, in readiness for the power cuts which invariably came during our more severe winters; the marvellous men who struggled, sometimes waist-deep, through the snow, to climb the telegraph poles and restore our power and our telephone – they were mostly, of course, Royal Signals ex-servicemen then, like the railway men, and it showed; the amiable road-men, one wielding a shovel, the other two looking on, always a trio; the radiance of a dawn sky as I, a determined five-year-old, trudged up the yard alone, to survey its wonder.

The romance of such a place caught at Vivian's heart. She was an incurable romantic, adoring the world of Lorna Doone and the highwayman Tom Faggus, and the delights of Surtees with his incomparable social observation of the world of nineteenth-century foxhunting. She had a quite un-English ability not just to observe (for the English are one of the most perceptive people on earth) but to express emotion at the smallest beauty of things. "I will lift up mine eyes unto the hills," she would say as we came back from a day spent away from the farm and on lower ground. Its periodic harshness told on her in later years, but for now she loved the farm and all the possibilities within it. From an early age, as we drove along Buckle Street from which you could see the house and its buildings, she would quiz me: "Now what's the name of that place over there? You must remember,

'Bourton Far Hill', in case you're ever lost you can tell people." That is home. I never was lost, but I quickly remembered.

"Wind, wind," I would cry on the stormiest days, as I tore round the garden, arms outstretched like aeroplane wings, relishing the drama of it all, adoring the eloquent moaning of a winter gale as it tore at the windows and doors of the house. The casement windows were never entirely draught- or rain-proof, towels being placed on the window-sills during the worst weather, which quickly became soaked. Vivian found the wailing wind and the exposure of the farm to bad weather harder to bear whereas Ted, despite periodic bouts of ill health and frequent discharge from his bad ear, relished the difficulties, although on social occasions at least, he was compelled to wear a hearing-aid resembling head-phones, the battery being carried in the breast-pocket, and which exacerbated his aural discomfort. The worse the weather almost the better he liked it. Perhaps he was reassured that he was still equal to the challenge. Conversation was littered with expressions such as: "We must tighten our belts/square our shoulders/grit our teeth/put your back into it/keep your nose to the grindstone/press on [with some task in hand]/gird our loins/put your shoulder to the wheel" and "Life is a vale of tears," he would quote, either from Robert Browning's *Confessions* or an anonymous eleventh-century author hymning the Virgin. His was an essentially dystopian nature, expecting the worst, and nicely surprised by the best.

Memories of wartime and its imperatives were still very close, and the farm provided the ideal battleground on which such conflicts and doubts as to whether he might 'come up to the mark' could be played out. Being invalided back to England and thus not having done much proper 'soldiering', i.e. experiencing actual combat, left him with a huge lack which was never really compensated.

When I was going through his papers after he died, I found a letter from the War Office dated 12 May 1949, turning down the offer of his services in the Territorial Army because of his deafness:

> '...You cannot be re-appointed to a commission in the Royal Army Medical Corps (R.A.M.C.) Territorial Army... you relinquished your commission on grounds of ill-health on 27 October 1945... you are still in receipt of a disability award... it is regretted that you cannot be accepted for appointment...'

Though he was reassured that his offer of further service was:

> 'Greatly appreciated and your name has been noted as a volunteer for service in the event of an emergency, subject to your medical fitness at the time.'

Two years later however, in July 1951, with the world situation once again threatening the necessities of war, a letter from the Central Medical War Committee stated that:

> 'It is now necessary to contemplate the possibility of a fresh national emergency [and to that end, had] been asked by the Government to reconstitute the emergency register of the profession on the basis of information voluntarily supplied by the doctors of this country.'

Mobility, the ability to be able to work away from home, to be judged entirely on grounds of physical disablement, had to be stated by the recipient. On the 21st of the month, Ted sent a suitable reply, volunteering his services. These services were never actually required.

Not to be able to serve in the postwar TA must have been a profound disappointment as he was a sociable person who would have relished the opportunities for camaraderie and the monthly escape from a sometimes grating domesticity. He was never happier than when having to perform some heroic deed, such as lighting a fire under the water tower right at the top of the farm in a raging blizzard so that the water would not freeze. In my later youth, when sometimes I was snowed out of the farm by the size of drifts, he would come looking for me in case I had expired, Scott-style, in the cold. Walter Scott, with the high romance of his novels, was favourite reading.

"There's a crisis!" he would exclaim as he came in from his early morning round of the animals. This was a favourite expression, conjuring up just the right degree of excitement.

Of course, Vivian simply hated it, seeing the disruption of her precious day already beginning. What woman wouldn't? Instead of inquiring what the 'crisis' might be she took to ignoring him, having first quickly muttered, "Oh God, not again." Sometimes this worked, as having given vent to whatever was worrying him he would retreat outside until breakfast. Or else he would console himself with expressing some lesser urgency and clapping his hands so that breakfast might be summarily brought – I was surprised when other fathers did not use the same tactics, or perhaps they did when I was not there. The aftermath of war brought out some truly strange behaviours and anxieties. At other times, all hell would break loose, every man was required on deck, not always for ungenuine reasons as when our entire flock of two hundred sheep were found wandering down the Five-Mile Drive, the stretch of main road running from Troopers Lodge Garage towards Fish Hill above Broadway.

Other farms, such as Farhill Farm at Salperton, a little nearer Cheltenham and just across the hill, were also in the running for purchase in November 1950 – Langley Hill Farm near Winchcombe too, and Heath Farm I know not where. Billy Fletcher and Ronald Brookes of Tayler and Fletcher, the local estate agents and auctioneers, were instrumental in the search. On 10 November 1950, Ted and Vivian met David Summers, the owner of Bourton Far Hill and its 230 acres at the Stow office of Tayler and Fletcher, to sign the contract agreeing to a price of £17,000 and to pay the deposit for the farm. The next day must have been something of a celebration as they had a busy day's hunting at the North Cotswold Opening Meet at the Lygon Arms in Broadway – this venue was changed only a few years ago for a windy hill-top and an empty field, far from the possibility of any madding and maddening crowds of anti-hunt protesters, at the end of the back drive to Spring Hill. So much for hunting being kept at the heart of the community. Apparently the police cannot cope with the traffic problems of the urban venue.

Bourton Far Hill, the 'Far' having been inserted only a year or two before, probably to prevent postal confusion with Bourton Hill House next door (having been known as Bourton Hill Farm on the 1946 Ordnance Survey map) was the eventual choice as much for its proximity to Midget (Uncle Arthur) as for any other reason. He had migrated to Gloucestershire in the '30s, after an unsuccessful farming foray in Kenya in the company of the Happy Valley set, and a soon-to-be ex-wife called May. He was childless, and more importantly, he was Ted's godfather. The house which he had built at Kildanes and its surrounding one hundred acres or so, lay close to the main road running from Broadway to Stow-on-the-Wold, and the land marched with that of Bourton Far Hill. The springs which fed the farm's estate, and therefore private, water-supply even lay on Midget's land but no matter, as the two properties were destined to be united upon Midget's demise, or if he chose to move away.

A few days after the contract for the farm had been signed, he visited Ted and Vivian in the bungalow to discuss finer details of their arrangement, and these became enshrined in his will. A few days later, just before the snow came, they visited Kildanes to inspect the springs, the ram which pumped the water and the water troughs. These were essential to the running of any farm and farming enterprise. It seems that I was left in the care of Mrs Johanson, the wife of Midget's butler, too small to play much of a part. Mrs Daves from Cutsdean was enlisted at this point as my main minder. Mrs Bandeira, also from Cutsdean, was to become a helper too during our early days at the farm – she was Portuguese and therefore a source of some fascination as I grew to awareness – her dark hair and exotic accent were not otherwise much encountered in my young life, and I was particularly interested in her heavy jewellery, alien to the rest of her hilltop *compadres* at Cutsdean.

Approached up a long, bare, pot-holed drive, which lay along one of the highest contours of the Cotswolds, the shape of the buildings at Bourton Far Hill was concealed by an impressive stand of beech trees that lined either side of the Rick Yard, running down to the back of the house. At the bottom and to the right stood a corrugated iron granary, set high above the ground and reached by a flight of concrete steps – it had been put up during the war when grain was being produced in serious quantities even on the hill. Opposite stood a Dutch barn for the storage of hay and straw bales. Attached to the back of the Dutch barn was the implement shed, filled with anything which might come in useful – hurdles, rolls of binder twine, barrels of sump oil from previous drainings, farm implements of course, spare gates, the governess cart (a pony trap with genteel sideways seats) which we used for blackberrying in the autumn, fencing posts. Round the corner of the main block of buildings lay a concrete yard surrounded by a cowshed and milking parlour which adjoined the end stone barn (within which dwelt a chaotic 'workshop'), while a bull-pen jutted from the cowshed out in to the orchard, its two halves described as the Bull-Pen Orchard and the Garden Orchard where some rather unsuccessful apple trees, and some rather more successful plum trees, yielded up their fruit each autumn. On the other side of the concrete yard were some pig-sties which lasted only a few years, as Ted did not pursue pig-farming for very long. These recent accretions had come during the war also, having been built by local prisoner-of-war labour.

The Snowshill Field lay to the left of the drive on the approach from the road, the Thirty-Acre lying beyond, while the Gravel Pit and the Lower Thirty-Acre intervened between these two and the Bank and Jockey Fields on the lower side of the farm, furthest from the Quarry. The Hastings and Brown (Frank Brown) Fields, with Midget's Field separating them from the Scrubs and Kildanes Valley, formed a spear whose point landed on the bridleway running along Bourton Downs to Bourton House. Eason's Field, alongside the Brown Field, ran from Midget's Field to the Downs just above the house and later came to belong to it. The Thin (Peter Thin) Field connected the Hastings Field to the Paddock, which ran down the side of the farm from the top of the Rick Yard to further along the Bourton Downs bridleway and nearer to the Quarry. The home ground intervened between the Orchards in front of the farm and the bridleway, and the circuit was completed by the Smallthorns Field the other side of the drive from the Snowshill Field, with the Quarry and its ever-diminishing field (no longer belonging to the farm) below it. A long field running below Spring Hill drive and the Dingles plantation, the other side of the road from the bank fields on the farm, had belonged to Bourton Far Hill before the Second World War.

The Farm Takes Root

The house looked across Happy Valley towards the horizon a couple of miles away; Buckle Street, the Roman road, runs along the top, its moving traffic clearly visible from the front windows. A pretty garden with a lavender path bisecting the lawn and running down to an ancient wooden gate giving onto the Garden Orchard, intervened between house and stunning view. An apple tree with gnarled limbs suitably close to the ground for the climbing thereof stood to the side of the path, while flower-beds containing roses and hollyhocks camouflaged the pump-house at the top of the lawn. A shrubbery, much expanded over the years by Vivian (who became an expert gardener, with an encyclopaedic knowledge of the Latin names of plants – *Hypericum* for St John's Wort and *Aqualegia* for Columbine she always insisted), surrounded the lawn on two sides, and a soon-to-be dug vegetable garden (which never seemed to produce much besides potatoes and beetroot, but was blessed with some good damson trees and a productive rhubarb bed) completing the circuit. A grass tennis-court, occasionally used but never properly maintained, lay on the open side of the house, later to be turned into a gravel sweep as part of the building-on. A walnut tree, suffering from a split trunk which had to be regularly medicated with Stockholm Tar, stood at the corner of the house; its nut-bearing abilities were negligible, but nevertheless Vivian bore it great affection, and it outlasted our time at the farm. Not so a rather lowering pine tree, devoid of branches at one side so that its appearance was more than usually gaunt as it towered above the house. Vivian, a little superstitious as well as romantic, stoutly maintained that for as long as the pine tree stood the farm would never properly prosper. It was felled, unlamented, in the early years of their tenure.

The farm buildings were conjoined by three fold yards, an inestimable benefit when dealing with livestock. These all possessed roofed-in shelters with long wooden mangers stretching their length, while the yard immediately below the cottage, and which opened into the cottage garden, had a row of five rather small loose boxes down one side which backed onto our front lawn. The water-saving tanks, for bathing during a drought amongst other things, were fed from the pump-house and conveniently placed by the wall next to the cottage garden. Two larger loose boxes lay between the cottage and the first stone barn, and more would be added later. These were topped by a loft containing the bales of straw for the horses' beds, which were released into the boxes below by means of trap-doors – though a common arrangement in those days it has long been recognised that such proximity to straw dust can lead to respiratory disease in horses. The first stone barn possessed an upper storey reached by a ladder; until the house was added on to, this was Ted's study where he could leave the cares of farming behind and devote himself to the study of his beloved centipedes and hours of microscope work.

The two stone barns especially provided nesting places for a multiplicity of birds – swifts, house-martens and swallows being chief among them – and any car parked within was prey to corrosion from their copious droppings. Bats too there were a-plenty, and even my father could hear their high frequency cries, sounds lower and much louder often eluding him. Their glimmeringly swift passage was a regular accompaniment to a twilight stroll.

A lean-to egg store midway along the back of the house housed a dark brown Belfast sink of large and shallow proportion, which was used for the egg-washing; eggs were sometimes picturesquely called 'hens' fruit' then. Opposite, and on the other side of the drive leading to the back door, was the garage, built at around the same time as the house. It was floored with ash, so that any car stabled there quickly acquired an ash floor of its own. Here was stored Ted's obsolete laboratory equipment – retorts and so forth, and also all his spare tubes for storage of his Myriapoda specimens. In winter a heater would be placed beneath the car to prevent the radiator from freezing. The end wall was later trellised with William and Conference pears, lovingly tended in after years by Richard Fisher, son of Don, he of the zipped boots described in another chapter. The newly erected wooden summer house, which housed Billy Roberts the stable-boy, and others before him whom I was too young to remember, surrendered its dual function of garden shed to the egg store quite early on, and finally became my private domain where I kept my hula-hoop, a tricycle and sundry wooden toys. Attempts to ride a bike were only slowly successful, and I distinctly remember my outrage when my mother took a picture of me lying on the ground beneath the bike after yet another failure.

All of this formed a marvellously compact and homogeneous unit, the older buildings being all of Cotswold stone as the new lodges, soon to be built, would have to be according to planning regulation. It was a poor fire risk though, as fire in one place could so easily have spread throughout. Fire did indeed come to the Dutch barn one summer – I think that bales had been baled and stacked too soon, before they had had a chance to dry out, thus generating heat within the stack. The Fire Brigade fought the flames successfully, the barn was not damaged enough to need repair, and unbelievably, most of the stack of bales was saved. But the luck enjoyed on this occasion by the wooden saddle room, a hut made black with regular applications of creosote, did not hold; it stood next to the granary and enjoyed the dubious privilege of receiving the ashes from the Aga right next to it, and these were not always as cool as they should have been. The inevitable happened: it burnt down, with every item of horse equipment in it. Midget came to the rescue as he had by then given up hunting and no longer had horses at Kildanes. We were the grateful recipients of some of the contents of his saddle room, fine quality stuff, some of it still in use today seventy years later – he never spared the expense.

The cottage, rather older than the actual house, provided the only staff accommodation, any other labour having hitherto been imported from the surrounding area; a man called Thomas lived there at the time of acquisition, but he did not stay. Ted went to view a possible worker's house at nearby Sezincote, the home of the Kleinwort family. Mr Pemberton, the architect, paid an initial visit before Christmas that year, both to survey the existing state of things at the farm and to begin formulating the plans for two semi-detached lodges at the end of the quarter-mile-long drive. By the 28 December 1950, Stewards, a firm of builders from Campden, had started work, Ted and Vivian having gained possession that same day.

The farmhouse in those days was quite small, consisting of a stone-floored kitchen with a passage and various domestic offices – larder, scullery, bathroom – leading off it. Here dwelt a multiplicity of coat-hooks accommodating a variety of mostly wartime clothing: great coats, Ted's 'British Warm', Vivian's FANY overcoat (a curious shade of grassy/limey green, if I remember) a heavy tweed hat with Arctic-style ear-flaps, endless dust-coats used as overalls when grooming horses, and many pairs of hunting-boots, mostly made by Peals of London. The rest of the ground floor consisted of a small sitting-room (later Ted's study) and a dining-room, between the doors of which descended a staircase to the cellar, an inestimable benefit to any house. Up the stairs, lined by a beautiful, sparely elegant pine stair-rail (the only one similar that I ever saw was at next-door Bourton Hill House, the farm almost certainly having been the outlying unit of a larger property and thus built by the same hand) were three bedrooms, one of which Ted used as a dressing-room later on but which was at first my nursery. The need to build on must have been immediately evident, but Vivian would have to wait some four years before her house could be enlarged into what might be regarded as something more easeful – a 'gent's res' was the common expression then – though in anticipation of our eventual planned move to Kildanes the additions to the house were relatively modest, enough so that a manager might eventually and comfortably live there.

Cecil Williams came from Longborough near Stow-on-the-Wold to embark on this, one of his earliest sizeable projects, Mr Pemberton again providing his services as an architect. The result was no more than satisfactory, a week's absence on the part of the parents and Mr Pemberton ensuring that at least one window was put in the wrong place. The drawing-room, extending from the original dining-room, was poorly proportioned and the windows were too small. My mother found the whole addition disappointing, and felt that it would have been better to have done a proper job, despite the expectation of our eventual move to Kildanes. "We shouldn't be counting our chickens, Ted," she would say.

David Summers had never lived at Bourton Far Hill, having bought it as a post-war speculation only some twelve months earlier. I have no doubt that he did well out of it, having an acute business brain. Before that it had been owned by Peter Thin, after whom one of the fields on the farm was named, who had farmed it throughout the war with the aid of his tenant Bertie Holder, whose much-later-on second wife, Nean Woolrich, owned the primary school in Bourton-on-the-Hill to which I went at the age of four and where she was the sole teacher. Jane, her step-daughter, was delivered on the kitchen-table at Bourton Far Hill a few years before the war began.

Apart from the inevitable teething troubles to be found on any farm at the outset, the only real nuisance lay in the presence of the

Quarry situated at the bottom of the farm, below the Quarry Field which remained in the ownership of Mr Slatter one of Bourton Far Hill's pre-war owners. This field was gradually diminishing in size as Huntsmans Quarries pursued their activities to support the rapidly expanding national road-building programme; regular blasting, in order to dislodge the precious limestone from its resting-place, blew out the windows in the front of our house on more than one occasion. In after-years there was some compensation when a rare dinosaur skeleton was recovered in its entirety, having been spotted by an alert quarryman and which now resides in the Museum at Gloucester.

Vivian's 'Boot's Scribbling Diary' for 1951 (or 'Scribling Dairy' as I termed it in an early attempt at reading) provides an account of our first twelve months at Bourton Far Hill. It is a record kept for practical purposes, and as such contains almost no personal reflection, but it offers a day-to-day account which is irreplaceable.

JANUARY

New Year, 1950/1, to be spent with David and Christine Marland, cousins of Elsa's and Sandy's was seen in at home as no baby-sitter could be found on such a night, but the next day the services of Mrs Daves were secured so that the evening could be spent with beloved Aunt Violet at Flag Close, consuming mince pies and copious drink. By the next morning heavy snow had fallen accompanied by much drifting, but Sandy crossed the road from Slade Farm for lunch, and the next day too (as no doubt the bungalow provided a haven in bad weather, the house at The Slade being not then built). A thaw came, just in time for the North Cotswold Hunt Ball in Broadway three days later. In those days it was always held on a Friday night rather than a Saturday so that any ill-effects could be blown away on a winter's wind during a good hunt.

The next two weeks or so were spent preparing for the move to the farm interspersed with days spent hunting, trips to Cheltenham for prolonged dental treatment for Ted – his teeth had never been good since the war and were not improved by incessant pipe-smoking – and hair-do's for Vivian with my *bête noire* Miss Clutterbuck in Cavendish House. Dinner was taken at Midget's, a man called Leonard Ascott came to the farm looking for a job, Bob Byng Morris (the artist Cedric's nephew and heir, married to Christine Field from nearby Toddington) came to size up a possible job as farm manager and most importantly, on 15 January the Aga was installed in the kitchen. What an event, what a luxury; it was expensive but became immediately a central part of our lives. Its four ovens – the plate-warmer, the simmerer, the baker and the roaster – together with two hot plates, one hotter than the other, provided our only means of cooking until the end of our days at the farm. Lambs, orphaned or otherwise disadvantaged, took their place in a sacking bed in the plate-warmer while clothes were dried on the airer which hung over the stove, suspended on pulleys. Adjoining the stove, and forming part of the same unit, was the boiler, fuelled by coke (a form of coal in small pieces, a pile of which resided in the cellar, beside the balls of anthracite which fuelled the cooker and which were poured through a hole in the middle of each hot plate).

Mr Johnsey, the coal merchant from Moreton-in-Marsh, would arrive wearing his leather apron which was indistinguishable from the rest of his body so moulded was he by coal dust, so that he might feed the cellar with Aga fuel through the coal-hole in the paving outside the kitchen window. I was fortunate enough, when I grew older, to sleep above the kitchen – my bedroom also had an open fire in the early years so that I was never cold. Nowadays Agas also fuel radiators but central heating in any form was not to come to the farm for a few years yet.

Mrs Bandeira continued her employment as home help during and after the move to the farm, having been deputed on 20 January, with Mrs Daves and a man called Graham to clean out the house and light the Agamatic, to give it its full name. The following day, a Sunday, Tony Hawkins began ploughing – there was not so much autumn planting in those days so that the land had a rest for the first part of the winter. At the start of the new week, Englands moved furniture from their store to the farm, and by Wednesday, 24 January 1951 Barnby Bendalls were moving our entire family and its belongings into the farmhouse. Perhaps the first lighting of the Aga had not been a success because the same day Mainwaring came from Radway with Granny to repeat the process. He was a genius, that man, who with northern guile could turn his hand to anything. I notice how often Granny (Mabel) was present in these days, always concerned to help and to look after me. Vivian's father rarely puts in an appearance, suffering no doubt from his widower status but also carefully keeping his distance, just in case he might be called upon.

FEBRUARY

The first building operations, of a minor kind, began immediately – making a lobby for the cottage off the back passageway so that it had a little hall of sorts, and excavating the entrance to the egg-store. Soil samples were taken so that new operations might begin suitably.

Vivian always said though: "It was like farming a quarry. There were only about three inches of soil on top of the hill, then stone, nothing but stone." Not for nothing had the Cotswolds been sheep country for centuries. Arable farming on these uplands had only really started with the food requirements of two world wars.

A week into February everything went wrong: phone off (it had been going off repeatedly], water off, egg-washing machine broken down, wireless broken, water pump hard to start. A few days later a mechanic arrived at Moreton-in-Marsh station to investigate the water pump. He missed his returning train in the afternoon but somehow Vivian managed to get him to Worcester in time to make his connection. There was much less traffic in those days.

Towards the end of that week things were somewhat ameliorated when Mabel came over with electric fires and cakes, etc. Mr Hay the electrician from Broadway, completed work in the cottage, and on the afternoon of 16 February 'Tom Hiatt [sic] called and enrolled us into the N.F.U. (Campden Branch).'

Ted's enthusiasm for working horses was already taking shape: on Sunday, 25 February 'Norman Crump, Bates and Harvey here to try Mary in gears.' She evidently showed some promise as a draught horse, being of a heavy type, or maybe she misbehaved, for two days later, 'Mary to Norman Crump for a week to be re-broken-in to gears.'

Life was busy, difficult, eventful, but never lonely. People were actively looking for work, and there was plenty to do on the typical mixed farm such as ours where almost every farming enterprise was undertaken at some time or another. Every day of Vivian's diary records the comings-and-goings of a myriad folk. The varied activities of the farm meant that there was plenty to go wrong too and that meant plenty of people to put things right. Rural life simply resounded with activity and personality; it simply could not contrast more starkly with today's rural desertion. There are plenty of urban visitors now of course, usually afraid to get even one wheel of their car wet or, God save us, muddy. Stock farming is too much trouble for most though, and the sight of a shepherd crook in hand and dog at his side walking rather than on a quad bike, is quite simply extinct.

Arable farming takes place during four weeks of the year, apart from applications of toxic sprays at intervals during the rest of the season– a hurried industrial-scale harvest replete with vast machinery churning at the edges of narrow roads, followed a few days later by cultivation of the ground ready for harvesting twelve months hence. The sight of a stubble field for more than a few days is a rarity, and is owed more to lack of available machinery and manpower than anything else; the soil is never rested, its structure is destroyed so that heavy rain means that the largest machines with the widest wheels still sink uselessly into the ground during wet weather. Maybe the land will have its revenge after all for agriculture has become for the most part more a way of death than of life, exacerbated by a Government which neither knows nor understands rural life and needs; it has no wish to either, joying in slaughter during the 2001 foot-and-mouth epidemic, and attempting the extinction of our ability to produce food by means of foolish legislation, such as the over-protection of disease-bearing wildlife, badgers in the main, and the banning of foxhunting, which sport does more for conservation of wildlife than any other.

MARCH
On 1 March Vivian went hunting on her beloved Rhythm at Mickleton Halt on the London-Hereford railway line, which in those days had a branch line to Broadway. 'Rhythm ill' it says in her diary. Three days later the mare was diagnosed with heart trouble and a 'long rest' was prescribed. She had been kept at livery in Broadway, a central point in the country as well as being where the hounds were kennelled, but on 9 March the diary entry reads, 'Box [load into a horsebox] Rhythm and move her onto our farm.'

Besides the ram-operated springs in The Scrubs at Kildanes there was also an emergency water supply which functioned for the house and cottage, the farm buildings and for the field and yard troughs adjacent to the house. It was operated from a pump housed in a wooden hut in the top corner of the garden. Mr Hay came on 12 March to instal its electric motor, and it proved of invaluable help over the years when the ram – or later the electric pump – in the woods fell prey to mechanical failure.

The following weekend found Ted in bed with a temperature of 105°. As was his habit, Colin Houghton, our doctor from Broadway, arrived at the cocktail hour to administer a penicillin injection to Ted, and to be prescribed a Gin and French for himself. These treatments became regular over the years, so much so that I later became allergic to penicillin, it being the only remedy then for many infections to which I was a martyr, while Colin's tolerance of his own medicine remained unimpaired.

Three days later Ted was well enough to leave his bed and descend for tea, having been called upon daily by either Colin Houghton or Mick Juckes from the Broadway practice. How different from the necessity nowadays to spread germs or even worse, risk health, by having to attend surgery. The following day, '507 hens' were collected at 2/9 (13.75p) per lb. Hens and sheep appeared to be the first livestock to live on the farm, around two thousand hens and perhaps a hundred sheep. The sheep had most probably been purchased with the farm. On 23 March, Good Friday, the eggs were collected. They were sold through the Gloucester Marketing Society, a co-operative which would then sell them on to the Egg Marketing Board (one of the few government agricultural agencies which did not continue far into the '50s) as distribution of essential foods was still tightly controlled by government. £3.4s.10d/24p was received for a consignment on 3 July 1952 – the quantity is unrecorded but small numbers would have been uneconomic for dispatch. Miss Hoskins also came for two dozen of them for her own private purposes. The following day Vivian cleaned the Aga flues, a regular job because of the soot resulting from fossil fuel burning. Matt, one of the farm workers got the sack, as the diary reveals that he was either 'throwing a sickie' or merely failing to turn up for regular work throughout all of the seven weeks or so since the move to the farm.

There is no mention of church attendance on Easter Day. Neither parent was overtly religious, although as I grew older we did go to church from time to time. Easter Monday was, and is, the day of the North Cotswold Point-to-Point held until the 1990s at Spring Hill whence it had moved from its pre-war location at Aston Somerville near Broadway. Predictably Vivian 'got absolutely soaked'.

Two days later 'five hundred more hens' came, probably ordered from Jimmy Walker – a wartime friend who had taken to chicken farming in Worcestershire. Lambing was obviously in full swing as a weakly lamb was brought into the kitchen – named Larry. The night of 31 March was spent mostly up, lambing with Ted and Hill, one of the more stalwart men (though he moved out of the cottage to work somewhere else in mid-June). 'Twins born, one dead. Skin used for Larry – ewe accepted him.'

APRIL

Two days later Vivian was wondering whether Howe was starting work, and Dow failed to turn up for work until midday as his bicycle was damaged. This must have been irritating in the middle of lambing but nonetheless Ted was away shopping in Moreton-in-Marsh and Evesham by 10am. That night Vivian 'retired hurt' with a slight temperature, which developed the next day into full-blown tonsilitis. The lambing continued unabated with Ted rising at 3am. Meanwhile I fell ill with a temperature of $102.5°$. The next morning Ted rose again at 3am, and for the next four mornings in succession. Luckily Vivian was up again after a day in bed, Sheila, my devoted nursemaid, taking the strain; I was continuing with illness and earache.

In the middle of these eventful and illness-filled days came a demonstration of the new David Brown tractor by Listers, the agents in Evesham – the tractor still ran in 2009. And on Saturday, 7 April the Grand National was run – 'Nickel Coin (a mare), Royal Tan and Denistown (remounted).' Nickel Coin won, the only mare to my knowledge ever to do so since the first running of the National in 1837. Royal Tan won three years later in 1954. Another mare, Tiberetta, put up several distinguished performances around Aintree later in the decade – third in the 1957 Grand National when the winning Sundew was never headed (my mother won a lot of money), second in 1958 to Mr What and fourth, just behind Mr What in 1959 when Oxo won it, besides having won a Grand Sefton and the Becher Chase run over the same fences; she never fell in her sixty-eight-race career. Kirstin too was a redoubtable mare running at this time. No other horse finished out of thirty-five starters. What an outcry there would be now at such a casualty list, but the fences were much tougher then, great upright walls of greenery with Bechers the most unforgiving of them all with its canted bank of a landing with a slope towards. It is formidable enough now, even after its (very proper) successive modifications.

Wilf and Mabel, 'the Easons' as Vivian called the grandparents, came for tea the next day, as they frequently did, and the following day Mr Collett delivered four tons of mangolds as cattle and sheep fodder from Hayway Farm just outside Willersey near Broadway, the same farm that delivered our milk and eggs well into this century. Auntie Violet arrived the next day to take charge of things as Ted's lambing duties seemed to have been completed, and he and Vivian went to London for three days. They attended a lecture by Steele Bodger MRCVS, a well-known veterinarian of the time, at Hyde Park Barracks, and missed the North Cotswold Hunt 8-80 Fancy Dress Dance at the Lifford Hall in Broadway. The next day they went to see Atkinson the stockbroker (no 'Mr' as in those days that was more an appellation for people who worked in agricultural or artisan business rather than for those in 'professional' occupations) and came home the next day to me with more earache, making it impossible for Violet to take me for the day to my aunt, grandfather and cousins in Leamington.

Summertime began on 15 April, later than now, and the next evening Sheila had off to go to her youth club. 'Men working again on windows' – to no effect, as they always leaked. And 'To Longborough for new ration books' as rationing of many things was still in force. 'Mr Apps came to value farm for Deed of Gift' – this makes me think that Grandpa (Wilf) must have bought the place and was now gifting it to Ted.

On 18 April, A. Howe finally started work, and the Olympic Horse Trials began at Badminton. I am not sure why they were 'Olympic' as the previous Olympics had been staged only three years before in London, the 'austerity Olympics' as they are now known. Ted and Vivian went to Badminton on the second day for the Endurance Tests, as they were called. Today's Cross-Country test has a much shortened form, having only a single jumping course to negotiate. In those days the Endurance Test, later known as the Speed and Endurance Test, was exactly that, still largely based on cavalry requirements, and the male competitors came almost entirely from a military background. There were five phases to the day – two Roads-and-Tracks stages of several miles (sort of orienteering tests to be performed at an ideal median speed), with one circuit of a steeplechase course over 'regulation' fences in between, followed by the Cross-Country course familiar to a good many people today (the ultimate jumping test), and then finally (this was abolished perhaps forty-five years ago) a Run-In or sort of winding-down after the Cross-Country, consisting of perhaps a mile of galloping to be performed again at an ideal speed.

Time was of the essence in all these phases, with penalties added for any excess taken as well as jumping penalties for any mishap.

That same day, 1100 yards of barbed wire, that useful abomination invented in the American Civil War as well as being extensively employed by the British in the Boer War, and so commonly used for fencing purposes, arrived from Claytons the agricultural suppliers in Moreton.

That Sunday, the invaluable Mainwarings came over from Radway to help with curtains, and two days later came stone for repair of the pot-holes in the drive. Some years later it would be tarmacked. (Mr) Archie Renfrew, the vet from Broadway, came 'to see house cow and to test for TB' during the week (it took three days for any reaction to show), and Granny (Mabel) came to stay for a couple of days. In after years Vivian would often complain of how hard it was to have been forced into such uncivilised living conditions, but I can't help feeling that they were rather lucky to have so much help, parental and otherwise. Midget came in for a drink while Mabel was staying, and afterwards she took them to dinner at the Manor House Hotel in Moreton. The next day she 'was busy in the garden' – their garden at Radway was very fine.

MAY

Grandpa (Alwyn) put in an appearance in the diary a few days later, but only as far as the Cotswold Lodge Hotel in Oxford's Norham Gardens.

The planning for building the lodges at the end of the drive was getting under way with letters to 'our MP and to Rural District Council re cottages.' And on 1 May a new wireless licence became due (one piece of bureaucracy at least which was done away with a long time ago), while Jimmy Walker stayed to lunch having delivered 'about 150 new eight-week-old pullets', and Mr Craft came to seed barley and oats. Two days later the 'hens were culled' and the cullings taken to Collins the Butchers in Broadway.

The following weekend Ted and Vivian went for a drink with Harold and Elise Pilkington at Hinchwick, the estate lying the other side of Bourton Hill. Harold was instrumental in keeping the North Cotswold Hounds in better shape than many other packs during the war, while Elise had a passion for King Charles Spaniels, not always shared by visitors. They were childless, and the estate was later inherited by Elise's nephew Stephen (Kipper) Asquith, a great-grandson of Herbert Asquith, Prime Minister during the early years of the First World War.

During the next week Bertie Holder, the wartime tenant, was consulted over the water piping on the farm, and a new telephone was installed to replace the 'candlestick' instrument – the grandparents at Radway held onto their old instrument until well after I was old enough to remember such things. Mr Bowles, the animal haulier from Ford, puts in his first appearance in the diary, 'delivering Sandy's [Marland] thirteen yearling heifers for us to graze' – the first mention of cattle on the farm – and that weekend a dray (horse-drawn farm cart) is purchased at Stow Horse Sales and Mary's recent breaking to gears is put to good use when Ted rides her over to fetch it, Norman Crump the horse-breaker supervising.

The lawn was mown for the first time the following week – how cold it must have been for the grass to grow so late, though Bourton Far Hill was always at least three weeks behind the vale in terms of growth. Dudley and Jeanette (Ryder), he of the breaking of the eggs in London's Spring Street, later Lord Harrowby, came to tea. By that time, he had overcome any qualms and they had been married for almost two years. And the next day Captain and Mrs Hannay called, the beginning of a fast and long friendship. A few days later Colin Houghton and his wife Barbara were entertained to dinner in Moreton. Mr Everett the farm manager at Spring Hill for whom Vivian had worked before she married Ted, came to demonstrate the 'castration of lambs', probably done with a rubber ring around the testicles. And during that week the Groves came to look at the cottage and accepted the job on offer, thus succeeding Hill.

Perhaps the most important event of May 1951 was that I stood for the first time on my own on the 25 May, very late for a girl, or for any child, but I had very bandy legs and can remember having to wear remedial shoes as I grew older. That same day the grandparents went to Eastbourne for the weekend, a favourite destination and where Great Aunt Edith, Grandpa's sister, lived. They retired there in the '70s. Pat Pringle (of egg-breaking fame), Julie and Penelope (later known as Snooky and my exact contemporary) came to tea on the last Sunday of May, having been north to see Julie's family. Her uncle was Edward Wadsworth the renowned artist and Vorticist associate of Wyndham Lewis, and who specialised in camouflage work during the Second World War, while Patrick was one of the unsung of the whole war, making many sorties over Germany as a pilot with Bomber Command. His talents excluded horsemanship though. Some years later he was visiting us and the Hannays, and having been loaned Donneybrook as transport, was making his way over to Bourton Far Hill – Vivian's diary entry for 18 September, 1954 reads: 'He fell off twice coming over, and Ted had to lend him the Jeep for return journey and ride horse [back] himself!'

The sheep-shearing, a backbreaking task undertaken by Ted until the flock grew bigger, was completed during the following week. Jimmy Walker came for lunch again, having delivered '100 more birds', and Mabel came again to stay for a few days, going to a sale where a Land Rover which might have done for the farm went for £600, quite a lot of money then. Their transport at this point consisted, as far as I can tell, only of a van, Ted having incomprehensibly disposed of his rather smart SS Jaguar some time before. The final day of the month saw a visit to Mr Firth the dentist, in Cheltenham – he was later most insistent, in the fashion of the time, that just about all my teeth needed filling as quickly as possible.

JUNE
Mabel helped with putting up an electric fence before she left for Radway. Until I read these diaries over seventy years later, I had no idea just how helpful she had been in these early days, and I suspect both parents of just a little ingratitude. During the night I fell over the side of my cot and was taken into bed by Mum, the first sign of any intimacy between us which is mentioned in her diaries – I was now almost eighteen months old.

On 2 June one Tony Chart comes to see the cattle, but they get out of the yard where they are to be drenched (dosed for worms) and 'escape across hay field and corn!'

Mrs Robbins, a darling apple-cheeked old lady from Cutsdean, enters the lists for the first time as darner of socks and mender of any mendable clothes – nothing, absolutely nothing, went to waste in those days. Recycling was a way of life, and the idea of wasting anything was absolute anathema: small pieces of soap unusable on their own were stuck together to make a 'new' tablet; plates were eaten clean at every meal – the idea of 'leaving a mouthful for Mr Manners' was greeted with the utmost contempt; parcels were dismembered for their saveable components of brown paper and string, the string carefully kept in a bag hanging on the back of the scullery door; worn-out clothes too would be dismembered for their remaining useable parts; jam-jars were kept in a cupboard in the back bathroom by the back door, a notice attached warning would-be intruders not to open the cupboard-door; sheets would be 'sides-to-middled', cutting out the worn portion and joining the two sound sides, and thus making impossibly narrow sheets.

I crept into bed with Mum again the following morning of 3 June, which she treats with merely an exclamation mark in her diary – intimacy just wasn't her bag – and on Monday, 4 June Ted went to London on the train for the day catching the 8.31 and returning on the 8.50 in the evening, while Vivian spent the afternoon mowing the lawns ('mowing hard'), something she did to perfection for many years, almost as if the 'hardness' of it justified her in some way.

The next day came 23 yearling cattle from Mr Kleinwort's (later Sir Cyril Kleinwort of Kleinwort Bensons the merchant bank) at Sezincote. He and Betty had visited a short time before to inspect the grass keep. Soon after Jimmy Walker came over with another hundred birds and stayed to lunch. In the evening Ted and Vivian took a chicken over to Mrs Robeiro at Cutsdean, and stopped off at The Plough at Ford on the way home. The Bowles transport operation, headed by Binks Bowles, ran out of the yard at the back of the pub, now a development of 'dinky dwellings', and they were the landlords of the pub as well which still belongs to Donnington Breweries at Upper Swell near Stow-on-the-Wold.

The following weekend the Willys' American ex-WW2 Army Jeep was delivered from London; Dick Lawson, an old friend, dropped in on his way to London; and on the Sunday evening there was a drinks party at the Cathies who lived in a magnificent Jacobean house at Barton-on-the-Heath the other side of Moreton. My contemporary Hamish Cathie lives there still. Their friends were many and various, including George Rainbird the publisher and founder of Octopus Books, and Roy Dotrice that fine actor.

Silage making started later in the week in a pit just beyond the cowshed. It was a smelly and highly labour intensive operation, but there was some light relief in the afternoon when the Jeep, being untaxed in Britain, had to go to be weighed in Moreton. The next day the police came out to inspect it. On Sunday Auntie Evelyn came for a picnic lunch with Caroline and Elizabeth, senior to me by a few years. The next few days were spent peacefully sewing and gardening; one evening Ted and Vivian went to Stanway Ash Plantation at the top of Stanway Hill so that he could collect some Myriapods (centipedes).

On 23 June, a Saturday, Groves and his wife moved into the cottage and Mrs Groves started working in the house for two hours every morning a couple of days later. That afternoon Ted and Vivian went to tea and cocktails on the lawn at Farncombe House above Broadway, a gorgeous spot owned by the Pembertons, he being their architect in the matter of the lodges. 30cwt (hundredweight) of coke arrived that week, preferable to anthracite as it was unrationed, and Mr Oughton brought '22 beasts' (young male cattle) from Lower Rye Farm to graze. The grandparents brought May (Midget's ex-wife of whom they were very fond) to tea on 25 June, and the next day Vivian contacted Hector Smith a local farmer and well-known hunter chaser owner, about using his sheep-dip 'any time after tomorrow night' as we had yet to construct ours.

The Aga went out at the end of the week, a terrible nuisance until gas pokers came in to make relighting so much easier. It was not relit until the next day, no doubt for that reason. A trip to Radway to fetch a trailer ended in running out of petrol on the way home, finally getting some at Stretton-on-Fosse. The sheep-dipping at Hector Smith's happened on Friday, 29 June, and on the return home sheep belonging to David Summers, which must have been grazing nearby, had got onto the Bourton Far Hill barley. Vivian says laconically, 'Rang him up about it.'

On 30 June Ray, who must have given his notice, asked to stay at Bourton Far Hill after all. Vivian mowed half the tennis court.

JULY

That first day Vivian finished mowing the tennis court; the mower was the most advanced Atco of its time with a powerful engine and a large roller which left a pleasing striped pattern on the grass, rather the same as a field which has just been harrowed. And on 2 July Mr Lush came from Temple Guiting to carry (remove from the field) twelve acres of hay on the Thin Field with his 'pick-up baler'. Mr Cowell of Listers in Evesham also came that day to advise on the electric fence – he stayed to lunch. There always seemed to be time then.

The Royal Show was at Cambridge, lasting for four days until 6 July. 'Ted and I to Ford pub [The Plough] for some gin at 2pm on 3 July, whether to consume on the premises or as an off-sale I do not know, but perhaps not unconnected with Billy Fletcher's and John Brookes' (of Tayler and Fletcher) visit later that day to discuss the coming sale of hay. About 14 tons of hay was in by that night.

Colonel (later Sir Geoffrey) Shakerley at Wells Folly the other side of Moreton-in-Marsh had a Hay Sale on the Wednesday, and on the parents' return they found the 'Little Grey Fergie' (Ferguson Tractor England - TE 34) being serviced by George Hart (one of the Harts silversmithing family who moved their business from London late in the nineteenth century as part of the Arts and Crafts rural immigration) from Cutts Garage in Chipping Campden. The Harts Workshop in Campden has remained unchanged today for well over a hundred years and is essential viewing for any visitor.

Vivian made a phone call that evening rebuking a neighbour for enticing Ray and Olive, two of their retainers. Enticing workers remains a cardinal sin in the countryside, the present employer always expecting to be contacted by a prospective employer before any concrete action is taken in terms of a change of job. It is a courtesy more observed these days in its omission.

Ray and Olive left three days later, and that afternoon, a Saturday, Peter Aizlewood (he of the wooden leg out hunting) married Phayre Standring with a reception afterwards in Warwick at the Park House. Their married life was spent at Brookend House in Chastleton near Moreton-in-Marsh. Phayre's father was the senior partner in Godfrey-Payton, well known land agents in Coventry and Warwick who still act for our family today.

The following week seems to have been occupied mainly with animal concerns: the walking (giving care, attention and lodging until the hunting season began) of a hound puppy was considered; Tinker, Vivian's beloved Border Terrier, was 'married to a bitch named Trixie', whereupon the two completed matters by clearing off for a twenty-four-hour honeymoon, necessitating a call to the police and a midnight search. Eventually Ted picked them up in the Quarry, a place that has always abounded with foxes; Bowles came to take 'four ewes and a ram' to Andoversford Market owned by Tayler and Fletcher; 'surplus' farm cats which had become feral were rounded up and destroyed.

That Sunday 15 July, there is the first mention of their attendance at the parish church of Bourton-on-the-Hill. The rest of the week was spent on farming and breeding matters: 'pulling charlock' out of the kale crop all one afternoon; both Ted and Vivian going to Stratford Market with Groves, and returning with eleven eight-week-old pigs, six of them Wessex and costing £19.17.6 in all; looking at a stallion for Rhythm, Bellman belonging to David Summers – she was 'married' to Jack Slatter that weekend (Vivian and Tinker in attendance), retiring to motherhood, while enjoying gentle hacks round the farm; talking to Midget about the loan of his lodge for staff housing. I am impressed by how much Vivian was involved at this early point in farming matters – one of my earliest memories is of her harrowing the Snowshill Field using the Land Rover as a towing vehicle, and doing it with a bad grace too. She fairly quickly dropped out of doing anything much in the agricultural line, preferring to concentrate on horsey matters and the house. Regular visits to Cheltenham to shop and visit the jeweller and the hairdresser were essential to her – she wanted the life of a lady, rather than a farmer's wife, and I remember her resting in the afternoons while scanning *Vogue* magazine. A thoroughly good idea – no one knows the meaning of rest any more in our restless age. Ted found all this rather difficult though, which must have contributed to the periods of breakfast tension between them.

Meanwhile they had gone to dine at Spring Hill with the Hannays, and on the Friday had taken me, with nursemaid Dorothy in attendance, to lunch independently at Radway with the grandparents while they lunched at Whateley Hall in Banbury and returned for tea.

The following week began with a bout of tonsilitis for Ted which kept him in bed for a couple of days, and the stable of lawn mowers was enlarged with the purchase of a Ransome Lightweight. The Tuesday evening was spent pulling thistles on the Snowshill Field; later on they would be cut with the Hayter cutter though I remember myself pulling whole fields of ragwort, preferably by the roots so that it was gradually eradicated through its two-year cycle. The next evening there was more charlock pulling, then listening to the wireless and sewing. Mrs Groves began to prove her worth by relighting the Aga and Mrs (Betty) Kleinwort came over to get the ear numbers of their Red Poll cattle – each was individually tagged for recording and health purposes – *plus ça change*.

On the Friday Midget must have been the cause of much rejoicing when he said 'yes' to farm use of the lodge at Kildanes. Maureen Valender from Cleeve Prior began work on the Saturday – much time was spent fetching and carrying people for work from some distance away as few had their own transport apart from a push-bike, though in this instance Maureen was living in. She gave notice the following week. On the Saturday evening Ted and Vivian went for a walk along Bourton Downs, at the bottom of the farm.

On the Sunday, 'Marian a devil today' – perhaps that is why Maureen gave her notice so quickly. On the Monday evening Midget's lodge was inspected – they must have walked over as he ran them home after a glass of sherry had been taken.

AUGUST
Vivian took Maureen home to Cleeve Prior on the 1st, saw her mother and obtained apology for letter, some altercation having taken placed – obtaining apologies was always important to her. 'Tinker cleared off hunting.' He was not castrated, which might have helped to keep him closer – few male dogs were then – and there was the consequent and constant worry that he might get caught in one of the many rabbit snares which then abounded. That first weekend in August, Auntie Violet and Grandpa (Alwyn) went to Bayreuth for a week at the Wagner Festival, something Grandpa did every year until he grew too old. Tinker was kept firmly on a lead when the parents went for a long walk that Saturday afternoon, returning home to find one McEnery waiting for an interview, he having cycled from North Cerney twenty miles away.

The following week saw Ted and Vivian at Gilberts Farm in Bledington – where our great friends the Bucklers lived nearly sixty years later – to inspect Geoffrey Giles, the son of the house, for possible employment. The rest of the week was spent preparing for a sale on the farm of surplus stock and equipment. This included Mary who had been shod the previous week in preparation, and for whom Vivian had borrowed a headcollar and a 'twitch' (a restraining device to be looped and twisted around a horse's top lip) from Basford, the groom at Spring Hill. This was so that her mane might be pulled and plaited, the latter by Vivian's great friend, Margot Partington, an expert in these matters. The sale had a 'large attendance – good results', which included getting sixty guineas for Mary from Mr Slatter of Quarry Field fame.

Pat Ascott, a new nursemaid for me, was engaged; Shell-Mex came to mend our farm petrol pump, and Arkells 'called again re more beer' which was sent a couple of days later. There was continual interviewing of prospective staff as Jack Dow had simply walked out, and forfeited his wages thereby – one Kennett, who missed his train connection at Cheltenham, arriving by taxi but having to be returned there later; a family named McFee brought by Mr Clifford of the Gospel Hall in Moreton; one Tomes from Idlicote near Shipston-on-Stour; Geoffrey Giles from Bledington who arrived with his father, a Sergeant in the RAF stationed at the US air base outside Moreton (now the Fire Service Training College).

The middle week of August saw Ted ploughing, obviously planning a winter crop – 'sorting out the elevator' which was used for stacking the higher levels of bales in the Dutch Barn, collecting parts for the 'binder' (early days still for the combine harvester) from Moreton Station whither they had been sent by Listers from Evesham further down the line. Ted and Vivian took tea at Childswickham with Derek and Billie Welton (he who later broke his neck out hunting) and looked at a horse for sale to replace Mary, and the next day visited Kersoe outside Elmley Castle (where our friends the Hobbs's now live) to see a horse of Bob Eaton's at Norman Crump's instigation. They took the time to buy some second-hand furniture on the way home at Mr Keyte's Little Collin Farm outside Broadway, including a chair, a washstand mirror, a chest of drawers and a large family Bible (a fine affair with copious illustrations which sits now in our hall), all for 45/- (£2.25).

On Saturday, 18 August Tinker won second prize in the 'Dog Most Like its Owner' class at the Comic Dog Show in Broadway, part of the North Cotswold Hunt Pony Show and Gymkhana. On Sunday, 'Busy on chores all day – Mrs Groves didn't come in at all so was singlehanded' – something which was clearly not usual. Ted spent the rest of the week ploughing with the assistance of Groves. Lady Clementi, staying with Grandpa in Leamington, dropped in for tea on the Monday as part of their tour of the Cotswolds. £125 was agreed as the price for Bob Eaton's horse at Kersoe subject to vetting, by Mr Gold of course. Bowles came for the rest of Sandy's cattle, and 'Mrs Kleinwort and a whole gang of helpers came to remove cattle. Ronald Brooks and Alfred Ellis called re ferreting our rabbits – engaged on ⅓/⅔ basis. Start right away.' Betty Kleinwort clearly took an active part in farming operations.

The following weekend 'Mabel [Granny] arrived to help all day.' And the next day 'Mabel arrived to help with Marian,' leaving that afternoon. That same day 'Geoffrey Giles moving into hut and starting job here' – she must have meant the wooden summer house in the garden, very primitive. That afternoon, 'Kennetts arrived from Blandford – moved smoothly into lodge [at Kildanes, which had had some re-decoration by now]. Mrs Ascott helped.' For the first time there is a reference to the weather – 'wet evening and night'. The weather continued stormy for the rest of the following week until the end of the month. Indeed, there was a power-cut all afternoon on Sunday, 26 August. On Wednesday, the only dry day of the week, Ted and Vivian went down to The Scrubs, the Bourton Far Hill side of Kildanes Valley, to 'cut rick pegs'.

The equine population of the farm began to expand with Rhythm's return from stud and a trip to Stratford to see a horse called Spoon Shot, who had run fourth in the Derby in his youth. It was a quick decision to take him on trial, apparently no vetting this time, as he arrived (courtesy of Bowles) the next day, while Ted went to Shernalls, a local covert, to catch some more centipedes.

SEPTEMBER
That Saturday, 1 September, Vivian 'tried out Spoon Shot – very well behaved'. Ted went by bike in search of centipedes in Dovedale above Blockley. The next day they went to see Mr Beaston's Guernsey cow at Compton Wynyates Home Farm near Shipston, and the wheat harvest began on the Hastings Field amid improving weather. Two schoolboys from the holiday camp held annually on Spring Hill turned up to help with the harvest.

On 4 September 'Ted fetched timber for sheep-dip from Kildanes' and Simon the next new horse arrived from Kersoe courtesy of Bowles. 'Harvesting in full swing' with which Vivian helped in the afternoon. Doug the farrier put front shoes on Spoon Shot and Simon and trimmed Rhythm's feet. 'Later I tried out Simon – very good.'

The next day Midget came to help with the harvest all day, joined by Mainwaring and Brown from Radway, while Ted and Groves went to a 'sale of Clun sheep' at Colesbourne near Cirencester. Vivian went to Moreton to fetch a wheel for the dray, which was fitted later that day. She rode both horses during the afternoon, taking Spoon Shot over to Spring Hill to see Basford whose opinion was always much respected, and somehow fitted in tea for the whole family in the harvest field too. Rain started early in the evening, and Mainwaring and Brown came in for beer and petrol before returning home. The

Hastings Field harvest was finished though 'rick-raking still to be completed'. At 8.30 that evening a new cow arrived, probably the Guernsey from Compton Wynyates. What a day!

Hind shoes were put on both horses later in the week, while Ted and Groves went to Tenbury Wells to buy more Clun sheep, forty of which arrived in a lorry the same afternoon. 'Men busy ratting in barn – Tinker killed one.' In the evening, 'Ted and I walked over to look at the Kildanes barley being combined.' On 8 September, they went for a ride on the two horses together. 'Sandy [Marland] arrived to start combining the barley – combine broke down' – a frequent occurrence in the early days of combining. 'Marian out late watching combining!'

The combine broke down again the next day, a Sunday, and a start was made on the 'oats with the binder'. The combine got going again the following evening – 'worked for three-quarters-of-an-hour and then broke down.' Things must have been getting to Groves as he gave notice on the Tuesday, and then withdrew it. Simon, having been on trial, was bought for £125 and then proceeded to go down with colic the same day, for which he had to be drenched by Archie Renfrew. He was better the next day. The barley continued to be harvested while the binder cut the dredge – a mixture of oats, wheat, barley and beans, used as an animal feed instead of manufactured cattle-cake, which was still subject to wartime rationing. The schoolboys went home without permission from the harvest field, and forfeited their tea.

'Thatching straw for the rick' was delivered later that week, and work began on stabling for the horses. Some horse clothing, now surplus to Midget's requirements, came from Kildanes. Ted spent most of the following Monday thatching, and Grandpa (Alwyn) came to stay until the Saturday, brought over by 'E+2', as we always termed it – Auntie Evelyn and my cousins Caroline and Elizabeth. At this point Simon was quite badly kicked on the knee, probably by Spoon Shot, and had to be rested and poulticed. Midget came to dinner on the Tuesday, and the next few days were busy with carrying the dredge until dark, and the oats, though Vivian found time to shop in Broadway with Grandpa one morning.

By the 21st the oats had been 'carried' but the combine continued busy with the barley on 22 September – a much later harvest then than now. For the next four days the rain poured down, a nerve-wracking business especially when harvesting the Jockey Field, a steep bank field on the far side of the farm, which they had to wait to do until the weather cleared. Nonetheless, Mr Wright from Scarborough above Cutsdean had his offer of 150/- (£7.50) per ton accepted, the crop to be taken by 16 October. By 25 October Simon's leg had grown worse, Cecil Williams delivered roofing for new cattle shelters and Vivian dislocated her shoulder – she doesn't say how – and had to go to Moreton Hospital for Dr (Arthur) Saxton to put it in again.

The alarm was raised the following day, as Pat (a girl from Blockley deputed to look after me) decided to take me for a walk in my newly purchased folding pram so that she might go to see her family. Ted rushed out in the Jeep to look for us only to find that Pat and I had safely returned. That Friday Cutts came to take the Jeep for repair and started the van whose ignition had been left on. Restored by a day in bed, Vivian spent the Saturday morning 'picking damsons' with Ted and taking 40lbs of them to Franklins in Broadway for sale. In the afternoon the 'carrying' of the wheat on the Smallthorns Field began, helped by Grandpa (Wilf), he and Mabel having arrived to stay on for harvest tea and supper. 'Furious arguments!' records Vivian, though we are not told why. I suspect that Grandpa was at his unsympathetic worst in the midst of such frantic activity – he would on occasion arrive unannounced to make sure that Ted was hard at work.

The last day of the month saw the end of wheat-carrying, made no easier by Geoffrey Giles going out for the day. Sandy brought his combine over to the Jockey Field and joined the harvest tea with Elsa.

OCTOBER
National Insurance contributions increased on 1 October, made by purchasing a weekly stamp to be stuck in a card designed for the purpose. That same day, 'Marian put to bed – overtired. Refused lunch and tea.' Sandy continued trying to finish combining the bank fields – 'net result for one day's work one ton approx. I cuddled M[arian] for an hour while the girls bottled and jammed damsons!' I was put to bed early with a cup of milk, and the barley already in the granary was found to be 'pretty dirty'. Not surprisingly the following afternoon 'Ted and I rested on our beds. Marian also to bed for good sleep.'

By 3 October Simon's leg was up again, and Sandy arrived to 'combine the dredge', abandoning the small strip of barley that was still left. Harvest tea was taken on the Gravel Pit Field, followed by a glass of sherry, Elsa also attending. The next day: 'Struggled with combine all morning – net result a quarter of a sack!... Further, combining and breakdowns. Wrights sent up re moving barley on Monday or Tuesday next. Combining finished – Ted and I out till quite late fetching up last few sacks of dredge off the field.'

On 5 October 'Sandy came and removed his combine', surely to every one's great relief. A fire was lit in the afternoon, a sign of autumn, and a decision regarding Spoon Shot is marked with a tick – his trial must have been successful. Ken, one of the men, 'made ultimatum to Ted – boss of machinery or else!' Perhaps he, Ken, thought he could have made a better fist of a harvest so delayed through constant breakdown. Two days later he gave notice, and was given a week's money. We went to Radway for lunch on the Sunday accompanied by Pat to keep me in order. That evening, after a talk with Vivian, Geoffrey decided that he wanted to go on working on the farm despite his sparse lodging in the wooden hut in the garden, and Oughton had been to look at the cattle during the day.

On Monday, 8 October, Mr Wright from Cutsdean came to take 'eleven tons of barley at 150/- (£7.50) per ton' – 88 sacks taken, the other 88 were collected the next day. 'Baked a batch of four loaves – most successful' – Granny would later praise the gritty consistence of Vivian's bread (an obvious sign of a healthy food to her) ignorant of the fact that the grittiness was largely owed to a fair amount of dirt, as the flour was home produced in rather dubious conditions.

Simon's knee was still a cause for concern and regular poulticing, while my legs, bandy as they were, were the subject of a visit from Colin Houghton. The search was on for a set of chain harrows (with which to refresh the grass in the spring by dragging it, thus encouraging worms and growth); a set had been inspected at Eyford Hill, the Kleinworts' farm, and another at a farm sale at Rollright by Chipping Norton, but both had been found wanting. Claytons in Moreton seemed a better bet for a new set. Mr Tidmarsh, the rat man, came on 10 October; and Vivian rode Spoon Shot for the first time since the dislocation of her shoulder.

The hen houses were moved later that week, from the dredge onto the spring wheat on the Smallthorns Field; and for the first time ever recorded, 'Mabel [staying for two nights] helped me with Simon – got down some more hay' – Granny had no interest whatsoever in horses, but perhaps the medical aspect of an injured knee engaged her kindly interest. She was rewarded with shopping in Broadway the next day while Ted and Groves had an unsuccessful trip to Hereford to buy 'stores' (young beef cattle to be overwintered and then sold on in the spring when they were 'finished' – grown to a size for slaughtering). That same Friday, the rat man came again, rats finding an ample food supply in such a place, and Doug came to take Simon's shoes off as he was not fit to work, and to 'remove' (take off and put on again after trimming the growth of the foot) Spoon Shot's.

That weekend Pat demanded more money after only six weeks and then went out for the Saturday night. Groves too was off, leaving Ted and Vivian with the evening chores of hens and horses and the egg-washing. A fox (or 'dog') 'had taken one or more birds at dusk.' And 'Mr Harris of Aston Magna called re wool – long chat about hunting and horses.'

Sunday was a sociable day with people coming and going for lunch and tea, and Mr Gold the excellent horse vet coming to see Simon's knee who was then turned out in the field with Rhythm – Spoon Shot had had to be kept away from her; perhaps he was something of a trouble-maker as horses sometimes can be. Later in the week he was found lame in the field and had to be brought in, having pulled a ligament in his back. These horses! But before then, having borrowed a twisted snaffle from Spring Hill (a bridle bit not much used nowadays) and Simon's knee obviously being better so that his shoes were put back on again, 'Ted and I went out on the horses on a glorious hot day' to a 9am cub-hunting meet at Hornsleasow, less than a mile down the road. The day before had been hot too – 'thick fog down in the Vale!'

The next day was spent bread-baking – 'I on my own – busy in house – put Marian to bed.' The mangolds (a root crop not dissimilar to swede and used for animal fodder) were pulled during the week. Granny came over for the day on Friday, 19 October, bringing my cousin Margaret (Margie) with her, some four years older than me, and Vivian's great friend Margot (Partington) stayed for supper and helped bed down the horses, saying her farewells before a six-month trip to South Africa. On

20 October 'a son born to the Johansons today' up at Kildanes. Summer time ended on 21 October, and the evenings grew darker as the clocks went back.

Then a sparse announcement for 22 October – 'pm – destroy Spoon Shot'. No reason is given though his lameness must have had something to do with it. That night Joan and Griff, her second husband, stayed in Moreton, and dropped in on their way home from holiday. The next day the hounds met an hour later at 10am, the Opening Meet being not far off. Ted was 'ploughing all day' but Vivian took Simon to the meet at Welshman's Hedge about three miles from the farm – 'Found – ran to Lidcombe. Hacked back to draw. Home.' The next day, 'hacked Simon out – did not go well, seemed tired and sick.' He probably was tired as he had not been got properly fit for the season; the next day 'he is better.'

That Thursday the faithful Groves gave notice – 'said it was only on account of Mrs G not liking the cottage.' He and Ted went to Moreton Station to collect two Clun shearling rams while Vivian went to Strongs the tailors 'for fitting and hacking coat, and to be measured for new cord trousers' – Mr Strong would work in the old-fashioned way as in The Tailor of Gloucester, seated cross-legged on his tailor's table with its yard-measure running to one corner of it, sewing by hand. It was Election Day, and they voted at Temple Guiting – Churchill once more became our Prime Minister. Pat was out for the night and the next day, a Friday, but that did not stop Vivian from going out with the hounds on Simon – '10.00 – Sheppey Pool, drew Sheppey Grove, ran thro' Bourne's Folly [on Snowshill Hill], across Smallthorns and Bourton Far Hill into Scrubs. Then to Kennel Hill, back to Scrubs, where abandoned. Returned to Kennel Hill to draw. Simon got sore back.'

A mysterious entry for Saturday, 27 October – 'Saw Mrs Groves re Geoffrey, and the truth came out re their leaving.' That evening, 'Ted and I to see Geoffrey's father at RAF Station, Moreton.' During the day, Simon was given an intravenous injection by the vet Mr O'Connor. The Aga chose to go out twice on the Sunday just as Elsa and Helen Syme (my Godmother, though I never saw her very much – she owned a café in Stratford-on-Avon) turned up for lunch rather than the expected tea. Ted went to see a man called Roy about the foreman's job on the farm in the evening. And on the Monday the delivery of a new Land Rover was discussed with Mr Gulliver at Steels Garage in Cheltenham. Thirteen Black Poll cattle were collected from Campden Ashes on Spring Hill, and some larch poles from Brough Wood were purchased at Brockhampton Farm.

The last Tuesday in October was a social day. They both went to Campden to collect the Jeep from Cutts, took Joan Donne (an old friend of Vivian's who I remember as having very large feet) out to lunch at the Noel Arms 'after sherry at Grevel House', then Vivian was left to shop and have tea with Pam Thin, Peter's sister. I am impressed by how much shopping went on then – was it for clothes? Food? A good deal of food was delivered by the baker or the butcher, or by Franklins from Broadway who took a weekly order and then toiled up the hill with it in a green van. Green was almost the only colour for a van then; the baker's van from Kineton, the next-door village to Temple Guiting, was driven by curly-haired Trevor and was green too. Our van was yellow.

The 31st was the last day for ordering three tons of fuel on licence – this must have been the anthracite for the Aga cooker. Williams the sweep came to do all the ground-floor chimneys, the upstairs and the cottage being left until 17 December. Mainwaring and Brown came over from Radway to dig the garden. The dray overturned with a load of the larch poles bought two days previously and had to be left until the next day. Geoffrey found lodgings with a family called Graham at Campden Ashes, the hut in the garden (the summer house) having obviously proved too spartan. He stayed for supper with them.

NOVEMBER

The first day of the month was celebrated with the delivery of the new Land Rover, shiny dark green with a canvas roof which could be taken off on hot days. It had cost £613-12s-4d, expensive then, you can get a serviceable car for £500 even now. It was equipped with a starting-handle (a bar with a socket at right-angles for insertion through the radiator and into the engine, and a right-angle at the other end from which to turn it) which was a quite generally supplied alternative to the self-starter (by means of the ignition) which was not always reliable. Sometimes, on ignition, it would take several vicious turns of its own accord, so that it was something of a skill to know when to let it go. The Land Rover became the family car, undertaking trips to Wales and beyond for holidays as well as being a farm workhorse, and it stayed in use until the mid-'90s when Ted no longer drove and a restorative home was found for it. I have no doubt that it is still serving its owner well. The remaining four tons of licensed fuel could be bought between now and the end of the following April. Ted and Roy went to rescue the dray and the larch poles.

The next day the 'thirteen Black Poll cattle were tested for TB' by Paul Stone from Renfrews – he was the best cattle vet around and had a prodigious memory for ear-tag numbers, a useful talent – and on the Saturday Groves' advertisement for a farm manager's job came out in the *Evesham Journal* and Geoffrey moved into his 'new digs'. A man called Ray came up for an interview on the Sunday evening. The Monday saw Pat get her desired raise, to 27/6 a week, that is £1.37.5 in present-day currency. One reactor to the TB test had to be returned to Spring Hill (collected by Bowles the next day) once Mr Stone had inspected the results. The telephone engineer came to instal an extension in the kitchen and Ted had to go and 're-start the ram', this on such a stormy day that it was too wet for Pat to go home in the evening.

The next day was the parents' third wedding anniversary, celebrated in conjunction with Guy Fawkes by a 'lovely bonfire and six Roman Candles for Marian in the garden.' Animals were moved around the farm that day, Rhythm into the Home Ground below the house and the chickens onto the Thirty-Acre above the house. They took all day to move. 'Mrs Groves not well again. Colin Houghton coming out to see her.' On 7 November, 'bread-baking today' and in the afternoon, 'I to Reggie Sherston to learn butter making.' Reggie lived at Sezincote Warren, just beyond Bourton Hill and towards Hinchwick. Recompense was made the next day when Vivian took him a bag of flour. 'Much cake-baking by the girls' – Pat and another called Dorothy; Vivian preferred the bread-baking. Arkells came with another beer barrel and the Weltons came to lunch. The next day they lent a numnah to Vivian (a soft saddle-shaped pad to go under the saddle, generally made of sheepskin in those days) no doubt to help with Simon's sore back. Two Minty bookcases arrived to house part of what was even then a large book collection, and by this time Vivian's hacking coat was ready for fitting at Strongs.

The Opening Meet of the North Cotswold at the Lygon Arms in Broadway was held on Saturday, 10 November at 10.45am, but Ted was busy all day seeing to the recalcitrant ram and ploughing, so Vivian went on foot with her parents-in-law and then had lunch at the Lygon Arms. 'Pat never came in all night' but the next night she stayed in while Ted and Vivian took supper with Helen Syme in Stratford. The following night she was out again and Ted got out of bed at 11.30pm to go and look for her. Once found, at Kildanes, she was told to stay where she was until morning. That same day poor Simon was threatened with stomach-pumping but recovered enough to escape it.

Troubles never come singly – Pat and Dorothy 'walked out on me the next day,' though the picture gets a little more complicated. 'Sacked Pat and sent her home with a week's money. Dorothy very upset. Pat tried to make her give notice too.' After lunch, 'returned home to find Pat back with offensive messages from parents. She took Dorothy home almost forcibly!' They must have been sisters. Mrs Groves came to the rescue over the next few days, having no doubt recovered a little, and on the Friday Granny arrived from Radway to accompany Vivian and me on a day in Cheltenham where I had a haircut – the first of too many – and Vivian had two fillings performed by the persistent Mr Firth.

The hounds ran over the farm on the Saturday, and poor Simon went down with a mild bout of colic again. 'Mr Eric Leigh [from Langley outside Winchcombe, and the grandfather of my contemporary and erstwhile neighbour Rex Bovill] called about Groves and his possible employment. Hard at work answering housekeeper adverts.' The following week was relatively quiet though the weather was stormy. 'Eleven fat lambs' went to Campden Market on Wednesday 21st – there has not been a market there for many years – and the next day Mainwaring and Brown came over to dig the garden again. Groves went to see Eric Leigh about a job on the Friday while Ted went to Moreton to fetch a chaff-cutter (for chopping hay to put into horse feed) and some disc harrows. The two horses were obviously living out in the field at this point, Rhythm an expectant mother on the Thirty-Acre and Simon in the Paddock 'for feeding', no doubt better for his health to be out in the field.

Katie came to stay on 27 November, arriving at 4.20 at Moreton Station to be met by Fry's Taxi – my Great-Aunt and

Granny's sister, she of *Radiant Health*. The next day Vivian took her to Cutsdean, delivering more socks for darning to Mrs Robbins and visiting Mrs Robeiro. The van went to Gloucester Car Auctions on the Friday accompanied by Ted and Katie; it was bought in at £370, a considerable sum in those days.

DECEMBER

Auntie Violet sensibly left these chilly shores on the first of the month to spend the rest of the winter on the Balearic Islands, accompanied by her cousin Bianca. Hounds ran along Bourton Downs having met at Broadway Tower, and two foxes were seen. 'The threshing machine moved in today ready for Monday.' Ted and Vivian went to tea with Dudley and Jeanette (Sandon) at Burnt Norton while Katie baked a cake for Ted's birthday on 3 December. Katie did not marry, but loved Ted to distraction, as well as fulfilling an endless round of family calls. Ted and Vivian – Katie must have been charged with my care – went to dinner with Midget at Kildanes that night of the 1st; Reggie (Sherston of butter-making fame) and Pam Colegrave with whom he lived, were also there. They got home at 2am!

The next day, a Sunday, Katie was taken to lunch at The Manor House in Moreton and I went too. Threshing started the next day, and Vivian had a 'perm' with Miss Clutterbuck in Cheltenham. Vivian, Katie and I visited Miss Woolrich in Bourton-on-the-Hill on the Tuesday; she ran the 'dame's school' there, somehow fitting around fourteen children into her tiny cottage. Perhaps I was being assessed for it, though I was not quite two years old at this point. On Wednesday 'the Guernsey cow went to the bull' of George Steele's at Bourton Hill, while Ted and Vivian were away for the day interviewing for domestic staff.

The Lifford Hall in Broadway was the scene of the North Cotswold Hunt Christmas Sale and the purchase of various gifts which were fetched the next day as 'forgotten parcels'. On 8 December Vivian visited Mrs Robeiro in Cutsdean and engaged her to start work the following Tuesday. Geoffrey left to return to Bledington, and Katie caught a bus to Broadway having to walk home a mile-and-a-half from Trooper's Lodge, the garage still on the main road above Kildanes. The local police inspector (was there less crime then?) called at lunchtime to inspect the *Animal Movement Book,* a precaution against disease. On Sunday evening Ted and Vivian went to drinks with the Marlands in Campden. Groves and Mrs Groves left on the Wednesday, and on Thursday Granny came over and gave her sister a well-deserved lunch out. Mrs Robeiro was being fetched daily, a mixed blessing when it was 'very foggy – roads iced'.

A Mrs John appears to have started work also, as well as Ida Slatter. Mrs John rang her sister in London on Saturday, 15 December – it cost 4/- (20p). Hounds had run right through the yard and the silage pit that day. The next day, Sunday, was again spent drinking at the Marlands where Ted and Vivian met John and Hilda Bourne from Snowshill Hill (to which Hornsleasow and Smallthorns belonged). Katie went too. Williams came to complete the chimney-sweeping on the Monday and Aldens came to instal a replacement for the troublesome ram in The Scrubs; it took them three days to complete the work. 'Broilers and cockerels' were collected for a poultry auction that Tuesday and on the Wednesday, having just spent a day in Cheltenham for the Land Rover to be serviced, Ted had to tow Alden's men out from The Scrubs, no doubt in the dark at 4.30pm, their work completed.

Ken and Jane Hay arrived at Bourton Far Hill on the Friday afternoon, just on the off-chance, but Vivian had to take Mrs Robeiro home and then go a few hundred yards further to Taddington to interview Ethna Brown who was to look after me. Ken by this time had only one hand, having blown the other off when dynamiting fish some years before on a poaching expedition. He often neglected to wear his artificial hand, which wore a black glove and was sinister in the extreme, but it was even more disturbing when he waved the bare stump of his arm during conversation, which he did often.

On 22 December the redoubtable Katie, who completely belied her fragile exterior, was fetched by Granny to spend Christmas at Radway having stayed with us since 27 November. A Mr Iles came to look at the bought-in van, and Roy ploughed up the water-pipe on the Hastings Field. Meanwhile, Vivian 'was busy in house all morning – making butter, roasting chicken, making mince pies, etc.' This comes as a surprise as by the time my memory begins, Mrs Leathers had taken over entirely and Vivian never cooked seriously again unless it was necessary. The 'pigs went for grading' on Sunday, 23 December.

A Mr Butters (tel: Cheltenham 2670) came to inspect the van on Christmas Eve. Christmas Day was spent at Radway with lunch cooked by the devoted Mrs Mainwaring, then at Leamington for tea 'to see Daddy, Elizabeth, Henry (Vivian's brother), Caroline and Binkie [the cat!]' Marjorie, Betty, Dick and Margaret (Tunbridge) – also relations – were there at first. We reached home at 8.40pm. This rigorous routine was adhered to throughout my childhood and adolescence, and Ted was a saint for putting up with it.

Boxing Day saw Vivian 'busy cooking family Christmas lunch' and in the evening they went to a cocktail party at the Adsheads in Campden . Mr Butters, who lived in Charlton Kings on the edge of Cheltenham, took delivery of the van on 27 December and for the first time I see that Mrs Rood had started to work for us. Midget meanwhile returned from a nine-day Christmas cruise. On 29 December Roy took the morning off to fetch his wife and new baby, and dear Ethna came with her mother to see the house and me, and was engaged on trial.

Vivian made butter which she completed the next day, and on New Year's Eve Leslie Exton started work and Katie came back from Radway to stay for another four weeks until 30 January 1952, seeing me through a fairly prolonged bout of illness before she left for London on the 9.37 train, arriving at Paddington at 11.30am (a very slightly longer journey time then).

Hunting had taken a back seat for both Ted and Vivian during the season of 1951/2; they were too busy establishing the farm and constant staff changes cannot have helped. Neither had they managed to organise enough fit horses. However, things were about to improve as Mr and Mrs Leathers and their daughter Jacqueline moved into the cottage on 26 January 1952, arriving from Oxford at 5.30 on that snowy afternoon. Once the snow had gone, Simon was brought in and placed under a proper routine, being lunged first by Leathers before Vivian rode him after quite a long break. He even went out for the odd day's hunting with Ted before the end-of-season meet at Trafalgar Crossroads on 22 March 1952.

5

THE STAFF

'All the world's a stage,
And all the men and women merely players:
They have their exits and their entrances;
And one man in his time plays many parts,
His acts being seven ages.'
– As You Like It (1599), Act 2, Scene 7, by William Shakespeare (1564–1616)

'...thy rod and thy **staff** *comfort me.'*
– Psalm 23, verse 4

One of the meanings of 'staff'' in the *Concise Oxford Dictionary* is listed as 'a person or thing that supports or sustains.' Some who we employed came nearer to the mark than others. But they all addressed my father as 'Doctor', and if anything was amiss and enquiry was made of my mother, she would always advise: "You'd better ask the Doctor about that, he'll know what to do."

My father had a policy of employing men on the farm who had been 'left behind' by the war. Many found it very hard to fit back into civilian life and having had a hard time of it himself, he understood the difficulty. They were not all saints of

The Staff

course, and Seymour Lane in particular gave cause for concern. Picture this: the grain lorry from West Midland Farmers at the mill in Bourton-on-the-Water arrived to fetch the (jute) sacks of corn. This was a hard job as there were no mechanical loaders then and each sack weighed a full 56lbs (about 25 kilos). There were, in those days, even heavier sacks of 112lbs (one hundredweight), to be handled generally by two men, and those of two hundredweight also – these were for economy of scale when handling large quantities and were normally moved by a pulley. However they were made illegal around the end of the decade for reasons of safety. Seymour had been suffering from appendicitis, ending up in the John Radcliffe Hospital in Oxford with acute peritonitis – his recovery was proving a protracted business. However, this did not prevent him from coming to observe the proceedings, my father sweating away with the rest of them.

"How are you, Seymour?" he asked him, between sacks, ever hopeful of a positive answer.

"Me wound's still weepin' Doctor," he replied, with a broad, toothless grin and the certainty that nothing could assail him. Permanently clad in a sort of sacking garment tied round with binder-twine, he seemed like the spectral figure at the feast, continuing to spectate and give advice: "More to the right – no, no – why, you've dropped it clean down the side there" – even harder to lift a sack from the ground than from the granary platform with the lorry close alongside.

Annoyance must, in the end, have given away to some sort of utterance – "Why don't you just bugger off?"

Anyway, Seymour's house became vacant for one more able-bodied soon after as he plainly did not intend to return to work.

Bill Mitchell and his wife, Mrs Mitchell, her Christian name is unrecorded, were employed as farm foreman and household help respectively. Bill wore thick glasses, and was well educated and dependable. His wife was rotund, short of stature and short of hair. She was a Jehovah's Witness, which entailed (amongst other things) disbelief in Christmas or in Christmas presents – this did not prevent her from accepting our Yuletide gifts without so much as a 'thank you'. She had an unaccountable enthusiasm for the Chinese language; my conversations with her often centred around this as she proclaimed that they had a fine way, linguistically, of 'putting it over'.

Leslie Ireland was an interesting character; he had a disconcerting habit of circling the farmhouse in the evenings while carrying a loaded gun. If the curtains were undrawn we were often surprised by his face pressed close to the window.

"Just keeping a watch," he would say, with every appearance of helpfulness. My mother did not quite see eye-to-eye with him over this, and two final straws in the end presented themselves.

One sunny afternoon during the working week Vivian was startled as she looked out of the window to see Leslie sunbathing shirtless upon the lawn in front of the house: "What do you think you're doing, Leslie?" she asked.

"What does it look like?" came the obvious reply.

I, as a four-year-old, was quite transfixed by the sight of this shirtless man speaking insolently to my mother, who was keen on her status and expected her 'inferiors' to behave in a respectful manner. Matters were clearly going to come to a head; my father was called from his study.

"Leslie, it's time for the cows to come in," he sensibly said.

"Right you are, Doctor," replied Leslie, arising from the newly-mown lawn and going on his way.

The fact that my mother did all the lawn-mowing had in all likelihood contributed to her ire.

My father, despite his deafness, was a past master at dealing kindly and straightforwardly with people in all walks of life.

Nearly all disputes with our labour force were caused by my mother's overweening regard for rank and for how people should behave. "Never feel your own pulse," she would tell me if I was being tearful or complaining – no one found it harder to follow their own instruction than she.

I was not allowed out on the yard while Leslie was at work, which made me perversely and inevitably eager to parade myself, chanting the catchy lyric, "*Odor-o-no, odor-o-no,*" this was an early brand of female deodorant, men's deodorant being as yet unheard of – soap and water must suffice for them. A sharp reprimand followed, not so much for the supposed risk which I had run, but for the indecency of my advertising a deodorant which my mother obviously used. Was Leslie any the wiser though?

The second straw with regard to his job tenure was the extension of his gun-carrying habit to the environs of his own house and that of his semi-detached neighbour, Herbert Gill. Herbert was a mild-mannered man of whom I remember little, but his fear of being shot, even inadvertently, and his care for his family led him to board up his windows. Clearly, such a state of affairs could not continue. Perhaps the police were called. At any rate, Leslie vacated his house, taking with him all fixtures and fittings: light bulbs and fittings, lavatory seats, door-knobs, anything remotely removable was removed. I believe that later on he ended up in jail. All this was especially galling as the lodges had been built to the highest specification in the belief that good housing would be appreciated and would encourage good work. Housing was 'tied' to the farm, counting, together with coal and milk towards a considerable increase on the weekly agricultural wage of £4 a week. Their rating (council tax payable) was settled on 2 January 1954 at the Magistrates' Court (closed early in the twenty-first century) in Stow-on-the-Wold, when Ted had to wait for most of the day before his case came on – there was a reduction to £3 gross, £2 net.

Bob Morris was a different man entirely. Leslie I remember as short and squat and given to sweating freely. Bob wore a moustache, was tall and good-looking. Born in 1913, he would have been a little over forty when I remember him. I have a feeling that his war service had been somewhat eventful and he came from immigrant stock, his father having left for Australia as a young man.

"I've got this nancy-ish uncle," he told us, "who does daubs and fancies himself as an artist. Queer cove, no doubt about it, and a baronet too. Not likely to have children, if you know what I mean, so I'm his heir. *Sir* Cedric Morris, you see. Hardly know him. Funny really."

Bob became the 10th Bart – the Morris family had started making money early in Welsh mining.

Cedric Morris and the artist Arthur Lett Haines lived at Pound Farm near Highnam in Suffolk. They ran an art school, their foremost pupil being Lucien Freud. John Skeaping, the sculptor, was a close friend. After the Second World War they moved to Benton End where Cedric's attention gradually turned more towards his beloved garden, horticulture and his motley collection of exotic birds, which had always been a fascination. Perhaps he and Bob shared some common ground after all. This is where they were living when Bob came to work for us at the farm.

The best of Cedric's pictures sell for well into five figures these days – landscapes, bright and sensual flowers, fritillaries being a favourite. Years after, I viewed a retrospective of his at the Tate in London, and later managed to acquire some of his pictures which now hang in pride of place in our house. Lett, for so long his devoted companion, was the more original artist, but his talent became forgotten as he was absorbed into domestic duties after an initial first flush of fame in America.

Bob had already been in our area for a while and had married a local girl, Christina Field, soon after the war had

The Staff

ended. They had three children, and keeping up the paternal taste for emigrant travel, they went to farm in Canada after leaving Bourton Far Hill. They did exceedingly well, as we were often told in a succession of Christmas cards. I think that Dad often thought of going there himself, and felt rather envious. He had always had dreams of exploration, not to be fulfilled.

Foster Russell, an obvious 'gent', had fallen on hard times, not helped by a volatile wife, Nan. He was rubicund, sturdy, with slightly crooked teeth revealed in frequent smiles, and a crown of dark curly hair just starting to be peppered with grey. Nan helped in the house, and being hotly temperamental she shortly came to virtual blows with my mother. I have an abiding memory of her running out of the house, blonde hair flying in the winter wind, tearing up the Rick Yard towards home, and then turning at the top to shout at my mother: "You bloody stinking bitch... bitch... bitch!"

Who knew what that was all about? But probably six of one and half-a-dozen of the other would have been close to the truth. Frictions between Vivian and the farmworkers' wives who cleaned were nothing unusual, and in the end Foster sadly gave his notice because of this, and was much missed by my father.I certainly had no rows with Willie, the Russells' only child. A year younger than me, at nearly three, he was my accomplice behind the cowshed in an endless game of 'dickies and botties'. Unburdened as yet by the demands of school, we spent happy hours at this wondrous game of discovery, watched over, when they were in, by Poppy a black cow, and Iris a blue roan, part of our small milking herd of five.

John Hiscox was another 'gent' hard done by in the war. He was serious and unsmiling, generally branded a 'bore' by my parents. He actually managed Snowshill Hill, John Bourne's next-door estate, and lived about a mile down the road in a newly built house named Hornsleasow. We came into contact a good deal with John and his wife Win as they had a son of my age, Jonathan. I think that he must have come on the scene a little later than Willie as there was no question of exerting ourselves behind the cowshed, or perhaps we simply weren't attracted to one another.

Both Foster and John contrived to send their sons to public school – Willie to Clifton and Jonathan to Rendcomb. Schools were much less relatively expensive in those days, and perhaps they had means beyond those of the normal farmworker. The social mix of those who came to work on the farm only shows how much society in general had been shaken up by the war. After all, it had ended only five years before we went to live there.

Some workers did, of course, come from a more traditional farming background. We've all heard the 'joke' question, 'When did you stop beating your wife?' Well, Groves (I never knew his Christian name) never did: she was regularly beaten every Friday evening, though he was a small, wizened man and she was a woman of generous proportion. I suppose it follows that this Friday night happening was more of a ritual than anything specifically corrective; it was a not uncommon custom in those days amongst working people, and for all I know, higher up the social ladder too. (This puts a 'gloss' on domestic violence, now so much in the news. It was customary and accepted, even if not acceptable to modern opinion.)

The Groves lived in the cottage adjoining the house, where Leathers the groom and his wife and daughter would live after them, and where we would live while the house was being added to later on in the '50s. The sound of blows, but no protest, would sound through the walls. My mother, quite naïve in some ways, was at first aghast. My father, as ever pragmatic, said, "Don't interfere. You won't be thanked for it."

Race, whose Christian name is similarly unrecorded, lived at the bottom of the drive in one of the lodges, built by the middle of the decade. He too had an earthy look, as became his principal function of molecatcher. "Catch 'em young," he'd advise, although I never could understand how you ensured the age of your mole, once caught. Their perfect little skins – Race had an excellent catching technique – would hang outside the back door for a while. What became of them afterwards is a mystery; perhaps they really were manufactured into garments. Who knows?

Race's other function was as tractor driver, able to assist in such matters as animal foddering in the fields, or sinking posts for gate-hanging. A man of few words, one morning he appeared at the back door, badly cut about the face.

"Ooh, Doctor, tractor's done for me," he exclaimed. "It were fair powerful up on field, just ran away with me it did."

Come to think of it, we had heard something of a crashing sound from up the yard minutes earlier. Upon investigation, the tractor was found, its radiator impaled upon the hinge-spikes of a half-hung gatepost.

"How did you manage it this time?" my father inquired, similar though not so serious accidents, such as falling off the back of the seed-drill, having happened before.

"Ooh, it were my right foot. It just stuck, so it did," clearly, of course, upon accelerator rather than brake. Race seemed certain that the accident was the fault of his foot rather than his own. In the end inquiries were made as to his health, and it emerged that he had been dropped on his head when a baby. Co-ordination thus impaired, he was removed from tractor driving forthwith.

Mrs Race came from the urban north and was used to trams passing the door. She sorely missed the town and its attendant delights, such as shopping. She was a keen dresser and liked everything to match: "the mooshroom 'at to go with the mooshroom coat" was essential in her eyes. She and Race left soon after the tractor incident. I do hope that she had more opportunity for snappy dressing wherever they went.

Although the men occur more frequently in my story, the women were no less important. Indeed, they were essential to the running of the place, and the wives of men working on the farm, Nan Russell among them, often came to work in the house, wearing flowered wrap-around overalls as all cleaners did then. Chiefest among them must rank Mrs Rood, floor-scrubber par excellence, laundress and silver-cleaner. How she achieved her 'targets' in less than a full day I shall never understand, ironing everything which had been hung to dry on the airer above the Aga as her final task, before being taken home to Cutsdean. She would scrub the stone floors of the kitchen and outer offices, using a sponge kneeler for support. Shrunken in an early middle-age, brought on by a lifetime of overwork, no more than five feet tall, the mother of five children (the youngest no more than two years my senior) she worked her fingers almost literally to the bone. I don't suppose that we were the only people to employ her either. Her husband Jim was the cowman at Lower Coscombe, so their working hours were early and long. They had a terrier named Waffles who ate grapes (I've since found that this is quite usual amongst terriers) and I stayed the night with them on more than one occasion when my parents were away and Ethna had ceased her duties as Nanny once I went to school.

All this domestic help may sound impossibly grand, but electrical aids were still few in houses then. Hoovers were relatively inefficient (though an upright one is included in Queen Mary's pre-war dolls' house at Windsor Castle) and a Bissell carpet-sweeper was just as often used. The twin-tub washing-machine, let alone an automatic (which my mother would never allow, believing it to use too much water) was bought only later in the decade, so that Mrs Rood must make do with a scrubbing board and a mangle with which to wring clothes out. The Aga, burnished to a loving sheen by my mother, its silvered hot-plate lids scoured so that you could see your face in them, and its proudly polished cream body topped with black and bearing the inimitable brown Aga signature on the door of the boiler, looking like new until the end of its days fifty years later, was the one modern piece of domestic equipment, and even so it must run on solid fuel (the only fuel for Agas then) and be stoked twice a day.

The Frigidaire Deep Freeze arrived on 6 June 1952 and at first lived in the cellar, taking three hours to instal. Later on it would have to work much harder as it moved upstairs into the kitchen, having to compete with the Aga, alight all the year round as our only means of cooking. Then was the heyday of my mother's delicious fruit lollies made from grapefruit or orange juice, a boon to us children when tired out from summer playing.

Mrs Leathers, her grey hair worn in a tight bun, cooked for us. She had large capable hands and a comforting manner, and she wore a great white apron to cover her ample bosom, as all good cooks must. I was allowed to lick the cake mixture from the bowl during her weekly baking sessions, and she made some especially delicious puddings, one being delightfully named Apple Courting Cake, a sublimely rich confection of cream, pastry, sponge and of course, apple. She was not above giving my mother the rough edge of her tongue when she felt it necessary, as was recorded in the diary – 'most insulting!'

At least we had electricity though; the farm must have been electrified well before the war, but it came to the whole of Cutsdean only later in the '50s. Many of the cottages then, though not the Roods', had beaten earth floors worn into an undulating, shiny, freckled surface. Quite beautiful. And Miss Wright, of the indigenous Cutsdean farming family, ran a tiny

Post Office on the far side of the village green, selling stamps and weighing mail from behind an ancient wooden counter. Now there is no Post Office in any of the eight villages running along the River Windrush from Taddington, making do with four hours of 'outreach' service for the week, as if for savages.

Ethna was a local girl from Taddington, the next-door village to Cutsdean, which I used to muddle with London's Paddington Station at my small age. She was freckled of face, red of hair, and you could say, a bit 'wanting'. She had a nasty and much-relished habit of chasing me up the stairs, just brushing my heels with her fingers, while she boomed "I'm a-comin!'" in her deep voice. She had an innate sense of what would please a child, being something of a forever child herself. Her kindness and capacity for affection were astonishing; I never recall a cross word or any irritation on her part; I truly believe that she saved my pre-school childhood from an otherwise great loneliness, as brothers and sisters there were none, and it became clear later on that my mother had never had any intention of having more than one child.

Riding for Darbys (the Rugby horse-dealers who mounted the Empress Elizabeth of Austria when she came to England to hunt) had been an incomparable experience for a highly competent rider such as Vivian, but her first love of music was never quite extinguished in the rough-and-tumble of farm life, and I shall always remember, as a small child, sitting quietly with her listening to Elgar's cello concerto, Grieg's piano concerto in A minor and Rimsky-Korsakov's symphonic suite *Scheherazade* – my staples still for a desert island if ever I were asked.

She found motherhood, at least in the early stages, a trying business I think, especially as I was a rather dreamy, remote little girl, not keen to be hugged too much in my early and more confident years. Hers and my father's marriage lay at the more complicated end of the relationship spectrum, compounded by his deafness. (Living with a very deaf person makes you realise how hard they must work to hear. Having a father who rarely 'heard' me as I grew older was a profound influence and a source of deep sadness to us both, I think, when he came to old age.)

Vivian's energies were absorbed by her perceived duty to be Ted's 'pair of ears' and by her longing to communicate with an often seemingly unwilling communicant – in fact, more often than not, it is just that deafness makes trying to hear an exhausting business. But one bright spot lay on the horizon: Maeve.

Maeve Horsfall came from Battle in Sussex where her widowed mother lived. She called me 'Fruitcake' or 'Small', and was endlessly kind and gently funny. She was a sort of groom, though she helped out in many other ways too, and had come to us as a replacement for Leathers, too old to work for us for more than a few years.

Perhaps Maeve's and my mother's relationship was made so easy by the fact that Maeve was a 'lady' and thus looked at life in much the same way. My mother taught her to drive on the farm, as I was to be taught later by my father, courtesy of the green Land-Rover. Impoverished and never married, though she had once been engaged ("Never marry a man if you begin to dread the sound of his footsteps," she once told me), she was very well connected and had worked for the Lawson-Johnsons, the family of Lord Luke in Bedfordshire. She was a great friend of theirs, as she became of ours.

"How are you today, Fruitcake?" she asked me one morning, an engaging habit of hers. I must have been feeling a bit low, or was just not thinking, in that childish way that children have. The light glinted off her glasses as she came towards me in the saddle-room and I stepped backward – straight into the tack-cleaning bucket full of water. My childish sense of propriety and self-importance completely took over so that the more Maeve laughed the angrier I became, stamping *both* my feet and screaming with impotent fury.

"Come on Fruitcake, calm down, calm down," Maeve soothed. "It's only an accident. I'll have you cleaned up in no time." I had a horror of being dirty or unkempt.

Things soon righted themselves of course, especially as she had a good story to tell me, about a cock on a dunghill made from a tree, who bestrode the landscape in great boots, which reminds me nowadays of The Ents in *The Lord of the Rings*. Perhaps she had read it, as it had been published for a few years by then. The figure of the cock was based on the shape of a tree which looked like a crowing cockerel, standing on the far horizon in front of our house. Maeve would walk over to inspect this tree on her days off, but I was too small to accompany her.

"He actually spoke to me this time," she told me after one journey. "He said that when you are bigger you should come with me as he has special things to tell you, things that only he could say, and no one else."

Maeve left soon afterwards as her mother had become unwell. I never made the journey to the tree, but often I would hear the cock crowing to me as I slept. I never learnt what it was that he would tell me though. The tree, and he, still adorn the skyline.

Maeve it was who gave me another valuable introduction. The television, won by my mother in a competition on the back of cereal packet, announced a forthcoming drama, *Huntingtower* by John Buchan. "*Huntingtower*! she exclaimed. It's one of the best books you'll ever read. John Buchan wrote *the* most exciting books."

She was right. Nothing can equal the pace and excitement of Buchan at his best, and he's no mean historian either. I began to devour his work at probably around the age of eight.

The Lloyds were a lovely couple, kind and gentle, and I suspect fallen rather below their original station in life. Mrs Lloyd was pretty even in middle-age, grey hair in a soft bun, with a soft voice and a natural courtesy. She baked fantastic cakes, and gave me some of the mixture. She had a comforting manner which unaccountably annoyed my mother.

"Stupid woman," she would say. "What use is it to say that the kettle *has* boiled?"

I knew that this had been meant as a kindness and a reassurance of imminent refreshment. What would we give for such a greeting upon returning home in these more comfortless days? But my mother, so sadly for her, was not easily given to accepting kindnesses. She had an extraordinary anger with the world and many of those in it, undoubtedly born of lack of love in childhood and compounded by a lack of patience and understanding on my father's part. I came in for my share of the anger, meted out as strict discipline: my hair was regularly cut unbearably short by Miss Clutterbuck (a foul woman, the memory of whom even now stirs me to disgust) on one of our periodic trips to Cheltenham. I would weep uncontrollably as my tresses, which I so longed to have in a pony-tail, were shorn to the floor, and I was left shaking with grief and counting the weeks until they might grow acceptably long again. This was all supposed to be good for my character, I suppose.

Years later, towards the end of her life, Mum wept as she lay in bed: "All I ever wanted was to be loved."

"I love you, Mum," I said, and as I said it, it became true; after years of enmity and misunderstanding, I was suddenly a little girl again, trusting and innocent still.

I had always respected her, feared her even, and sometimes loathed her for the weight of expectation that she had placed upon me, but for that one instant those barnacles laid by time's hand had vanished, and we were re-made for one another.

Mr Lloyd was a World War I veteran whose duties were confined to shoe and boot cleaning.

"Poor old Lloyd," my father would say. "His breathing is very bad today," as Mr Lloyd (as we always called him to his face) wheezed through his work. He was a short, stout man with a pugnacious face and a discreet smile, who had been gassed while fighting in the trenches and had been in ill-health ever since. He had been a young man then, but some forty years later you would have guessed him to be well into his 70s. He was lucky, though, to have kept his sight and his mobility, and indeed his life.

They constituted a veritable gallery, our band of helpers. From high to low in social caste, from the semi-criminal to the right-thinking undaunted, exaggerated by the fortunes of war in almost every case, they were indeed a passing show to 'the little girl with the kirby grip', so absorbed by the doings of her elders.

*Ted in uniform as a Captain in the RAMC
(Royal Army Medical Corps) c1940*

Grandpa Eason (Wilf)

Granny Eason (Mabel)

Ted winning the mile at Malvern 1933

Ted leaving a 'sitz' (sauna) Barosünd, Finland 1935

Ted prospecting in a stream near Wellington, Somerset 1935/6

Ted doing a 'roll' over a rail, Newmarket c1936

Ted, Ken Hay and Joan (Ted's sister) at Oak Brow 1936

'Pixy', Joan, Chris Smalley (her fiancé and later, first husband, killed in the raid on St Nazaire in 1941) and 'Jill'

Marian at seven months old at Chapel Lodge at Heightington, Worcestershire 1950

A family group at Chapel Lodge, Heightington 1950

Aeriel photo of Bourton Far Hill before building on, early 1950s

*North Cotswold Hunt Opening Meet, Broadway, November 1950.
L–R: Vivian, Johnnie Pearson, Fairlass Harrison, the Revd Hodson
(Rector of Stanton)*

Leathers holding 'Rhythm' and Vivian holding 'Cresta' at a local show 1952

Vivian and Marian 1953

Marian in the Apple Tree at Bourton Far Hill 1952/3

Maeve and Marian with lambs, Bourton Far Hill 1954

Marian on 'Polly' with 'Cresta' (aged two) 1954

Combining oats on the Thin Field, Bourton Far Hill, August 1955. Lush (?) and Ted on combine, Foster Russell down below

First load of barley away from Bourton Far Hill, August-September 1955

Sheep-dipping at Bourton Far Hill, Summer 1957. L-R: Bob Morris (?), Bill Mitchell and Ted

Billy Roberts with 'Cresta', March 1957

Patrick Pringle and Ted at Bourton Far Hill, Julie Pringle to the left, Spring 1957

'Kep'

'Shadow' in the Governess Cart with Marian outside the Stone Barns at Bourton Far Hill, with 'Tinker' and 'Tailor', Spring 1957

Ted, Vivian and Marian with 'Tinker' on the hayfield, 29th June 1957

Marian with 'Tinker' (right) and Tailor, Bourton Far Hill, Spring 1957

The water tank to the rescue! Ted and Marian at Bourton Far Hill, June 1957

Wilf and Ted with 'Tinker' at the ford at Castlett (the Vanguard in the background), Guiting Power, 5th June 1957

Ted and Vivian carrying the hay with 'Bounce' on the Snowshill Field, Bourton Far Hill, 25th June 1957

Picnic lunch at Dunraven, Lansdowne Circus, Leamington Spa, 4th August 1957. L–R: Evelyn, Caroline and Lizzie (Haynes) and Marian. 'Tinker' and 'Tailor' too!

Bill Mitchell sitting on 'Cowslip' (?), July/August 1957

Diana Colegrave's Picnic at Sezincote Warren, April 1958. L–R: Glenda Hannay, Marian, Susanna Gilmore, Fiona Hannay and ?

Grandpa (Alwyn) Haynes at Dunraven, Leamington Spa, late 1950s. He died in 1963

6

FARMING MATTERS

'Look after the land and the land'll look after you.'
– Old country saying

"We need rain!" my father's constant refrain, even when an untimely or unseasonal downpour looked set to ruin everything. Rarely would he retract from what amounted almost to a mantra – probably hay and harvest were the only times when even he would have to consider rain as an undesirable element in the scheme of things. Nothing delighted him more than to stand at the dining-room window as it streamed with drops of water through which the view to the horizon was just visible, sucking on his rather malodorous pipe stuffed with Three Nuns Empire (particularly hard to take in the back of the car with all the windows shut) and clasping his hands behind his back as he rocked on his heels with satisfaction.

"Good, good!" he would exclaim, as my mother relayed a wireless forecast of wet weather to come – his deafness made him prefer the television to the wireless. The springs in The Scrubs would remain 'fit for purpose', and he need not worry, at least for another week or so, that we might run dry. Rain was the key to everything and it was a source of constant amazement to him, as it is to me, that stock farmers can chance their arm in Australia as a Big Dry slowly kills their cattle, their sheep, and their livelihood.

The Roman road running across the Snowshill Field and into the far side of the Rick Yard (so called as the straw ricks, which we still thatched for their own protection, used to lodge here rather in their fields of origin) was next to the spot in the Paddock containing mounds and hollows which I was convinced concealed Roman treasure. In fact they indicated much more recent slate workings – Cotswold slate is famously hardy and good for roofing, though too expensive now for most people – it was visible from the air, and if you looked hard, from the ground also. It was a magnet for the more educated walker of those days, now the Right to Roam ensures a more aggressive stance, encouraging those who count it their 'right' to be able to exercise a leadless dog even when close to a field with livestock.

Walkers in those days bestrode the hills, as their Roman predecessors had done, along ancient routes which crested hills with uncompromising directness. The Snowshill Field was so high, nearly nine hundred feet above sea level, that its surface would lie bare of all but the lightest snow covering in winter, leaving short blades of grass to be driven by the wind, while the drive the other side of the wall would be drifted sometimes eight feet deep. This drifting was helped by some rather ill-advised tree planting, around the middle of the decade, on the other side of the drive from the field. My theory was that if the trees had been planted within the field the drive would have been better sheltered against the stormy blast. As it was, the belt of trees was some fifteen yards wide, consisting of soft woods – mostly larch and spruce – and containing within, a line of beech trees which, seventy years later, are well grown enough for the protecting soft woods gradually to be felled.

The farm was fenced almost entirely by dry stone walls, that is to say, walls which contain no cement. There were few hedges on the place but for a straggly affair which divided the Bank Field and the Jockey Field (opposite the jockey stables), and one which ran along the top of the Jockey Field all the way to the bridleway running along Bourton Downs. This contained some ancient iron railings which had probably formed an earlier barrier. Otherwise, only a few artificial fences of wire or timber made convenient, and more recent, divisions in the fields nearest to the farm. Dry stone walling is almost an art form, now firmly back in fashion due to environmental and conservation considerations, and the consequent availability of public money for at least partial payment. But in those days many walls were allowed to collapse as they were costly and time-consuming to maintain, and required wiring with barbed wire in order to contain the sheep who enjoyed jumping from field to field.

The black-faced Welsh sheep and the Kerry from Ireland, white-faced with black eyes and muzzle, were regular offenders and some people shied away from buying them for this reason. Not so my father, and not only did he wire his walls when necessary but he made a good stab at maintaining them too. Not for him the careful staking out of a base area with posts and string – he worked entirely by eye, grading the stones for satisfactory building and keeping the small ones for 'filler', and always without gloves in the coldest weather, 'walling' being a winter job in general when there was less other work to be done. I think that he found it relaxing, almost therapeutic: "I'm going out to my wall on the Thirty-Acre/Snowshill /Brown/ Smallthorns," he would say. "I'll be back for tea."

Of course there were times in winter when work was hard and long, during snow. Every winter would see at least one serious fall in those days; cattle and sheep would take much longer to feed, it was difficult to get round the farm, and harder still to get out onto the road as the drive drifted so easily. During one snowfall, Rhythm and Fanny, who were on the bank fields furthest away, had to be rescued through a raging blizzard and rapidly increasing drifts, Rhythm with a seriously cut pastern (the connection between hoof and leg); they were lucky to get home. We never had a snow-plough of our own, which could have gone onto the front of the tractor, which meant that once the snow came our only hope of getting to the outside world was by riding out. More than once the local council offered us an airlift by helicopter, but this was quite impossible as animals still had to be fed and water-troughs still had to be kept working despite their frozen state.

One particularly hard winter, we were offered the help of the council snow-plough – its usual non-availability was spectacularly compensated for when the driver succeeded not only in clearing the drive of snow, but in skimming the ground surface free of its newly applied tarmac surface – he had set the blade too low, it being hard to judge with such a weight of snow before him. Although the ploughing had been done as a favour my father took the council to court in a negligence suit and won, thereby winning himself no friends 'at court' and earning the lasting displeasure of the County Council's Chairman, Geoffrey Shakerley, later knighted for his public service.

Cattle, on the whole, were less work than sheep. They overwintered, generally without health problems, on our windswept, limestone upland, so good for the rearing of all animals. They suffered only a little at Bourton Far Hill from husk, a bovine cough which is dealt with by drenching; and gadding (when they could be driven almost mad in the summer months by the attentions of the gadfly, galloping wildly and sometimes smashing fences) for which a remedy, Ivermectin, became available during the '50s. This is now administered externally along the backbone, but back then was used only in drench form, necessitating the use of the cattle-crush, an essential for any bovine treatment, holding the head of a beast in an effective armlock. Occasionally one would panic and have to be quickly released to avoid strangulation. If there was no reaction to the compulsory TB test, they would remain until the following year when they were ready ('finished') for market. This would vary of course from beast to beast, entailing several enjoyable, pub-bound trips to Gloucester, Stratford, and Andoversford, amongst others, to sell them on. My father bought an early Ifor Williams trailer, suitable for transporting cattle as well as horses, so that he could take up to four animals himself, rather than using Bowles. The trailer, whose purchase gave such initial joy to my mother, was soon a bone of contention as cattle left huge traces of their occupation, rendering the trailer quite unsuitable for its alternative use as a horse transporter without much laborious cleaning. He took sheep in it too, usually tegs (overwintered young, and therefore lambless, ewes – he turned to these once he found lambing too arduous) at around twelve at a time.

"What a hell of a day!" he exclaimed upon his return one day from Banbury, not without a trace of a smile. He was later than usual, and told us why.

"I'd just got to South Newington when I noticed a couple of sheep galloping into a garden alongside. A woman was shouting and waving her arms. So I stopped."

"It must have been that door again," my mother interrupted. "It's never shut properly since you hit the side of the trailer on the wall." Having managed to insert a small accusation into the account, she must have been satisfied.

"Oh no, worse than that," my father owned, never one for a cover-up if events revealed an amusing story. "I'd forgotten to latch it. Those bends in South Newington slowed me up enough so that the sheep could jump out. About half of them made it into the woman's garden, and then they started to spread out to her neighbours."

"She must have been furious, I would have been," my mother said.

He looked at her: "No, not really. She joined in with a few others, and we managed to corral them in a closed space. Luckily, one of the men was used to sheep. It was a job getting them back in though. We had to let the others out."

No self-respecting sheep is going to go back the way it came, especially when an inconvenient jump through a high doorway is involved, unless you don't want it to, that is.

And then, reflectively, "She even asked me in for a cup of tea afterwards. We all needed it."

"How kind," Vivian said, suddenly relenting.

You would be lucky now to find such understanding householders, or to find a sheep-friendly person at home during the day.

There is no doubt at all that sheep are a lot of work. Why else are there full-time shepherds? Only in deepest winter perhaps do their demands ease up, though lambing now starts as early as Christmas, ensuring that a ewe can produce lambs twice in a twelvemonth. Lambing was a sleepless business, and hard work, even for two people, when the flock was two hundred strong. Multiple births of more than twins could be a problem, with the third lamb nearly always suffering rejection, though luckily there were usually enough ewes with singletons who could take on a second responsibility. The rarer quads, and very occasional quins, rarely survived in total. Occasional freak births, such as two-headed lambs and those born with more than four legs, were dispatched immediately – they would not survive anyway. There had to be a lot of manual intervention to ensure a maximum survival rate, sometimes aided by a dog standing near, which was known to encourage a reluctant ewe to foster an orphan lamb; there were always some bottle-fed lambs in any lambing season but the satisfaction of rearing a healthy flock of sheep was huge.

As the lambs grew to a few weeks old, they would be 'tailed', and the males, apart from the odd chosen one, would be castrated by means of a tight orange rubber ring placed around the infant testicles. Many farmers used this method for tailing also – Herdwick, the parti-coloured Jacobs and Portland are three of the few breeds which keep their tails. We never had such special sheep – but my father would heat up an ancient brazier into which he would put his tailing-irons until they were red hot, and the lambs would lose their tails in a single hygienic flash. They were extraordinarily quick to heal, and the tails would burn in the ever-faithful Aga boiler, the incinerator of much else that would otherwise have gone in the dustbin. I believe that lambs' tails make very good eating, but they must be troublesome to prepare.

Now it was the turn of the ewes for attention: 'Harris came with the fleece sheets' on 1 July 1952 so that they could be shorn of their weighty wool. The weightier the better, as wool was worth money in those days. A petrol-driven clipping machine was used for this back-breaking task, in later years performed by intinerant Australians perfectly honed for such work. Any shearing cuts, and there were always some, were immediately dressed with Stockholm Tar ('train-oil) to prevent 'fly-strike'. Once the ewes were shorn they were put through the sheep-dip – we constructed one at the bottom of the bull-pen orchard early in the decade. This was filled with a stringent organophosphate solution, murky grey and utterly opaque. Organophosphates had been licensed for use by the Agriculture Act of 1947, in the full knowledge that they were highly toxic to humans and could cause permanent damage to the nervous system. Many years later I sat next to Lord (Solly) Zuckerman at lunch – he had been the chief scientific adviser to the government when the act was being drafted. I wish that I had known then what I know now, as my father on one occasion, too enthusiastically wielding his dipping paddle upon a sheep's neck to ensure immersion, fell into the dip and totally immersed himself. How lucky he was to suffer no after-effects – others have not been so fortunate.

Sheep need worming at regular intervals, and this dosage was administered in drenching bottles which were designed to hold the exact measure. As many as possible would be brought into the bull-pen, making them easier to catch. Although sheep are large and quite heavy, once up-ended and sitting between your bent knees they are quite easy to handle. They would also be ear-tagged in this way, a lead-based, flexible tag being inserted with a special tagging device. This is now compulsory regardless of cost to the farmer, but most farmers tagged their sheep then for reasons of domestic identification and so that one batch of sheep was not confused with another. The tags were often removed when quick progress was being made through undergrowth, and ewes with torn ears were a common sight, which makes a nonsense of any idea that tagging provides a full-proof method of identification.

The sheep throve on our uplands, for it had been sheep country for centuries. Such complaints as liver-fluke, contracted more usually when sheep are kept on unsuitably damp or low-lying ground, were rare. But the twice-daily farm round was made for good reasons – sheep are prone to 'fly-strike', when the eggs of the bluebottle hatch out in the fleece and the resulting maggots can eat the sheep alive; and they get foot-rot, even on the best ground. I remember one ewe who had a large hole in her head, probably caused by a pulled horn which had not been spotted in time, and enlarged by maggots; she recovered. Sheep suffering from diarrhoea ('scouring') needed 'dagging', as flies would otherwise attack their hind parts, and my father always carried one or two sheep-knives in his pocket, horn-handled and stout-bladed, ready to pare away any defective horn from their feet. These knives needed only a quick wipe on the trouser leg before being used to slice an apple or a piece of cheese – the way to clean a knife when outdoors is to plunge it into the earth and immediately withdraw it; it will come out clean. Indeed, slightly tarnished metalware will emerge quite shiny from a short immersion in the ground.

The shepherd's crook was the other essential tool in the field; as long as you could get close enough to the designated sheep, a skilful wielding would draw the sheep to you by capture of a hind leg. And if a sheep needed an injection, there were syringes and needles for the farmer to use himself without recourse to the vet. These same needles, of a much coarser gage than those for use on humans, were used by my father on us if the need arose. The pain was intense.

Dead animals, 'fallen stock', were collected by the North Cotswold kennel huntsman as food for the hounds, as were any horses which were humanely destroyed by the huntsman by means of a captive bolt, or pistol bullet, fired at the exact crossing of diagonal lines drawn from the ear to the eye. One or two horses, especially loved, were buried on the farm – something forbidden by modern regulation for fear of fouling watercourses, a rule disregarded by anyone with any sense, who would never foul a watercourse anyway.

Bounce was our first working horse, acquired around the middle of the decade. She was not tall, around 15.2hh, and she was black with a blaze of white down the front of her face. Her legs carried a fair amount of 'feather', and I should think she was part-Shire, though her breeding was unknown. She was used for carting muck, of which there always seemed to be plenty – a man would actually come with a cart periodically to remove the mud from the farmyard – and for foddering animals in wet conditions, much easier than using a tractor. Later on, when our labour force diminished, she and my father would 'carry' the hay to the Dutch barn between them, a horse being much easier to use than a tractor as he merely had to say "Whoa!" to her when he needed to stop by a stook. She would also take us on blackberrying trips to the Purple Rough (long since grubbed up) on the far side of Happy Valley, which formed the boundary between Bourton Hill and Hinchwick. An enemy plane on its way back from a raid on Bristol had ditched its superfluous bomb load in the Rough during the war, to lessen its weight and enable it to reach home safely. It was said that there might still be a UXB (unexploded bomb) out there awaiting the unwary, so we had to be careful.

The first of the tractors was the 'Little Grey Fergie' (the Ferguson TE34), revolutionary in its time for its many attachments, some thirty in number, rather like a large Meccano set, which made it the first true 'jack-of-all-trades' on the farm. Later on, we acquired a red Massey-Harris (later Massey-Ferguson), and then a blue Fordson-Major which stayed on the farm until its dispersal at the end of the century. A red Nuffield was also part of the stable at one point. To Vivian's constant horror, an unguarded circular saw, its naked and viciously serrated blade turning fast, would run off one of the tractors; it was used solely by Ted for ensuring our domestic wood requirements, as legislation prevented any farmworker from using such a dangerous piece of equipment. Even the protection of gloves was refused, in the coldest weather too.

The resulting logs, to be burnt in an open fireplace in either the study or the drawing-room once the house had been built on to, would be carefully placed outside the kitchen window on top of the high wall, thus entirely exposed to the elements. Still very possibly damp, having been moved to a secondary storage in the hall fireplace they would be expected to burn once arranged to make a fire. Instead, they produced a steady sizzle, exuding water in the form of a light foam, and as the fireplace in the drawing-room smoked due to imperfect installation, the top window behind my father's chair had to remain open, ensuring that he sat in a persistent draught. Not surprisingly, neither my mother nor I tended to share these comfortless sessions, which he spent mostly behind *The Daily Telegraph*.

Once the harvest was over, at some point during early winter, Mr Lush from Temple Guiting, a small, olive-skinned man with a pock-marked face, would arrive to occupy the nearer stone barn with his threshing machine so that the grain might be separated from the straw stalk. Even now I can remember its unbelievable clattering noise, as he presided over its inner workings like some latter-day wizard. He did our combining too in the early years, combines in those days being much smaller and towed by a tractor – ten acres a day was regarded as good going then – as I think that first struggling harvest of 1951 had left Ted feeling that further harvesting was best left to the professionals.

On 6 October 1954, he was paid 55/-(£2.75) per acre for combining forty-five acres, a total of £123.15s/75p. I was reminded by our neighbour and erstwhile farmer Chris Hickman that harvesting would sometimes go on into November, the tractor driver stoutly wrapped against the cold, so perhaps we got off lightly after all.

This was the time of year for 'dressing' the fields with basic slag, a by-product of the coal industry, which left clouds of black dust trailing behind the tractor. Failing that, the muck spreader would flail its contents over the soil, thus maintaining a flourishing ecosystem. Even then Ted was nurturing an interest in the Soil Association and in natural ways of doing things, going somewhat against the grain of prevailing thought, which by the end of the '50s was becoming more and more in favour of chemical methods of cultivation in order to ensure larger yields. We, on the contrary, greeted the poppies and the cornflowers naturally occurring in crops with pleasure, and remained content with yields of around one-and-a-half tons to the acre, all that could naturally be expected on such stony upland.

"Good Lord, you'll never guess what I've just found in the silage pit," Ted exclaimed one morning as he came in, sweating from his laborious turning of the silage with its necessary dosing of molasses, a most foul-smelling business, as the grass steadily matured over a period of days.

My mother looked suitably enquiring, as he dug around in his pocket: "What on earth…?" she almost shouted. This as he produced a set of false teeth (his bad teeth having finally got the better of him), still much discoloured from a year outside their proper station, and popped them into his mouth.

"Oh Ted, how could you?" she remonstrated. "Where on earth did you find them?"

"In the silage pit," he grinned, delighting in her, and my, consternation. "I think they'll do. A bit bent though. I may have to straighten them. Saves getting some more."

He had endured a toothless year, determined that he would find his teeth again having lost them during the previous silage-making.

Another heavy horse called Molly came to us a few years after Bounce. She was of a nervous disposition, and had proved unequal to the task of being a dray horse at Vaux Breweries in Sunderland. She arrived by train one afternoon at Moreton-in-Marsh, sent down by Douglas Nicholson the Brewery Chairman – horses could still be transported by train until 1965 – and quickly proved herself no less nervous with us. One terrifying day at Evesham Show she almost wrecked the pageant as she ran away with her smock-clad crew of passengers, including me, screaming in the cart behind her. And my father's complaint to the visiting Master of the North Cotswold that the hunt had smashed several of his walls was entirely negated by the sight of Molly climbing over a wall to get into the field where they were observing damage, which was previously thought to be the responsibility of the hunt.

"Come and have a drink," was all he could say after that performance.

Most of the horses, at one time or another, were pressed into service for shepherding or cattle-herding, thus contenting my father in his desire that horses should be not just beasts of pleasure, but useful too. Some horses started by being rather wary, especially of sheep, but they soon learnt to be light and quick enough to deter even the most determined steer from evasion. One or two could have competed quite satisfactorily on the Western Riding circuit, Tich being something of an adept with Maeve on board. The smaller horses were also broken to harness so that they could draw the governess cart, which had been bought at Stow Fair as an adjunct to Shadow and Tich, and this vehicle too would go blackberrying in the Purple Rough.

'Farmers' Friend' it is called, and not just farmers' but hunt followers' too, as no hunting person should go out for the day without a knife and some string in his pocket, so that gates can be opened, and if necessary re-tied if any string has had to be cut. But not just any string – I am talking of binder twine, or baler twine/string as it is nowadays called. Today's twine, nylon, slippery and coming in various colours, is nonetheless a pale imitation of the redoubtable sisal twine of the '50s and before. This was straw coloured and hairy, and any strands kept together would cling mightily to each other – they could almost have been the prototype for Velcro. It was extremely strong and could be used for the making of halters for horses, for ropes, and for the repair of haynets, or anything really, a craft at which I became adept at an early age. It seemed to have a life of its own which lay far beyond its primary purpose of tying hay-bales and sheaves, and was so-called because it was the original twine used by binders before the baler came in. I mourned its passing, yet another example of the crazy passion for oil-based products – nylon string is no substitute at all when it comes to making things. Binder twine had one further use at Bourton Far Hill, as a belt for keeping up working trousers which had lost most of their other attachments. It vied for this use with the odd worn-out tie, and when trousers became worn at the knees Ted would turn them round so that his flies adorned his posterior.

He was not musical, and never had been, even in the days of his hearing, but sometimes, as he drove the tractor in its duties on the top fields of the farm, I would hear him 'singing it' along at the top of a tuneless and rejoicing voice. Despite, or more probably because of, the challenges and frustrations of the agricultural life, the farm made him happy in his solitude.

7

SPRING HILL

> '*The year's at the spring*
> *And day's at the morn;*
> *Morning's at seven;*
> *The hill-side's dew-pearled;*
> *The lark's on the wing;*
> *The snail's on the thorn:*
> *God's in his heaven –*
> *All's right with the world!*'
> – From *Pippa Passes* (1841) by Robert Browning (1812–89) –
> a favourite poem of Ted's

More than a house, an estate or a family, Spring Hill so named (like many other places, such as the former Home family home in Roxburghshire) because of its situation atop many springs, lay athwart the lives of all three of us – my father's, my mother's and mine. Walter and Kathleen Hannay – he a scion of an old Scottish merchant family, one of whose ancestors was painted by Batoni as he progressed on the Grand Tour; she a sister of Valentine Fleming (friend of Winston Churchill and killed in the Great War while his famous sons, Ian, Peter and Richard were still boys) and a member of the great banking dynasty founded by her grandfather Robert in Dundee in the 1860s – were the first to greet us upon our arrival at Bourton Far Hill.

"Of course," I remember Dad telling me when I was a little older, "they were both very grand in the very best way, kind and considerate, and eager to welcome newcomers: I think they thought that we were a little mad moving to such a bleak place, but it was next door to Midget so it made perfect sense. Do you know the convention governing calling cards?"

These were still in use in 1951, at least by my grandparents' generation and by a good many of my parents' too.

I always loved these conversations, when I would be vouchsafed some titbit of information not easily gleaned anywhere else and known by few of my contemporaries. My father and I interacted well when I was little despite his deafness; he was always the one who read me a bedtime story, and who even taught me for one term when I had to be taken out of school.

"No, tell me," I replied.

"I remember it so well, because I don't think anyone else actually paid an official call. Mum and I were both in the house when a large black car, a Bentley or something like that, rolled up at the front door. We must have had someone to answer the door; there's not much point in paying official calls if you're going to open it yourself."

"No, I suppose not," I said a bit doubtfully.

"If we had not been 'in', in other words, not receiving callers, the calling card would have been left with the top right-hand corner turned down to show that they had called in person. If someone working for them had brought it, just to make contact, the card would have remained unfolded at its corner on a card tray in the hall, and it would have been preceded by the announcement of the name of the caller in any case, whether the caller had come in person or not." Cards were the size of a business card, generally engraved in copper-plate and engraved, of course; nowadays, engraving comes rather expensive so that any formal invitation, which is becoming increasingly rare anyway, is more often printed.

I could see now why calling cards needed a door-answerer. They were a sort of signalling device, preserving distance between caller and called-upon until the latter felt like bridging the distance.

What would many of us give for such a barrier these days when every knock on the door, welcome or unwelcome, opportune or inopportune, timely or untimely, has to be answered without any possibility of cover?

"So did they come in? What were they like?"

I could, in fact, dimly remember Walter, with a full head of white hair and a large moustache – he died while we children were only two or three – and the rather younger Mumpsy (Kathleen) rather better as she outlived him by ten years or so. She was reminiscent of Queen Mary, frequently dressed in the Edwardian manner and with ropes of pearls adorning her on official occasions; otherwise, she tended to wear shorts in the summer, and being of a practical nature, used a Boy Scouts' belt with a pen-knife and sundry other handy tools attached to it.

"They came in, sat down, and from that first moment it was as if Mum and I had known them all our lives."

There was, in short, a magical connection, though my father described it in more prosaic terms.

From that day forward we were *persona grata* at Spring Hill. The place became my second home, and Alison, Mumpsy's daughter-in-law, described me as her fifth daughter until she died in my middle age.

Spring Hill was what would be described as a small Georgian mansion; four-square, built around a central courtyard; possibly begun in the reign of George III it served as a hunting box during the hunting season 1872/3 for the 9th Earl of Coventry towards the end of his Mastership of the newly formed North Cotswold Foxhounds. His seat was at Croome Court in Worcestershire; it was sold in 1948, the 10th Earl having sacrificed himself during the Battle of Dunkirk in 1940 in order to prevent the village of La Bassée from being razed by the SS. Instead, they shot him. His memorial can be seen in the church of St Mary Magdalene at Croome and he is buried at Givenchy-lès-la-Bassée. He had inherited the earldom from his grandfather, his father having predeceased him in 1932.

The approach was from the back through an archway into the courtyard, and from the front from lower ground to an oval sweep leading to stone stairs sheltered by a stone canopy, and a front door with glass in the upper panels. You stepped into a spacious hall with a metal-balustraded, wide and shallow staircase curving up from it.

On the left was a dining room with a dining table that could seat around twenty-four; portraits of Walter and Mumpsy looked down on us, as well as a number of pre-Revolutionary Russian paintings done in traditional style. (Walter, through Fleming investment, had done much business in Russia and the Baltic in the 1930s, as had Grandpa, and he was a partaker in the Kraenholm Mills cotton-spinning enterprise in Estonia, mentioned earlier. They might even have met during this time which, perforce, ended with the coming of the war.) To the right lay the drawing room, filled with fine furniture, and at the end of the passage off the hall was a music room, a later addition to the house, whose walls were lined with portraits of hunters past and present by the horse artist Mabel Hollam, each individually named. This was the scene of many a fine party over the years, from when we were very small until adulthood and later decades.

The house was built on three floors and with a considerable basement, which housed a fine (wine) cellar and a necessarily gargantuan boiler. Twelve or thirteen bedrooms, counting the nursery wing, and all that goes with that, takes some heating. The ground floor accommodated a kitchen, which was then a monument to Victoria – dark paint and woodwork everywhere, a huge wooden kitchen table, rows of heavy cooking pans hanging on hooks from the ceiling, and a cook named Aggie. Her husband Ernie Pru was the head gardener, and they lived in a cottage alongside the back drive and amid a formidable walled vegetable garden, furnishing all domestic requirements in the way of *legumes*.

Next to the kitchen was the billiard room, another later addition further along a stone passage, and next to that was a similar size room containing a ping-pong table. I became quite good at table tennis, though I was never what you would call a good games player. At the end of the passage was a door leading to a large enclosed yard at the back of the house, and a stone stairway led upwards from here to the nursery wing of the house. The children's bedrooms were rather similar to school dormitories of the time, with metal-framed beds, eiderdowns, a lino floor with rag rugs beside the beds, high windows with rather inadequate curtains. In short, every expense was spared, a far cry from the almost compulsory designer-ism of today's juvenile accommodation.

The nursery itself could have come straight from the pages of *A Secret Garden*. It contained a battered rocking-horse, an elderly upright piano, a wind-up gramophone and a quantity of children's books, mostly (as I remember) of the illustrated variety, rather different from the classics which I was beginning to devour at home.

Nanny in her starched uniform presided over a strict tea-table, which I approached with trepidation.

She was exacting in her requirements of us: "Now children, *no* talking while your mouths are full, and Fiona, most certainly no icing until you have finished your cake. Elbows *off* the table if you please, Marian" – we had laxer standards at home. "Sit up *straight*, Glenda, if you please."

Even grown-ups were not immune from her admonishments. Robert, the girls' father, and Alison would frequently visit us while we were at tea, sometimes partaking of the goats' milk that we were all-too-often served with. If they were caught in any lapse of behaviour they too were for the 'high jump'.

"Mr Robert, that's a terrible example you're setting there," she would remonstrate as Uncle Robert leant across the table to pick the one remaining cherry from the iced cake. He would be abashed and rebuked, and look suitably ashamed.

I loathed goats' milk and the whole discipline that went with teatime, and when asked over only for tea would passionately and tearfully beseech my mother that I should not have to go. The commands of straightly grey-haired Nanny were reinforced by a nursemaid called Valerie, so there was absolutely no escape. Mum rarely gave me a get-out, though as she thought it (quite rightly) a good thing for me to mix at every available opportunity, rather than secluding myself in my bedroom with a book – I began to read at an early age in typical only-child fashion.

My parents and Robert and Alison became fast friends, and an agreement was reached whereby I would go to live with them if anything should ever happen to both Mum and Dad. How thankful I am now that nothing did, as I would have been consigned to a diet of goats' milk. I am told that it is not nearly as health-giving as it might be, as the excretory organs of the goat are rather too close to the udder for comfort.

During Mumpsy's lifetime, and for a good many years afterwards, the girls only came to Spring Hill during school holidays as their father was a practising barrister in London. They lived in a tall house in SW10, which became a bolt-hole during my teenage years. Robert's younger brother Lennox, a soldier in the Scots Greys, became the full-time incumbent at Spring Hill upon his mother's demise, when he left the army to return to the estate as a full-time farmer. 'Flashing Dashing Lux' we called him. Tall, good-looking, eternally affable, we adored him as an elder brother.

"Oh, *please* Lux, can we come with you?" we would beseech him; however seemingly boring his errand might be, he held always the promise of excitement and glamour. His friends were no less fascinating to us, coming mostly from a military background: Norman Arthur was one, who competed regularly, while a serving officer, at Badminton and encouraged Lennox to build wonderful fences to jump all round the estate, which greatly improved the hunting.

Charlie Douglas-Home, later editor of *The Times*, was another. "Hi, girls! Great to see you," was his enthusiastic greeting. He never patronised our junior status, and always had something amusing to tell us. He had a shock of blond hair and a smiling face, and a deep intelligence and sympathy for others. His widow, Jessica, is one of the prime movers in the attempt to conserve the few traditional Saxon farming areas left in Rumania, also including the renovation of country houses devastated after their Communist confiscation in 1947.

I was almost exactly halfway between Fiona and Glenda in age and two years lay between them. We described ourselves as the 'highest' (that was me as I was always tall for my age and reached my full height by the time that I was twelve), the 'middlest' (Fiona, the older of the two girls) and the 'lowest' (Glenda, more slightly built than her sister). Fiona was an extrovert, curly-headed and even then showed great musical ability, as well as being strong and athletic. Glenda was the more intellectual of the two, though no less musical, and to this day they both play regularly to a professional standard, Fiona being a teacher of music.

Our time together was spent roaming the garden and the adjoining woods, which lay within the wall encircling the house and its grounds. We built a den in the yew trees with its back against the wall and furnished it with all that we could scavenge from the kitchen – broken cutlery, dishes with bare patches where the enamel had been lost, saucepans lacking a handle, together with rugs and blankets that had seen better days. Away from the constraints of the nursery and the possibility of goats' milk, we whiled away the hours in stories of the ponies and the pets which shaped our lives and governed our imaginations. Mine was actually a racehorse, *Baron de Cur*, who had a silvery neigh (he was inspired by Cresta, bred by my mother to achieve fame as the 1959 winner of Badminton Horse Trials) and ran faster than the wind, while theirs were even more fantastic. Sex and boys were as yet beyond our ken; boys were rather an unknown quantity, although I had plenty of experience of them at primary school and thought them pretty loud and somewhat stupid. Our feminine circle suited us well, and was no less active for lacking the male element, which would arrive all too soon. And as we talked and expanded our world, a peacock would interrupt us with a his raucous, melancholy cry. More than one cock and several hens lived in the garden, though I never discovered where they spent the night.

Ted's deafness looked as if it might replicate itself in me when I was five or six years old. The colds of childhood invariably turned into the most solid and persistent catarrh, which left me presiding over a steaming jug of Friar's Balsam for much of wintertime. Earache was an all-too-frequent accompaniment to this and often one ear would become blocked so that hearing was difficult. Oddly enough my father did not seem unduly alarmed by this possibility; perhaps he was so accustomed by now to his own disability (and it most certainly is, especially when deafness comes in adult years, whatever deaf campaigners may say) that he saw the chance of it in others as quite normal; anyway, my condition worsened sufficiently for me later to have to spend two weeks in hospital before things began to improve. This meant that the swimming pool set in the park below the front of Spring Hill and beyond the ha-ha, was out of bounds for me except as a spectator dabbling my toes in the dark green water, it being strictly forbidden to have my head under water.

"Oh, Marri, please come in, give it a try, we'll help you," came the siren cry from either Fi or Glennie.

"No, not today. I'm too cold," or "I'm not feeling well," I would say by way of excuse.

Actually, it was not much of a siren cry as the cold green water with plenty of algae and frog spawn thrown in did little to entice me, afraid as I was of water anyway. I remained firmly ashore while they, with typical Scottish hardiness, enjoyed every minute of their cold immersion.

Although a strong swimmer himself, my father did not seem to be concerned that I was to be firmly classed as a non-swimmer until I learnt in my late twenties, taught by my then husband in the more salubrious setting of Dolphin Square in London. Parents cannot see to everything.

We all had ponies from an early age, and enjoyed the freedoms and rural pursuits of children then generally available without the hindrance of any whiff of the dreaded health and safety. As a result, we were no strangers to bumps and bruises. One of our number, Susanna Gilmore, the daughter of Eddie Gilmore and his Russian wife, Tamara (more of them in another chapter) had an especially obstinate pony called Horace. Susanna spent most of her school holidays with her American 'aunt', Diana, by now Jock Colegrave's widow, at Slade Farm.

"Gosh, you're brave riding him, Sus," I said loftily one day, being used to somewhat more reliable mounts myself.

"What do you mean?" she rather sniffily replied.

"You must be a stranger to fear," I said. Hearing so much grown-up chat gave me a rather precocious way of expressing myself. "Horace is so ghastly, I wouldn't climb on him if you paid me."

"No one is asking you," she said, and with that she turned Horace's head and gave him a kick. He responded in a way which entirely bore out what I had just said: against any direction of Susanna's, he galloped headlong towards a nearby clump of trees. Having reached the trunk of the nearest, embellished with exceptionally low-hanging branches, he proceeded quite literally to scrape Susanna off his back by passing the trunk and leaving no room for her leg. Not only was it crushed against the trunk, but the overhanging branches gave her no chance of staying on his back. She suffered a wrenching fall and some serious cuts to her face and her leg.

I do not remember how we got her home, but she was also quite badly concussed and to this day says that she cannot remember anything of the actual accident. The grown-ups involved were not unduly concerned, and before long Sus was reunited with Horace. Such happenings were not unusual, just part of the rough-and-tumble of life. After all, a world war had not long finished, and there had been many worse hazards than a bruised leg and a cut face then. It was regarded as healthy and normal to be put at some physical risk, and we all lived to tell the tale.

Ted was frequently asked to shoot at Spring Hill. I never remember him shooting anywhere else, except at home on the farm where he would on occasion come back of an evening with a rabbit or pigeon in hand for the pot. He had a rather battered Stensby, a Manchester make of gun probably now defunct, which he used in preference to the Churchill, one of a pair belonging to Grandpa which had been specially made for him as he had short arms, and which had been foolishly split up. Grandpa was a keen and quite good shot who was asked to big shoots such as the Brocklehursts at Stokesay in Shropshire, where he helped to bring up the average. My father, on the other hand, counted it a cruel sport, more of a necessity if food was needed than anything else. Hunting was always his passion, until he gave up in his seventies. As he saw it, "You risk life and limb out hunting, but you have to be unfortunate to risk yourself when shooting. It seems a cowardly pastime to me."

I am not sure that the Hannays were particularly keen either, but they kept a shoot, entirely uncommercial as was often the case in those days, and a gamekeeper of course, who lived in a lodge at the near end of the front drive. It was built in a sort of Hansel and Gretel gingerbread style, and is now let to likely tenants. Lennox was not a shooting man, so that the shoot ceased upon Mumpsy's demise and the estate was given over entirely to hunting, which was Lennox's passion. Robert too was known in after years as the Hunting Parson in the Beaufort country, but that is another story.

Mumpsy was the most elegant of horsewomen; she stuck to riding side-saddle in a tight-fitting habit, never, so far as I know, being tempted to ride astride. She was fearless like all the women in her family, and had good horses about which she was entirely unsentimental.

This is Vivian's story: "We were hunting down in the Vale one day [a stretch of land running roughly from Broadway in Worcestershire to Stratford in Warwickshire]. I was on Spade, a strong-pulling horse, so that I was well up in front where Mumpsy always was. We came to a rather wide, deep ditch, somewhere on Bickmarsh [near Bidford-on-Avon] I think. Hounds were running and no one was going to be stopped by it, but it was a nasty place [term used for a fence, usually unpleasant, when hunting]. We were just behind her as her horse slipped on take-off, his fore-legs could not gain a foot-hold on the further side and he was straddled across the ditch. His back must have been broken instantly, as he fell into the ditch and just lay there after a few struggles, obviously in great pain. Mercifully, they found someone with a humane killer quite quickly and the horse was destroyed. I've never forgotten it; Mumpsy just stood there, and said, 'Never mind, plenty more where he came from'." These words were not meant to be harsh, but were said almost as a statement of comfort. Such happenings were looked upon as the fortunes of war – I suppose most people had seen far worse things then. John Jorrocks' likening of hunting to 'the image of war', came to mind, and Mum was a devotee of Surtees, devouring his works when she had lived in a room above Cyril Darby's stables before the war.

We were rather more emotionally attached to our horses as we did not have so many of them. That, however, did not stop my mother especially from being asked to hunt the horses in the stables at Spring Hill, as neither Lennox nor Robert were at home for much of the time. Donneybrook and Hunt were two that both parents rode from Spring Hill. They would exercise them sometimes too – "Ted and I to Spring Hill… Round by Hornsleasow, Toad Corner and Hill Barn to Hinchwick. Back through the Warren [Sezincote] onto the Downs [Bourton] and through the Quarry." This must have been in preparation for the North Cotswold Opening Meet a few days later on Saturday, 8 November 1952. Mum took Hunt for the day, hacking him down to Broadway from Spring Hill. "At 4pm, got back to Spring Hill with Hunt lame in o/f [right front] knee. I rang for

Ted who came to fetch me home." It is striking, but entirely true of the time, that Basford had total authority over which horses went hunting and with whom. He was absolute ruler in the stables, as trusted grooms were in those days.

The aforementioned Spade was a horse who has always stuck in my mind as Mum told me that one day he pulled so hard that she felt her heart 'go' – I am not sure what exactly she meant but it did not sound good. The horse was hunted in a fantastic amount of paraphernalia – martingales, strange bits with devices to stop him getting his tongue over them and thus getting even more out of control. My guess is that he was in a fair amount of pain, probably from his teeth, or maybe from his back – people in those days paid little heed to these possibilities and horse dentists and chiropractors were almost unheard of then. Thus there were many horses who came out hunting in quite devilish devices. Mum was one of the first people to use a horse dentist, probably tracing back to her experiences with Spade, for which she was roundly derided at the time, even by my father, who was both a doctor and a graduate of Weedon (the pre-war Cavalry School).

Basford and then the soft-spoken Irish Noctar, the grooms at Spring Hill, would have been mortified if they had thought their horse management was anything but beyond criticism, but the hunters were turned out without rugs and still with their clipped coats as soon as the hunting season finished, usually during a bleak spell in March or April. We used to gaze at them horrified as they stuck it out in some of the bleakest fields on Spring Hill. They came in hale and hearty though in early August, ready for another season. Perhaps we are too soft nowadays; certainly we are too much inclined to anthropomorphise, a consequence of one-horse ownership by those with no history of such.

Noctar was succeeded by Drage, a saturnine man of small height and spare proportion. I am not sure how kind he was to the horses as my recollection is that he was not employed at Spring Hill for long. His chief attraction was his son – though we were too young, as yet, for romantic entanglement, young Eric was an object of our attentions as he had a motorbike.

We were hanging around the stables one day in an idle fashion and sure enough, the devil found work for us to do. Eric and the motorbike hove into view. He was obviously much older than we were, and delighted at the prospect of getting the boss's children into some kind of trouble. He had lank, dark hair, which hung dashingly low over his forehead and gave him a mysterious air.

"Feel like a ride?" he asked with feigned insouciance.

Fiona was the first to come forward. "Oh, yes please," she so politely replied.

He leered; I could see him thinking, *got a right one here*, but I was too young and out of my depth to say anything, instinctively knowing that we were heading for disaster.

She climbed aboard the pillion and was swept off immediately at high speed, first around the stable yard and then away down the drive. None of us had been on a motorbike before, and I never have since. I could hear Fi shrieking, at first with delight, as she enjoyed high activity, and then more ominously, with fright. The engine roared, though I don't suppose that it was a very powerful bike, as it came back towards us, Fi ashen-faced.

"Right, who's next?"

This had turned into something of a challenge, almost a rite of passage, but I hung back. Rites of passage simply were not in my line. Glennie was next, and somewhat cooler in her demeanour. She has always exhibited considerable self-control when needed, and never more so than on this occasion. She was not going to give Eric best, and neither did she. He looked a little abashed as he returned from his foray.

Now it was my turn. I knew that I could not duck out though I was sorely tempted. I did not like the idea of a landing on hard ground though, and told him so.

"OK then. Let's go into the park," he said.

Little did I realise what this would mean as I gingerly climbed up behind him and planted my hands on his waist.

With seeming kindness, he asked, "Ready?"

I suppose I said yes, because the bike suddenly gave the impression of exploding. The wheels dug deep into the turf before splattering it far and wide in a shuddering dash forward. It was the closest that I have ever been to hell. Ducking and diving in what seemed like all directions at once, the bike angled so steeply that my body seemed at times to be touching the ground. I screamed unashamedly, completely terrified. There were glimpses of the other two girls, their mouths wide with astonishment and fear. But Eric would not stop until it suited him. My ordeal seemed to last an age. I had no option but to cling on, bailing out was no alternative.

Then, above the turmoil came an angry cry, and my rescue was effected. Uncle Robert stood there, his face a blank of fury, and when he was angry he was formidable.

"Get off that bike, now," was all he said.

The turmoil ceased, I inwardly gave some kind of thanks, and dismounted trembling in every part of my body. The ground around us was as if it had been under the plough, a terrible devastation.

"Give me the bike," Uncle Robert ordered. Then he turned to us and told us to go and wash, having first made sure that we were unhurt.

Eric was left to face the consequences. He said nothing, simply hanging his head, defeated, as we looked back. Robert was speaking very quietly. The bike was not seen again, and we were left to reflect upon our foolishness. Any connection that we had with Eric after that was fairly perfunctory. He must have been punished in some way, and several times in the succeeding days I heard his father speaking sharply to him and threatening to cuff him round the ear.

Christmas came and with it the estate party for all the staff and their families, and in which we children were included. The music room was hung about with tinsel and a large and liberally decorated tree presided by the window. Party games, which I hated as I always was the one left without a chair, and dancing, which I was useless at, were the order of the evening. No one asked me to dance but for the egregious Eric, by this time back on form and out to create a stir. I would much rather have been out in our stables with my pony Shadow, or sitting by a roaring fire reading a book.

"Want to dance then?" came Eric's unceremonious invitation. His hair seemed lanker than ever, and his smile even more uninviting than before.

I tried to look confident with all the experience of my nine years. "I suppose so," was my studiedly ungracious reply.

"Come on then," and with that he roughly grabbed my hand and we joined the maelstrom of some fifty others in a whirling dance whose name and patterns I did not know. To say that I was swept off my feet would be no exaggeration, though not in its customary sense. The bare, and polished, floorboards provided no purchase at all for leather-soled party shoes, so that I was at best only precariously balanced as we swung round in a circle, hand to hand, Eric and I. Then he let go.

Our speed sent me flying to the outer edges of the room, knocking over a few other youngsters on the way. I was stopped from hitting the wall and all its pictures by a table, whose edges hit me hard on my shoulder, lucky not to have hit my head. Very bruised and not a little shocked, I picked myself up from the floor, not making any kind of a fuss, as we were expected to be entirely uncomplaining in those days about physical injury. Other participants in the collision did likewise, and the party continued uninterrupted. Eric must have known that he could thus get away with it. I did not see him for the rest of the evening, not even his nasty smile. His revenge upon me was complete, and we saw little of each other after that. Never was I so relieved to see my dear father coming into the room to collect me. He was never demonstrative, but there was an extra long story that night – even at the age of nine he would still read to me if I was sick or sorry, and I was certainly sorry that night, though honour forbade the mentioning of names.

The Spring Hill estate consisted, as it still does, of around eighteen hundred acres – the 'in-hand' land with a manager by the name of Everett (my mother had done his farm accounts when she left the FANY – First Aid Nursing Yeomanry – at the end of the war) and about half the land tenanted by a Scotsman called John Prentice who lived at Far Upton Wold, a fair Cotswold house about a mile-and-half from the main house. He wore thick glasses and had a thick accent, and he was my introduction to Scottishness. The dairy in the farm buildings was our collection point for mail when heavy snow prevented access to Bourton Far Hill.

On the rare occasions when we entered into conversation, he would greet me with old-world courtesy: "How are you this morning, missy?" Always, the 'missy'.

And I, in similar fashion, would reply with what I hoped was a stately nod of the head, "Well, thank you, Mr Prentice."

"That's good then," was how the conversation invariably ended.

Such ceremonial did not exist in our humbler establishment. In fact, my father was a little inclined to mock such niceties, as I think a lot of people with a rough war experience and having had close contact with their men were inclined to do. Formal manners were from a gentler age which had miraculously survived, in part, the decimations and depredations of World War I, but were not to last long after the next war had finished.

When John Prentice retired his land was taken in hand to form the present holding which Lennox then farmed as a single unit. The land immediately adjacent to the house and surrounding it on three sides was known as Hare Park, and the woods surrounding it as the Hare Park Plantation. Within these woods lay a spot of infinite fascination situated beside the main ride, The Dogs' Graveyard – cats did not seem to enter the picture, though there must have been some in the stables for mousing purposes. This was a little formal spot containing headstones properly engraved with their incumbents' names and dates. Many of them too, perhaps twenty or thirty, at Mumpsy's instigation, for there were many dogs resident in those days and dogs do not, after all, live for long. I was vastly impressed by this, and rather hoped for something of the kind at home, but our animal burials took a more commonplace form.

The front and back drives were both possessed of lodges consisting of one storey and built in solid Victorian style, set back behind iron railings. Meadows' Lodge at the end of the back drive, and lived in by Tom Meadows, was pulled down at the time of which I am telling, while the front drive lodge survived for a little longer. It fronted a turning off the public road leading to the Jockey Stables, so called because Frank Brown the racehorse trainer had lodged his lads there. There were some five or six cottages, only two of which are now habitable and let out to tenants, but in those days they were all occupied by people more or less connected with the estate, the most prominent family being that of Nobes. Mrs Nobes was the mother of no less than thirteen children, though she looked old enough to me to be my great-grandmother.

"'Ow are you today, duckie?" she would enquire, the gaps in her mouth accounting for a greater area than that filled by teeth. "Like to come and play, would you?"

Definitely not, I thought to myself, though I would manage a wan smile in reply. The thought of their chaotic house, and all those children, was not one to be entertained. But one curious day, having developed a rather persistent habit of wandering from home – I must have been four or five – I found myself sitting on the bridge, which spans the source of the Dikler (after which the great 'chaser' was named) looking across the road towards the Jockey Stables, and carrying my knickers in my hand. There must have been some underlying attraction to the house of Nobes, so very different from my own, though I am at a loss to explain the significance of the knickers.

"Oh child, what are you doing? We've been so worried, and you've come such a long way [all of a mile]. You could have been run over, anything, anything could have happened," cried my mother when she found me.

"But I wanted to find the Nobes, Mummy," I said.

"What on earth for?"

I didn't know, but I must have been dreaming some strange waking dream, as children do. My mother was wise enough not be angry; I think that perhaps she understood something which I was too young to understand myself.

Ethna had left by now and I was not so closely supervised as before, a situation which suited me perfectly. I continued my wanderings on an *ad hoc* basis, though never again to the bridge over the Dikler. Parental concern over contact with the Nobes was not ill-founded – their health regime was obviously poor as one of their sons had to be operated on a little later: he had not been to the lavatory properly for twelve months.

Campden Ashes, further towards the big house, was a second conglomeration of buildings that lay only a short distance away from the Gamekeeper's Lodge. Two or three houses accommodated itinerant workers, one of whom, Percy Hill ('Persil') managed our vegetable garden. He was an inveterate smoker with appallingly bad lungs; nevertheless, he walked the weekly journey of two or three miles over hilly terrain which would have taken its toll on sounder people than he. Others who helped in the garden, once the first emergency diggings of Mainwaring and Brown had ceased, were Messrs Box and Reeves, both from Moreton-in-Marsh. Both had to be fetched, and Mr Reeves had never been in a car until then; he lived in what must once have been a lodge for Batsford House, on the turning to Batsford just before the railway bridge going out of the town along the Fosse Way.

Other outlying houses were scattered over the estate, and of course Mr Everett the farm manager had a farmhouse to himself, Seven Wells, which was on the road to Chipping Campden and formed part of the surrounding border. The Polish Camp, further along the road at the crossing with the Five-Mile Drive from Broadway to Stow-on-the-Wold, marked the limit of the Spring Hill domain in that direction. Its cluster of concrete buildings roofed with corrugated iron had been erected by German prisoners-of-war, and after the war it served as accommodation for displaced Polish persons, mostly refugees from the ensuing Communist occupation of Poland. By the end of the 1950s these families had either been integrated into the wider community or had returned home, but as a small child I remember being out hunting with my father one day; as we stood during a check (when the hounds have lost the scent during a run) in the middle of the camp, a little Polish girl came rather too near to the back end of my pony.

"Be careful, he may kick," I advised with childish imperiousness, more concerned to appear important than out of any real concern for her safety. The little girl looked blankly at me.

"She won't understand you, darling," said my father.
"Why not?"
"Because none of the children here speak English."
"Why not?" again.
"Because they're Polish, that's why they live in the camp."

This seemed a bit unsatisfactory to me, offending my over-tidy mind.

"But why do they live in a camp?" I persisted.
"Because they have come here as refugees from Poland."
"Is that something to do with the war?" Light was beginning to dawn; I listened to a lot of conversation to do with the war at home.

"Well, partly, but not only that. The poor old Poles not only lost to the Germans, but to the Russians too, later on."
"What do you mean? Did they have a war too?"
"Not exactly, but two or three years after the war was over, the Russians came into Poland because they wanted to protect their Communist homeland in Russia, and they thought the best way to do that was to make their land bigger by extending their borders."

This was history and politics at its absolute best, told to me by my father who knew all things and who always explained them clearly. When we were alone he treated me as an absolute equal, and helped my early understanding of much of which my contemporaries were completely ignorant.

"Hang on," he said. "Can you hear? Hounds are speaking again. We'd better pay attention."

The lesson was over for now, but the many Polish camps, then and since, which I have come across always remind me of that first conversation.

I dream of Spring Hill still and often. The house and the people in it were a second home and a second family, providing all the companionship of others of my own age which was at least partly lacking at Bourton Far Hill. It was a perfect childhood containing the best of both worlds, that solitude so desirable – and now so sadly lacking in so many young lives – and a community of friends providing adventure and a richness to childhood, and that is to be prized above rubies.

8

THE HUNT

'A sacred occupation'
– my mother Vivian

*'It keeps all in life and motion,
from the lord down to the hedger'*
– William Cobbett's *Rural Rides* (1813–30)

With rather more than a whiff of exaggeration, Noel Murless the racehorse trainer chose to emphasise the superiority of hunting over shooting by apostrophising shooting as a 'sport for shits' – as quoted in his obituary. An off-the-cuff utterance, an inaccuracy even – hunting people shoot as well, so anyway it cannot be entirely true. As John Jorrocks said though, in R.S. Surtees' Handley Cross, "'untin' is the very h'image o' war with only five-and-twenty per cent of the danger."

If 'guns' will pardon me for saying so, shooting has none of the neck-risking elements of hunting, requiring a facility of technique only – unless you are standing in the wrong place, that is. It is a fact that few, if any, shooting people also go hunting, partly of course, because the keeping of a horse, with all its attendant expense, is a large commitment. Shooting in the '50s was a very different pastime from that which passes for sport today; it was based upon the country estate, with coverts used jointly for the harbouring of pheasants and the pleasure of seeing the resident foxes. It was even thought helpful to a shoot for the birds to be 'shaken up' a few days beforehand by the passage of the hounds. There was little, if any, commercial shooting; farmers and landowners would enjoy 'walked-up' shooting as well, claiming game from the hedgerow for the pot, as well as rabbits, pigeon and even rooks (for a pie). Shooting and hunting co-existed for the most part happily, and when the Bournes (of Bourne and Hollingsworth, then in London's Oxford Street) came to live at Snowshill Hill early in the '30s, turning it into a high-class shooting estate, it was made clear to them, especially by the Hannays at Spring Hill who were neighbours with only a road dividing them, that hunting ruled supreme and that shooting must be arranged around hunting days, rather than the other way around as it is nowadays. Any deviation from this, or any suggestion that hounds might not be allowed on a particular day, would ensure social exclusion; John Bourne, Christopher's father, even went hunting during those early years. Some keepers, even now, are known to take to the saddle for a day with hounds or follow enthusiastically in a vehicle or on a quad bike.

All this, of course, is now subject to the Hunting Act 2004 which bans the pursuit of live quarry by hounds. This legislation is liable to become more restrictive at the time of writing if there is a change of government in 2024.

Only some twenty or thirty years later did shooting become the domain of corporate entertainment, intent on shooting as many birds as possible, and that includes the delightful partridge earlier in the season. A large 'bag' is a necessary accompaniment to a day spent on one of these shoots, where a good few of the participants will never have handled a gun before. I cherish an unkind hope that present economic circumstances may put a break on such activity. Shooting affects hunting adversely in such circumstances, some areas of the hunting country being denied altogether to hounds until the shooting season ends on 31 January, which leaves only six or seven weeks for hunting until the season ends around the middle of March. There is no official end to the hunting season, as foxes (before the current ban) were, and still are, classed as vermin and could therefore be hunted legally at any time (hares, though, are classed as game). They never have been for obvious reasons of conservation. The inescapable fact is that shooting brings money to those who own the land while hunting does not, and foxes are exterminated on most commercial shoots.

But, *plus ça change*: *The Guardian* newspaper of 12 January 2009 recalls the same date 110 years ago in *The Manchester Guardian*, complaining that 'the position of Masters of Foxhounds seems every year to present more difficulty. With the increasing popularity of covert shooting, the tendency is ever to close more coverts to foxhounds. Wire fencing, also, is a continual source of anxiety, for which, however, tenant farmers cannot be held altogether responsible... a popular Master generally contrives to get his own way in most things...' This last clearly foretells the career of our recent Joint Master, Nigel Peel.

Our recreational life in the '50s centred around hunting with the North Cotswold Hunt, our local pack of foxhounds. This was not an old pack of hounds; a few, such as the Duke of Richmond's Charlton (no longer extant), the Barlow in the North Midlands, the Duke of Beaufort's (for which no records exist to tell us when hounds were first kennelled and hunting from Badminton) and the Berkeley (the then Lords Berkeley were known to have hunted huge tracts of land between London and Bristol throughout the second half of the sixteenth century and into the beginning of the seventeenth) had been founded before the end of the seventeenth century. Yet it was really the Enclosures which encouraged the coverage of most rideable country in England and Wales, and to a lesser extent, Scotland, with the territories ('countries') being hunted over by packs of Foxhounds, and also Beagles and Harriers (hounds hunting hare on foot and on horseback, respectively) and those of Otterhounds (voluntarily ceased, owing to the increasing scarcity of otters, long before the current general hunting ban came in). The planting of hedges and the erection of wooden post-and-rails and stone walls, all according to the character of the area to be fenced, led quickly to a realisation of the enjoyment that jumping (or 'leaping' – 'lepping' it was called then) could afford, and then there was the galloping.

Not all hunting involves jumping fences, certainly not on Dartmoor or Exmoor where bogs are the main hazard, but it certainly does on the top of the Cotswolds, where stone walls and post-and-rails prevail, and in the well-hedged Vale country surrounding the Cotswold escarpment from Winchcombe and Broadway, and then on towards Stratford-upon-Avon and the famous Pebworth Vale, which curves back towards Chipping Campden.

The two Vales, of Wormington, near Broadway, and Pebworth, were considered in the '50s to be 'prime' country in the hunting lexicon. Indeed, Hill Farm at Pebworth, the traditional meet on the Wednesday following the Opening Meet of the season in Broadway, was attended by 'thrusters' from all over England – 'top sawyers' indeed, determined to jump the famous Pebworth hedges. As yet unspoilt by industrial farming methods which never rest the land and lead to bottomless ground, and the huge unjumpable irrigation ditches dug to accommodate the water such injured ground cannot absorb, the hand-laid hedges and their adjacent ditches lay invitingly, or sometimes loomed challengingly, not yet grubbed up to create the prairie land encouraged by government food-producing policy as the 1960s began. Now, revised policies encourage the planting of new hedges, even the re-wilding of food-producing land which is perhaps an over-compensation.

The '50s were definitely still within the heyday of twentieth-century hunting, the traditional social framework was still (just) hanging on – in short, everyone 'knew their place' and acted more or less accordingly, in a sort of rural symmetry. And yet, hunting was and is the most democratic of pastimes – anyone from a dustman to a duke may take part, money is not the defining element – some of the most enthusiastic and knowledgeable hunt supporters come from the humblest backgrounds, and while only those with money can afford the smart horses, anyone with a bicycle or a pair of legs, or if disabled, a car, can follow the way of the hounds and have a sociable day out to boot. In pre-decimalisation days – before 1971 – from the gate-opener receiving a silver sixpence (a coin similar in size to the present-day 5p), from a pocket correctly filled with such change for tipping throughout the day, to the boldest rider up front, all were assured of amusement and good fellowship during the day, and now also.

The Dummer Beagles provided, then and now, local hunting on foot, following a trail rather than the hare during the current ban. Indeed, the ban threatens the social life of the countryman far more than that of the wealthy, though ways have been found to carry on, always under the threat of an ill-aimed prosecution which affects the hunt staff more than anyone else – the law of (un?)intended consequences is vividly demonstrated.

There are plenty of entries in Vivian's diaries of the time, referring to days out with the Beagles as well as with the

Foxhounds, though Ted was the keener Beagler of the two from his early days in Cheshire. Sir Newton Rycroft, Bart was the Master then, having founded the pack in 1939 and continuing in his post until 1963.

Dick Fanshawe – unjustly nicknamed 'Daffodil Dick' because he had not served *sufficiently* in the war, ensuring the continuation of hunting instead – and Major David Mitchell served as Joint Masters of the North Cotswold from 1950-2. For much of WWII Dick was in fact away doing undisclosed war work while his wife, acting as sole Master of the South Oxfordshire Foxhounds, hunted the hounds herself.

For those two seasons in the early '50s Dick also hunted the hounds as amateur huntsman, as many other Masters did and do now. His Kennel Huntsman was the legendary and affable Albert Buckle who then went on to hunt the Whaddon Chase hounds successfully for many years under the Mastership of Dorian Williams, also famous for so many years as an equestrian broadcaster and as a sponsor of adult education.

In 1952 Major Mitchell was joined by Mrs (Ruth) Fanshawe and the Hon. F.A.H. Wills, later the 2nd Lord Dulverton, and in 1953 Major Mitchell resigned from the Mastership leaving Mrs Fanshawe and the Hon 'Tony' Wills to serve together. Romance between them blossomed; this led to one of those scandals which tore the country in two, some siding with Judy Wills, while others (with probably a hint of wanting to be 'in' with the local aristocracy) backed what would eventually become the *status quo*. Ted and Vivian were definitely in the former camp, it being seemingly mandatory in those days that sides should be taken in matrimonial disputes. Judy, regarded by many as a much wronged wife not deserving of her fate, was ousted by the ruthless Ruth Fanshawe (I thought in my infancy that this was where the word came from), and Tony Wills' heart was torn in two. He was a good man, much respected, who was conscientious and kind in all he undertook – indeed, in later years he personally sponsored the Overlord Tapestry commemorating the D-Day Landings (now on display in Portsmouth) as well as planting hundreds of acres of trees on his Batsford estate near Moreton-in-Marsh. These days such goings-on are commonplace, and although they cause just as much personal pain as they ever did they do not cause nearly the excitement.

"I'll never forget seeing him, in a cloak, walking up Fish Hill [out of Broadway] in a storm," I remember my mother telling me.

"Why was he doing that?" I asked.

"It was when things were at their absolute height. He must have been in turmoil."

I had only the vaguest idea what she meant, but two divorces were eventually granted, one to Tony and Judy, and one to Dick and Ruth. The marriage of the latter to Tony took place finally in 1962. Judy did not marry again, devoting herself to looking after her four delightful children, while Dick went on to marry Di Edwards-Heathcote who made her name as a brilliant point-to-point rider on Scarlet Lancer, the most gorgeous chestnut horse you've ever seen, and named after her glamorous husband who had served as a professional soldier in the $16^{th}/5^{th}$ Lancers – they wore scarlet tunics in full dress review order.

Ted and Vivian rather unkindly thought that the whole thing had served the wayward Dick right, and said so. He was thought lucky to have found such a beautiful and talented second wife. Di still follows the Heythrop on foot, having been long widowed.

As for Ruth, Ted always said, "It must have been like riding a bicycle!" A tall angular woman, the daughter of Sir Walter Farquhar, Bart who was killed in action just before the end of the First World War, the sister of Sir Peter Farquhar, Bart, renowned foxhunter, and the aunt of Ian Farquhar, who served as Master and huntsman of the Beaufort hounds, she ruled Batsford, a house originally built by my mother's ancestors the Freemans in the sixteenth century, with natural authority, outliving Tony by a number of years.

The North Cotswold was hunted for the first time as a separate country in 1868 by the 9th Earl of Coventry of Croome Court, Severn Stoke in Worcestershire. Before that it had been hunted as the 'Campden Country' from 1772 for twenty-four seasons by Bulkeley Fretwell, a Yorkshireman who came to live at Upton Wold above Chipping Campden. Succeeded by Mr Corbet of the Warwickshire, some of the country was then taken by Lord Fitzhardinge.

In 1806 Lord Fitzhardinge began his forty-year Mastership of the Berkeley, establishing three kennels, one of which was at Buckland near Broadway. In 1839 these kennels were replaced by those at Broadway, the stables of which form the present-day kennels.

The Cheltenham and Broadway countries became the Cotswold Hunt under Mr Cregoe Colmore when Admiral Berkeley, Lord Fitzhardinge's brother, succeeded to the Mastership of the rest of the country upon the latter's death in 1857. Colmore remained master for thirteen seasons, during which time the 'Cotswold Controversy' raged. The main complaint was that Mr Colmore did not visit the Broadway end of the country sufficiently often, despite the raising of a local subscription of £400. Apparently by way of compensation, Admiral Berkeley (by now the 1st Baron Fitzhardinge) occasionally brought his hounds to Broadway in order to keep the country open, and was even assisted sometimes by the 9th Earl of Coventry as Field Master, the same as he who took on the Mastership in 1868 of the newly minted North Cotswold hounds. My four-greats-uncle on my mother's side, Tom

Shekell, was a founder member of the hunt. He was the owner of the Pebworth Estate in the Pebworth Vale, three farms of which still remain in our family.

The Broadway kennels, together with a new stable block were bought at a cost of £3000, raised by Committee. This Mastership continued until Lord Coventry found the distance travelled from Croome Court to Broadway, and back again, on hunting days too tiring, thus renting Spring Hill as a hunting lodge during his last season. He established 'Lord Coventry's Hounds', later the Croome Hounds, in the southern half of the country while the Mastership of the North Cotswold passed to Mr Algernon Rushout in 1873. He served for twenty-three seasons, ten more Masterships intervening between his and that of Major Dick Fanshawe and Major Mitchell in 1950.

The piecemeal hunting with different packs of hounds which is indulged in nowadays was regarded then as rather poor form. The parents were keen on loyalty to one's own hounds, so that any proposal of hunting with an adjacent pack, such as the Heythrop, was met with a look askance. Hunts were much more divided, jealous of their borders, politics not having introduced the need for solidarity: the postwar attempt to abolish hunting had failed, roundly. Hounds finding themselves in another country at the end of a run would have to return to their own before they could draw (to find a fox) again. This rule is in abeyance now of course and hunts are much more supportive of one another.

Dress codes were strict. Gentlemen wore a black coat unless they were invited to wear the hunt button, which would then entitle them to sport the hunt livery, usually a red coat. (A coat is always described as red; 'scarlet' and 'pink' are used as nouns, never as adjectives, when describing the hue of the coat; Thomas Pink was a actually a tailor.) Ladies wore black coats, perhaps made by Mr Busvine, with a black 'hunt button' (bearing the hunt's crest) if invited. Gentlemen (subscribers and landowners) wore top hats, sometimes secured by a connecting string 'guard' to the collar (that being considered somewhat provincial as the hat should fit well enough in the first place not to fall off), while those hunting as farmers and their wives (the odd gentleman landowner has been known to join their ranks so that he might hunt for free) wore a hunting cap. It was just about permissible by this time for ladies too to wear a hunting cap. Only the Master and his hunt servants (hunt staff as they are now called) would keep the ribbon hanging free at the back, others must sew it inside the hat, and that included ladies unless they were wearing a bowler hat, also an option for gentlemen when wearing black, which was also the obligatory dress for an unliveried groom.

Side-saddle habits, also made by Busvine of Brook Street if you were very smart, were in tweed ('ratcatcher') or dark blue or black melton cloth with matching breeches; the dark habit could be partnered by a top hat, or a bowler and the hair would be held in a bun, false if necessary, often with a veil to cover the face. Breeches for ladies riding astride were generally drab Bedford cord, a sort of dark fawn, yellow being thought a bit 'fast', while men would wear the same, of cavalry pattern if using 'butcher boots' made from black calf leather and topped off with a similar gaiter strap. The 'permission' for ladies to ride astride had come in with the sexually liberating influence of the First World War – it would have been unheard of, almost scandalous, for a lady to ride thus prior to 1914. Staff shortages too played their part – with so many men away fighting, the side-saddle rider could no longer be accompanied by the necessary groom, it being fairly impossible to do anything practical, such as getting on your horse or opening a gate, while riding this way. Top boots – never worn by women unless the tops themselves were black, or unless a lady was also (very unusually) a huntsman – came in various shades, the boot itself being black while the top was usually mahogany, or more dashingly champagne or even pink. These latter are seldom seen nowadays as the work involved in keeping such a light colour is too great. White breeches should be partnered by top boots. Brown boots were worn only for cub-hunting (now known as autumn hunting), before the Opening Meet, together with 'ratcatcher' for both ladies and gentlemen.

Hunting ties (not to be confused with a hunting stock, which is made of leather, and now almost completely obsolete) were always white or cream, or very dashingly, blue with white spots, after the Opening Meet. Before this day, a coloured hunting tie or even an ordinary shirt and tie would be worn with a tweed hacking jacket and cavalry breeches. Gloves were generally of string or leather, not brightly coloured, and if you were sensible, you would put a spare woollen pair inside your horse's girth on a wet day. Spurs, worn in the groove above the heel of the boot, and usually on a spur-rest already provided, had a longer shank than the 'dummy' spurs in use today, while a hunting whip consisting of a handle with a horn hook at the end of it, a leather thong and a string lash (for the purpose of 'cracking the whip' when necessary; although that was discouraged and still is unless you are very knowledgeable) was *de rigeur*. This was because the hook, generally made of antler horn, was useful for opening gates and holding them open, while the thong could always be used for holding a hound which had been injured or otherwise needed to be detained – mounted followers, even when they have paid a subscription, are supposed to be useful when the occasion demands. Permission to carry some other kind of whip, generally a 'cutting whip' when riding a young horse, had to be sought from the Master – this nicety generally goes unobserved these days, except by my husband. I speak somewhat in the past tense on matters of dress, not because any of these rules are obsolete, but because they are now so often disregarded, often in a mistaken attempt to adopt a low profile because of the hunting ban. This is quite unnecessary as long as the hunting on the day is being legally conducted.

The only great change in the past fifty years has been in the matter of hats – top hats, if they are worn at all, are now often fitted with a safety standard skull cap inside which makes them look ridiculous; hunting caps are frequently worn with a securing head-harness, more than just a chin-strap, while naked skull-caps (hideous in the hunting-field, or anywhere else) are frequently seen, as are other weird and wonderful cycling helmets. Safety concerns have penetrated even the confines of 'the image of war', although none of these are mandatory, the older ones amongst us carrying on much as before.

The liveries of the different hunts, worn by the hunt staff, provide a clue as to their origins – the yellow livery of the Berkeley Foxhounds is that of the Earls of Berkeley; although the title is no longer extant the hounds are still owned by the Berkeley family. The Heythrop livery is green with buttons attaching to the tails of the coat, stemming from the days when the Heythrop country was a subsidiary country to the Beaufort, and hunted as such by the Duke from Heythrop Park in Oxfordshire, built by him as a hunting box. The 'outside' livery at Badminton, the principal seat, was green, and thus worn by the hunt servants of both packs, whereas the inside servants' livery was blue-and-buff which is still worn by the mounted field of the Beaufort, and as evening dress. Some of the Heythrop masters, even when not hunting the hounds, in recent years have adopted a green coat; I know not why as it is incorrect, being the staff livery.

The North Cotswold, in common with most packs of hounds, wear scarlet, but they sport the distinctive primrose yellow collar and the coronet of the Earls of Coventry on their hunt buttons. Pleats and buttons on the tails of their coats were eschewed by the enlightened Joint Mastership of Nigel and

Sophia Peel for reasons of economy – when staff move on to their next appointment with another hunt it is better that their coats should not need complex alteration. This continues to be the case.

Members of a hunt are divided into three categories: farmers, over whose land (generally a minimum of fifty acres, though these days this is no longer rigidly applied) *all* hunt followers and Masters alike should be grateful to ride – they do not have to pay a subscription, though many generously do; landowners, whose generosity with land should be similarly respected and considered – hunts have different rules as to the minimum land holding necessary for membership of this category, generally around two hundred acres; subscribers, which covers the rest. Subscriptions should be paid on time, that is by the 1 October, though hunts have a myriad of rules regarding this. Children below a specified age will often be allowed to hunt for free. I hunted little, apart from on a leading rein, until the age of nine or so, as Ted and Vivian correctly thought it a nuisance for small children to be getting in the way of adults, as they will do even when accompanied by an adult, as they had to be then. They probably did not want their sport for the day to be spoilt either, and there was always the possibility of being kicked by a much larger horse with what could easily be devastating effect. Or the reverse even.

"Take not out your hounds on a windy day" – so spoke Peter Beckford, the doyen of hunting writers in his seminal work *Thoughts on Hunting* published in 1781. Much has changed in the course of over two hundred years – long hunts then were decried as lack of skill on the part of the huntsman, and of course the breeding of hounds and thereby the encouragement of particular qualities at the expense of others was still in its infancy, so that the actual killing of the quarry was important in keeping the hounds regularly focussed – but this particular piece of advice still holds good, for the very sound reasons that hounds are difficult to hear in the wind and because the fox's scent becomes dissipated in such weather. Nonetheless, people nowadays are concerned to get their money's worth so that hunts in general, apart from the rare packs which are still privately owned, are more prepared to disregard this advice than once they were. The artificial trail which we are currently compelled to follow is probably less easily interfered with, too.

'Get your hunting in before Christmas' was another wise saw. Winter weather in the '50s being much harder than it is now, it was advice more closely followed then. Besides, other distractions now intrude much more: the attractions of the ski slope (never great for me); perhaps the thought of a tropical break (but what do you do when you come home to an English winter?); the possibility of illness or accident, which always seems to be greater as winter proceeds; a waning enthusiasm – it is well known that grooms especially become tetchy as January draws to a close. The dark mornings and cold weather, with all their attendant difficulties, do eventually take their toll on even the hardiest. In January 2009, we enjoyed an object lesson in the advisability of pre-Christmas hunting – a 'proper freeze-up' with even our lake frozen, and no date set for a let-up. Hunting is quite impossible in such conditions as the ground is too slippery for horses and too jagged for hounds' pads (feet). Only if snow comes might hunting in freezing weather resume, more probably on foot.

Very few people 'did' their own horses in those days. There were still male grooms a-plenty, the necessity for girls to take on the job (there are few, if any, male grooms outside the racing stable now, and they are 'lads' anyway) did not really bite until a decade later. As there were few mod-cons it was a much harder physical job than now. The materials for saddlery required careful and lengthy cleaning – linen linings for the bottoms of saddles, for instance, needed scrubbing, being left to dry and then an application of white chalk ball to bring up the whiteness. The rugs that horses need in winter were of heavy materials such as jute and wool, with none of the wicking properties to dispel moisture which are so freely available today. Horse were 'whisked' with straw upon their return from the day's exertions, and the straw was then left beneath the rug so that their bodies might dry. As a result, 'breaking out' into a fresh sweat was not unusual, and neither was the consequent attendance, sometimes late into the night, of Leathers, our aptly named groom.

Bringing two or more horses back to the stable at the same time at the end of the day was simply not done. A half-hour gap was the norm, so that each returning horse could be seen to undisturbed. Washing a horse after hunting was unknown – picking him over for mud and thorns with the fingers was the only way, and actually much more thorough. The legs were then bandaged, as they are now, and brushing off waited until the next day. Half-an-hour these days will probably see your horse rugged up and with his feed. The hunting was much harder then, with hacking to the meet as well as home, often leaving horses thoroughly tired, if not exhausted – one day's hunting a week was regarded as a horse's normal work quota if no second horse was used.

Leathers was quite old when he came to us at the end of 1951 – he had served in the Gallipoli Campaign in the First World War, and I never remember seeing him without his puttees (military leggings used for riding). His summers would be spent whitewashing the inside walls of the stables, doing small maintenance jobs, repairing and washing the heavy jute and woollen horse clothing then in use, perhaps doing a small amount of gardening. He would rasp the horses' teeth too, a six-monthly task, and even more essential when horses were stabled and not wearing their teeth naturally while grazing. He undertook the worm-dosing too, creating balls – whence the beneficial 'Birtwick Balls' in *Black Beauty* – out of black treacle and a green powder called Phenothiazine (PTZ). Once he had left, my mother took on these tasks. We did not subscribe to the practice, common then when riding in the summer was much less frequent, of 'turning away' stable staff until the autumn, so that we did not have to pay them. My parents felt that it was not fair, especially on older people.

Motorised horse transport, though it had become available during the time between the two World Wars, was still something of a luxury in the '50s; hacks to meets and upon leaving hounds to return home could be twelve miles or more, the hack home frequently conducted by torchlight in order to read the signposts in less familiar country, and often accompanied by singing in order to keep up the spirits of weary horse and rider. Until the following decade with the axeing of the railways and the accompanying refusal of the railways any longer to transport horses, more distant meets were reached by train, and were often arranged near to the train station. Indeed, Lord Redesdale at Batsford had permitted the original railway line running from London to Hereford to cross his land on condition that stations should be located at suitable hunting intervals along the way, and other landowners would have almost certainly acted the same – hence we have Handborough (on the Duke of Marlborough's Blenheim Estate), Charlbury, Kingham, Moreton-in-Marsh, and further west, Honeybourne and Ledbury amongst others, no doubt located for similar considerations. Ventilation shafts above the disused railway tunnel on the Badminton estate are still visible.

The coming of the railways had at the time been decried by hunting folk, but in fact it was turned to good account. Railwaymen, and in particular train drivers, were not uninterested in hounds themselves, and any train driver having to stop for hounds on the line on Lord Redesdale's land, something which a huntsman would always try to prevent for obvious reasons, would be handed a ten-shilling note (equivalent to a day's pay in the '50s) on his instructions, and be thanked. Train drivers were frequently tipped by their disembarking hunt passengers. Huntsmen in those days rose 'through the ranks', often starting out as puppy boys – an advertisement for such in the Beaufort Kennels in the early '50s attracted no less than fifty-four applicants. More hounds were bred then because of the depredations of distemper for which there was no vaccine. From puppy boy, he might climb through the ranks of second horseman, second whipper-in, first whipper-in, kennel huntsman to the often highly lucrative post of huntsman, his 'perks' including the skin of fallen stock, while the bones went to the first whipper-in and the offal to the second, or the kennelman. These were worth real money in those days.

The grander huntsmen, such as Will Pope of the Grafton, would rule the kennels, doing little of the unpleasant day-to-day work themselves, requiring a kennel-boy to test the heat or coolness of the hounds' porridge (pudding) by plunging his arm into the steaming cauldron up to his elbow; when the great man telephoned from some other venue he would then instruct the whipper-in to feed the hounds. Non-hunting days would be spent racing or shooting with farmer friends.

By the early 1990s huntsmen were on an agricultural wage, as well as being able to make a business out of running a second flesh-wagon for the collection of carcasses from farms and selling the skins thereof, perhaps twelve pounds for the skin of a cow marking the top of a descending scale down to four for that of a sheep. Tom Normington of the Grafton had had a trial for Northampton Town Football Club as a professional, but turned to hunt service for its better wage and conditions; five shillings a week more, with the eventual hope of getting the 'real' money. Those were truly the days.

We were not grand enough to have second horses, and we hadn't the staff anyway. A second horseman was distinct from a groom, as he had to be out for much of the day. The era of mobile phones has vastly simplified the task, and the fact that foxes do not run so far, or perhaps so fast when they are mistakenly hunted. In those days any second horseman would ride under the direction of the hunt's head second horseman as he, more than anyone apart from the actual hunt servants, knew the pattern of the day and would ensure that none of their number got in the way of hounds. They might carry a welcome sandwich flask at the hip for the refreshment of their employer, and generally wore a highly polished stirrup leather as a Sam Brown to indicate their function, as well as being properly turned out, without the oft-seen baseball cap of nowadays!

The hunting characters that people my first decade crowd in: George Coles, now there was a man – rich, loudly spoken and vulgar to a fault. He was Hunt Secretary, and a very good job he made of it, being vigilant in financial management and also extremely kind, so that those in need of special consideration in the matter of their subscriptions always received a hearing. He had married 'above himself', to Helen, whose family owned Campden House, a fine Jacobean dwelling with its own estate just outside the town. It suited her that he should be her spokesman while she performed a retiring role, and this he fulfilled to perfection.

'The finest view in England!' (no doubt a paraphrase of Snaffles' picture-title, *The Finest View in Europe* – the prospect between a horse's ears while galloping across a well-hedged vale) he would frequently exclaim while out hunting on his beautiful grey heavyweight, Jumbo. He loved the Cotswolds, and especially our part of it. He was a good friend of the parents who were very fond of him, disregarding any snobbery expressed by others.

George was one of those grown-ups to whom children felt they could talk on an equal basis. I remember even now: "Germany before the war; it seemed like a good place then. The trains ran on time, the roads were new, quite unlike anything anywhere else. We never saw anything wrong. They seemed to be clearing up a bit of a mess." Hardly a unique view in the '30s. "How wrong we were."

I was early introduced to some intuition of wartime wrongdoing and wartime conditions as much of Vivian's difficulty was, I think, guilt at one (or more) removes, a kind of German-ness impossible of expression. I was an only child, and as is the way with only children, early aware of grown-up difficulties.

George gave Ted good advice on money matters, and later proposed me for membership of Lloyds, ultimately a dubious privilege. He suffered much unhappiness in his relationship with his son Bobby: "Too much, too soon," he would often say in a rueful tone.

Don Fisher, now there was another man. He had zips up the backs of his hunting boots; this never failed to impress me, marking him out as someone different, though perfectionists in matters of hunting dress regard them with distaste. Now, in middle age, I realise what a sensible idea it was, especially as he had been wounded in the legs during WWII. Grey-moustached, sharp of wit, he rode quality horses, and was one of my earliest amours.

John Greenwood intrigued me too. Master for only one season at the end of the decade, he refused to wear a hat out hunting, something quite unheard of: "I have a scalp problem, my head needs to keep open to the air," he would explain to anyone who cared to listen.

"That chap's not right," Ted observed, a favourite theme mostly with some medical connotation. Indeed, John wore a constantly strained expression and looking back had probably had a tough war. Perhaps that is why he lasted only the season.

Tony Binney, Roger Leadley-Brown's employer and incumbent of Kiftsgate, I remember for one story of bad manners, related either by Ted or Vivian, I forget which: "He had fallen off and I went to catch his horse for him [a common courtesy out hunting]. He stood there scowling, without a word of thanks. 'Bring the horse nearer will you? I can't get on from here.'" Said with a scornful air, doubtless to cover up his feelings of foolishness at having fallen in the first place.

He was met with an unexpected response: "Catch the horse yourself then." The horse received an encouraging 'haroosh' from the rescuer, obligingly cantering away across the field. Binney stood there, now bereft of both horse and catcher, his fury unrestrained as he shouted at a retreating back. The account was repeated many times with relish. Roger, as Binney's groom, was ten times the gentleman and was treated accordingly by his employer.

Ma Binney as we called her, rode side-saddle maintaining a lantern jaw and an unsmiling countenance at all times. Ted found it hard to be courteous in her presence and was sometimes uncharacteristically rude in his observations.

Miles Clifford was the District Commissioner of the North Cotswold branch of the Pony Club by the time I grew old enough to be an active member. His bristly moustache and loud manner concealed a great fragility. He had gained a Lt-Colonelcy during the war years, no mean rank, but had been doing a staff job during the later years of the conflict. He rode well on a 'tubed' horse which almost drowned one day when falling in a watery place – owing to 'wind' trouble it had undergone an (now long outmoded) operation enabling it to breathe through an externally placed tube in its neck – a permanent tracheotomy in fact. Tubed horses were a constant worry as the tube had obviously to be kept clear at all times, and not just of water.

All his military inclinations were now towards the Pony Club, which he liked to think he gripped more firmly than he did. Vivian's secretaryship under his command lasted the inside of a year, and they almost came to blows. To be commanded in a military manner was simply not to her taste. He would give us Pony Club children 'pep talks' at the beginning of every summer camp, calling us all 'chaps' irrespective of gender. For some reason he was very fond of me, and I of him. He tried too hard to run a tight ship, as so many ex-service men were wont to do, his pale blue eyes sometimes protruding with the effort of it all, but our branch of the Pony Club prospered under his command, increasing its membership and excelling in all its competitive efforts. In after years, as he grew old, I saw Colonel Clifford as often as I could, and it was a sad day when he died. His son, Richard, was an early idol, an impossibly good rider, three years older than I to the day. Sister Diana, older yet, was by common consent the most glamorous girl in the Cotswolds, even if she did wear too much make-up for North Cotswold tastes.

The Hannays at Spring Hill were of course contemporaries of mine and my parents. Fiona and Glenda were bold riders, always prepared to show us young the way on ponies of all kinds, though I should say that children then were required to keep at the back of the field and to be in control at all times. Getting in the way of elders and betters, or even worse, causing an accident to themselves or others (as not infrequently happens nowadays in these foolishly lax times) furnished a very good reason to be sent home by the Field Master, who was responsible for enforcing proper behaviour on the part of all those followers of hounds mounted on horses. Children were expected to be accompanied by a responsible adult anyway.

Lennox (Hannay), the 'flashing-dashing', was too impossibly glamorous and senior to us even to be approached out hunting, while Robert rode more slowly and on heavier horses, but to equal effect, always there at the end of a hunt, while their mother was the ultimate in side-saddle elegance, and had only the best of horses.

There were too, as now, some professional riders to hounds, that is to say, those who were showing horses to clients in order to sell them (as my mother had done with the Pytchley), or who were producing horses for other purposes, either to 'qualify' them as point-to-pointers (twelve days proper hunting then, not just unloading them from the lorry for the meet or as now, simply making a seasonal payment) or to educate them as show horses. Farmers' sons too played an extensive part in bringing on young horses, a sideline which fitted in easily with the farming practices of the day.

Tim Holland-Martin was a great 'qualifying' follower, an accomplished rider in both point-to-points and in Hunter Chases (a sort of halfway mark between point-to-pointing – races organised by the hunts – and full-blown steeplechasing – so-called because such races were originally ridden from one highly visible landmark to another – and conducted under the same rules as the latter). He was impossibly good-looking, some fifteen years older than I, and fulfilled for me something of a godlike role. Curiously though, his horses did not always jump out hunting, often having to be given a 'lead', a frequent fault with racehorses out hunting. Despite the strictures upon children being up at the front of the field, I found myself one day in the position of going ahead of him, the proudest moment of my young life. Point-to-pointers are not always good hunters as the two disciplines had, even by then, become so different, not just a matter in both cases of galloping and jumping to the finish, but much more specialised.

Why do I use the word 'impossibly' so often when talking of these men? I longed, even at such a young age, to ride horses as they did, to be tall and elegant, in short to 'cut a dash'. A certain romantic inclination was in the mix too. The idea of riding side-saddle, no matter how beautifully, never did it for me though. Many years later I learned how to, but perhaps it was too late by then.

Nat Tollit, the mother of one of my dearest friends, Niccy, educated show horses to perfection, both her own and other people's. For years she rode champions at Dublin for Nat Galway Greer, the renowned breeder and producer, and Niccy too would later judge Ladies' Hunters, under a side-saddle of course. No mean feat, as not all horses shown in the ring are as well mannered as they should be.

"I'd better gather up my knitting now," Nat would say, as she sat calmly on a four-year-old. As the huntsman blew Gone Away she would shorten her reins just enough, ease the young horse along just enough to give him confidence, and be found after a five-or six-mile point (the direct distance run between the start and the finish of a hunt, the actual distance ridden could be more than twice the length of the point) perfectly unruffled, as if the horse had been hunting every day of his life.

Others too I remember: old Fairlass Harrison, a colonel with a ready smile, and his wife Kathleen (a bridge partner of Nat Tollit's) who used a sheepskin upon her saddle to improve her grip; Peter Aizlewood, our Hunt Chairman in later years, who had lost one leg above the knee in the war and rode in a specially adapted saddle – I always waited for his wooden leg to fall off, and it did once; his father, Aldham, a Major-General in the First World War, who inspired me with true terror, especially when once I found myself all alone with him hacking home – he did not unbend; Mrs Hornby, a redoubtable side-saddle rider – there must have been half-a-dozen or so who still rode only in that style when I was a child.

Another of these was Miss de Havilland, one of two sisters who lived in Blockley near Moreton-in-Marsh, our borderland with the Heythrop, but she chose to come out with us and rode loyally into her sixties. She died out hunting, trapped beneath her horse in a ditch as the water rose. The horse was eventually pulled off her.

"Get him off, get him off!" she had cried, as the water rose. "I'm going to drown!" By the time they did she was dead. Ted was out that day, and came home much upset. Miss de Havilland with her grey bun and her grave demeanour was much respected, and much missed.

It was not so uncommon for people to be killed out hunting in those days; it is less so now as hunting, even before the current ban, had become much tamer with foxes running less far by virtue of more intensive farming methods and much busier roads, and with the country becoming fenced with 'made-up' (purpose-built) fences for jumping rather than the field being able to 'take their own line' as you can see in sporting pictures by artists such as Lionel Edwards. These painters usually hunted themselves, representing things pretty accurately. The 'broad front' presented by a field of riders in those days helped to push the fox along; latterly he is more able to duck and dive in front of a bunched group. Taking your own line could be a sobering experience – once I saw a horse straddled on the sharp toppers of a stone wall; he must have been dreadfully cut, and the risk of infection from a stone-cut, accompanied by lichen, was almost invariable. You never knew what lay the other side of a fence either – a set of chain harrows did not ensure a soft landing. Still today, some hunting countries to the east in the Shires, and further north, retain much of this open character.

Derek Welton was one of our number, the father of Antony, for many years Treasurer to the Heythrop. Derek was a fine and brave horseman who lived at Childswickham in the Wormington Vale; he quite simply broke his neck one day in a fall along the Rushbrook in the Wormington Vale, though he did not die until a few days later on 28 December 1952, in Oxford's Radcliffe Infirmary. I too suffered a potentially fatal fall along there many years later when my faithful Fudge put his foot in a rabbit hole and turned a somersault landing on top of me; I was surprised, as my spine tingled, that I was still able to move; now I am in my seventies and suffer arthritic pain in my neck. Jock Mann, the father of Liz Wills who later became a master of the Heythrop, met a similar fate when we were still children. Jack Starkey, a neighbour of the grandparents at Radway, and grandfather of Jane Starkey the international event rider, fell off his horse stone dead at his own meet at The Grange, the perfect end I always thought. After my fall it took two years to regain sensation in one of my index fingers.

Foxhunters, and hunting people in general, learn to think quickly and to take the most direct route if the Field Master permits, sometimes even when he doesn't. They must keep their eyes open at all times, so that a change in the going or an unexpected drop the far side of a fence does not take them too much by surprise. They must, as when driving, pay attention to 'the other fools on the road', as Vivian would have it. Get too close to the man in front when you are jumping, 'jumping in his pocket', and you risk being baulked as he refuses and probably (such is the way of these things) runs along the length of the fence. It follows that you should be in reasonable control of your horse – it takes a special skill to ride a strong horse, so that it does not inconvenience others, and comes only with long experience. Thinking ahead and concentration, apart of course from being physically fit enough and being able to ride well enough, are the main requirements. 'Fox sense', an understanding of how the fox will run, comes only with knowledge and understanding, and some people will never acquire it. It does, however, make hunting much more interesting. Ted and Vivian were neither of them expert in this regard, 'hunting to ride' rather than 'riding to hunt'. My young life was thus spent in shameful ignorance of matters of venery, and it was always something of a fluke to be able to find hounds if once I had lost them. Needless to say, the hunting ban and the mobile phone at first stoutly resisted by the 'old and bold' has reduced the need for native cunning.

A story told to me by John Redfern, who farms in the Pebworth Vale, illustrates perfectly the much more war-like nature of hunting forty or fifty years ago. One stormy afternoon he and three friends were speeding four abreast up a private roadway in pursuit of the Warwickshire hounds, close to Blakemore Covert. Coming towards them was a gentleman follower on a grey horse, garbed in the obligatory top hat and cutaway coat. Evidently not in his first youth and not large of stature, he nonetheless shouted at the approaching four, "*Out of my way!*"

Fernie, disinclined to obey, rode straight at him as if in a joust. "Our horses came wither to wither," he recalled, "and the other horse came right over the top of us, its rider left flat on his back in the plough by the side of the road. I remember he left a perfect imprint in the earth, top hat and all, as he rose to his feet! Well, I had a bit of a conscience after we'd ridden away. I confessed to Beryl Buckmaster [Master of the Warwickshire in the 1950s] and said that I thought I should really go home [this was what you always did when you had committed a misdeed]. 'Not at all,' she replied. 'He's had it coming to him for a long time.'" Rank did not count for everything – Fernie's victim was Sir John Wiggin, Bart, who lived at Honington Hall near Shipston-on-Stour.

As in the heat of battle, words exchanged out hunting which would be regarded as rude or aggressive in 'civilian' life must be immediately forgotten at the day's end. Never comment upon another's misfortune, except to commiserate, and never say any but the nicest things about another's horse, unless of course it kicks you or your horse, or misbehaves towards you or others so as to create a hazard, in which case the wisest words are probably, 'Why don't you take it home?'

As there was such emphasis on good manners fifty years ago, instances of bad manners were much more memorable than they would be today. Some people did behave unaccountably badly, their horse not merely kicking another without consequent apology, or indeed kicking a hound while the horse's heels rather than its head was turned towards the pack (a sin for which they would be sent home in those days, though sadly not in these) but committing intentional actions rather than having accidents.

The hounds were on Bourton Far Hill one day, at the top of the Rick Yard. They were running fast, and some of the field had become embroiled in the Paddock alongside the house, a field bounded on its far side by a strained wire fence. Something was clearly amiss; Ted was on his horse at the top of the yard, shouting at the top of his voice.

"What the bloody hell do you think you're doing? You fucking bastard! Get off my land, and don't come back!" This last is the worst thing you can say to a hunt follower – he must wait to be told before he can come back again.

He then urged his horse aggressively towards the offender. I heard more shouting, and later on, the reason for it. The gate in the strained wire fence was old and not easy to open. When this happens out hunting there is usually a lot of cursing, plenty of imprecations uttered against the landowner or the farmer, (the gate is possibly jumped – you hope that you don't break it) or another way to go is found, certainly when a boundary fence is involved. Not this time: he who shall remain nameless (I know who it is over sixty years on) had taken his wire cutters from his pocket and proceeded to cut his way through the wire of the fence. You might think this a small matter, but because the wire was strained in a continuous line for its entire length, some four hundred yards in the case of the Paddock, this meant that the whole fence consisting of some four or five strands of wire (2000 yards, 6000 feet of it) would have to be replaced. Still to this day, I find the whole episode quite inexplicable.

In those days a pair of wire cutters were commonly carried in the pocket in case of emergency; nowadays the North Cotswold discourages the practice. Many people are much less self-reliant and knowledgeable nowadays, and most could be not be trusted with such an implement. Better to wait for an expert, though the timely use of wire cutters can be vital if a horse is trapped in wire, for instance.

Injury to both horse and rider was frequent in such a risk sport. I was out one day with Ted at Temple Guiting, further over towards the Cotswold country. He was riding Fanny (her 'stable-name'), Rhythm's at-times rather disobliging daughter. She was brilliant when she wanted to be, but only then, a real 'little girl with a curl'. Coming to a fence with a large drop on the other side she had made as if to jump it and then done a particularly 'dirty' stop at the last moment. Ted was a hard man to dislodge from the saddle, being long of leg, tenacious of grip and a well-trained horseman withal, but he was unlucky this time. Over her head he went to the other side of the fence, and as he fell his right wrist took the impact and snapped clean across. My abiding memory was one of surprise as I surveyed the damage and saw his hand dangling uselessly at the end of his arm. It must have become painful quite quickly as I remember a good deal of anger on his part, a useful cover-up for physical shock, and for hurt pride too. My poor mother, quite unfairly, bore the brunt of it, Fanny being 'her' horse of course. A sorry little party arrived home later at Bourton Far Hill, courtesy of someone's kind lift.

A recent conversation with a renowned Heythrop huntress and hostess sums it all up: "Hunting is a training for life. You can always tell by the way someone drives or dances whether they go hunting, and whether they'll be any good in bed."

9

ANIMAL FARM

'Animals are nothing but heartbreak, except when they're not.'
– My own saying.

"Orses is 'uman, just like us.'
– One of the men under my father's command in the
Cheshire Yeomanry.

No farm in the '50s was complete without a full complement of animals, domestic and agricultural. The mixed farm meant a plethora of pets as well as an impressive array of cattle, sheep, pigs and their attendant offspring. The hens did not breed with us, that was left to the specialists. They were housed in mobile wooden houses with slatted floors through which their droppings could pass, and beneath which a solid floor would be slotted for nocturnal protection, chiefly from 'Charlie Sox'– chickens are a magnet to foxes, providing an easy meal or just the fun of depredation, making a total nonsense of the modern preoccupation with their protection. While their beauty and their fascinating ways are unrivalled in the English countryside, they are, nonetheless, a menace to stock (they will take newborn lambs, too), and are controlled more humanely by hunting with hounds than by any other cruel methods such as shooting and poisoning, which so often result in slow and agonising deaths. When hunted, the sick, halt and old are quickly killed by a hound-inflicted broken neck, and the best get away; even shooting is inaccurate and unselective, the diseased tending to be the ones left, while some are wounded and left to die in agony.

One disease was restricted to the animals outside our immediate family and beyond our control – Myxomatosis, which had arrived in Britain from Australia early in the '50s, introduced (believe it or not) on purpose as a rabbit-controlling measure. Hence the Australian film title *Rabbit-Proof Fence*. Its results were devastating, and it achieved the intended result of almost exterminating the rabbit population by infecting 95% of them with a disease which made their eyes pour with mucus, immobilised them and eventually killed them as they sat, eerily still – I remember crowds of them, like statues, all over the Smallthorns Field, an obscene spectacle but one much enjoyed by the dogs who would roll on their dead bodies, as they are wont to do when they come upon carrion. Rabbits, of course, did survive, but changed in appearance: that sweet powder-puff-like scut for a tail became much smaller and was no longer a distinguishing mark. Even today, more than fifty years later, you will see the occasional 'myxy' rabbit, lingering unsafely in the road, evidence of a permanently infected population. "Much better to have shot them," my father said at the time, not practical perhaps considering their numbers. Only in the last twenty years has rabbit made a comeback to domestic and restaurant tables.

Vivian came home from exercising a horse in great consternation one day: "It's dreadful, we must do something," she cried.

"What's the matter?" asked Ted.

"I've just been across [a nearby estate] and found a fox in a trap. They're using gin-traps over there. His leg's half off." By this time she was weeping. "How can they? How can they be so cruel?"

Gin-traps were peculiarly vicious, having jaws which snapped tight shut on any limb which sprang them, and which left the subject animal in a torment of agony and terror as it fought to free itself, even on occasion tearing the limb off in an effort to escape. They had been illegal for some years even then, the larger version for capturing humans, the man-trap, having been outlawed in the nineteenth century.

"We must do something," and with that Ted got his gun, they climbed into the Land Rover and sped away to the rescue if such it can be called. To take a gun onto someone else's land without permission is just not done and the purpose of their visit, with its declaration of the discovery of illegal trapping, led to something of a row. I doubt that the matter was brought to police attention, country people on the whole preferring to solve their own differences, and I do not know if it was Ted or the keeper who ended the fox's misery, but no gin-traps were henceforth seen on the offending land.

How verminous foxes truly are was graphically demonstrated not long after. "My God, you'll never guess what's happened," shouted Ted as he tore into the house one morning from his early round of the farm.

Another crisis, Vivian must have thought, but this time it was for real.

"That bloody man! I always said he was useless, and now look!"

"What is it, Ted darling? Do stop shouting," pled Vivian.

"He's forgotten to put the floor in one of the chicken houses and the fox has taken all their legs off in the night! Christ, what a mess!"

'He' remains nameless as I do not know which of the men on the farm was the guilty one. But the oversight was costly – some fifty legless chickens had to have their necks wrung, a beastly task, and probably at an age where they were not very saleable. Boiling fowl – we had chicken for weeks!

There are gruesome happenings aplenty on a stock farm, inevitable where animals are concerned, as when a hundred yearling birds suffocated in the trailer on their way to market at Stratford-on-Avon, but this next incident concerned one of the cats. Our sympathies were once extended to one mother cat who was non-feral, of Tabby hue and without her tail, discourtesy of Tinker, a year or two before (naughtily encouraged by my mother to 'chase the pussies!'). The mother cat and others were fed every day in the granary to keep up their strength for vermin control (it is a common, and inhumane, fallacy that cats must be unfed to make good mousers and ratters). She was at this time fulfilling her description by rearing a litter of seven, doubtless fathered by an itinerant tom. As with any good mother she was eager to find the snuggest nesting place for them.

"Oh my God!" Ted again, as he came in for a late breakfast. "The tractor was so hard to start this morning. It just wouldn't turn over. You know what? That bloody silly cat put her kittens in the fan belt. What a bloody mess!"

Vivian must have gone pale at this news. "Are they all dead?"

"Oh yes," he replied. "It's going to be pretty horrible clearing it up. I'd better go out and get it done now." And with that he went out to do the necessary, farm life being never short of necessary tasks.

Tinker the Border Terrier was my childhood companion in most things. Also known as 'Beegee' or 'Beej' or 'Ulla-Culla' (Malay words from Vivian's childhood), he was of the long-legged, old-fashioned variety, bred to run with the Lakeland packs of hounds, and so having legs proportionate to his body which was clothed in a springy brindled coat that was delightful to the touch. He had a fine, broad forehead, indicating a greater intelligence than that of the average terrier (they generally rate around four out of ten on the canine intelligence register, if you are lucky) with marvellous dark eyes, the mirror of the soul, and perfect triangular velvet ears which I would rub against my face and kiss with delight. They were known as his 'handkerchiefs' by Mum because they looked like the leaves of the handkerchief tree which she had so lovingly planted in our arboretum (The Spinney) beside the garage. He was two years older than me in human years, but my mother always said that we 'grew up together' – while I was a baby, I gather that this meant a good deal of prowling around my cot on his part in the misapprehension that I was a rat, and thus worthy of his attentions. Later, he and I would play tag around the drawing-room furniture. According to Vivian, "You were a bit lucky sometimes!" But then we all are lucky to make it to adulthood, sometimes through the direst of circumstances, which make a mockery of contemporary nanny-ish proposals that no alcohol should be consumed by anyone below the age of fifteen. People need to be left alone more unless they are in obvious need, much of which is produced by daft politics anyway.

My mother would 'strip' his brindled coat in the summer, standing outside the back door by the set of steps beside the rainwater tank, built for this purpose and as a mounting block. I believe that she loved Beej more, even, than any of the horses. Particularly when he was galloping joyously around the garden, I would shout 'teapot handle' to him – I had noticed that his tail arched on such occasions to exactly that shape.

Later on in the decade, the decision was made that a younger dog, also an uncastrated male, should be introduced as a companion. Thus came Tailor onto the scene. He was a similar type of Border, though somewhat lighter in build with lighter eyes (his 'mirror of the soul' should have been a warning) and a slightly narrower head. He had none of the unique charm of Tinker though he would have thrived more, I am sure, if he had received individual attention. My parents never warmed to him and I don't think I did either. Tailor received a bit of a raw deal.

One day both dogs went missing, and a search party went out. I only remember a great cry that went up from the middle of the Thirty-Acre at the top of the Rick Yard; my mother had found them both, fighting as to the death. She had arrived in the nick of time, and had been able to separate them as the fight was almost over. Tinker, as the older of the two, had had the worst of it; he was brought back in her arms, a pale shell of a dog, limp and almost lifeless, his eyes cast back in his head, covered in blood pouring from the many bites inflicted upon him. He was lucky to have survived, but was never the same afterwards; he was never quite steady on his legs, and I never shouted 'teapot handle' to him again. Tailor came back later in the day, bearing more minor wounds and otherwise little the worse for his successful challenge to an older dog. I do not remember his fate and now I hope that he was found another more suitable home where he could reign supreme.

Besides the outdoor 'mousing' cats, we had one who lived indoors; he was black with immaculate white paws and a mew of white on his nose. He had been christened Thompson by me, possibly because I heard discussion of the merits and otherwise of tomcats, of which he was one. He demonstrated this on a fairly regular basis by 'spraying' and now I simply cannot understand why he was not neutered. The difficulty of having a tomcat in the house was also frequently demonstrated by another most unpleasant habit. We all of us one day noticed a malodorous smell emanating from the new spare bedroom. The beds therein bore comfortable, soft, candlewick bedspreads with a sort of fluffed-up cotton fringe pattern set on a fabric base, and rarely seen now. These were the ideal setting for cat shit, even more foul smelling than that of dogs because of its fishy origins. All attempts to keep Thompson away from the candlewick proved unsuccessful so that we were left to periodic martyrdom in the matter of his lavatorial exploits. Once I was caught in a childish act of cruelty, swinging him round by his tail, perhaps in retaliation for his misdeeds upon the bed. For that, and for throwing stones at Cresta to see him gallop, I was locked in my room for the afternoon.

We kept no small animals, such as guinea pigs, rabbits and gerbils. Dogs and cats were enough to be going along with. Caroline and Elizabeth, my Leamington cousins, kept goldfish and stick insects as well as cats; Elizabeth had a strong predilection for spiders, which she would allow to run freely up and down her arms while she played music to them. This was strongly approved of by Ted who would naturally pick up a spider in his long, sensitive fingers without hesitation, being called urgently to perform the task when one had arrived in the bath. He was called upon throughout his life to identify creeping, crawling and flying things invariably produced in a matchbox by a trepidatious friend. I was not so apt, and for a long time resorted to the common remedy of washing invading spiders down the plug-hole, although with only limited success in the case of the larger ones, which formed a partial haunting blockage for days. I have reformed now, but still use a flannel rather than just bare hands when picking them up, unless they are very small.

The farm animals remain mostly anonymous of course, apart from the Shorthorn-cross cows which assembled themselves for milking every morning and evening. They were Shorthorn crosses, back in fashion as an all-purpose breed, and were up to six in number, the maximum that the cowshed could accommodate – Poppy and Buttercup were sleek and black,

Iris, Bluebell and Cowslip were purple or blue roan, and Daisy I think was brown. They developed highly individual characters, being in such close association with humankind; Poppy behaved much as she appeared, sleekly and smoothly, while Iris was shouted at a good deal for kicking over the milk bucket full of milk. Their milk would be poured into metal churns which were left on a wooden table opposite the end of the drive by the entrance to Smallthorns Farm, ready for collection by the Milk Marketing Board, the last government wartime agricultural agency to survive, only disbanded in the late 1990s.

A few of the steers and heifers (the young cattle being overwintered) were named by Ted, more for identification purposes than anything more intimate, but he was a good stockman and fond of his animals. The discovery that a livestock market was sending animals abroad for slaughtering would preclude his attendance, and he won a number of market prizes over the years for the production of his stock. He was never happier than when doing the farm round, especially in the peace of the evening, shepherd's crook in his hand and dog by his side.

The sheep dog was, and is still, an essential component of sheep farming. Nowadays, Australian Heelers are popular – so-called because they will actually nip the heels of recalcitrant sheep – and perhaps because they enjoy the ride on the inevitable quad-bike. 'Cum bye' (circling the flock to the right), 'cum away' (to the left), 'lie down' (to halt the proceedings in mid-flow) and 'that'll dae' (it's all done now) were all familiar and universal words of command – in parts of Wales though, 'bye' and 'away' were sometimes reversed in direction! 'Split 'em' (split the flock) and 'look back' (for a straggler) were too sophisticated for my father though, who was not always exact in his usage; Vivian would berate him: "You're just confusing the poor dog."

Many farmers will have their sheep dogs living in the house with them. We did not, perhaps for reasons of cleanliness for their coats are long, but more probably for reasons of discipline. Working dogs, be they for shepherding or shooting, tend to work better if they live separately in a kennel. Just the opposite of a guide dog, of course. But this only works humanely if there is more than one dog – surprisingly, our one sheep dog was subjected to a solitary existence in the top loose-box of the five along the side of the fold-yard. Kep, from the Lake District, a gorgeous black-and-white Border Collie bitch, must have been able to hear our domestic doings sometimes and would howl mightily, especially at full moon.

"Please bring her in, Ted. It's so cruel to keep her alone outside," Vivian would implore, but Ted would have none of it and I never really knew why, or why discipline should be such an overriding concern. Nellie, Kep's successor, a black Collie from Wales of uncertain breeding was kept in the same way, and also howled at her loneliness. For that reason only it was a relief when Ted stopped keeping sheep.

My first pony, called Polly, was iron grey and far gone in years. The usual way of telling a horse's age, by the growth of its teeth, becomes less useful after the age of eight (thus a horse or pony over this age is often described as 'aged'). In Polly's case, the technique was of no use whatever as she had lost most of her teeth, resulting in the impaction of grass and other rotten matter in the gaps – once this had been dealt with, she was fed soft food and any grass consumed was carefully monitored.

"Really, what a disgrace, sending her to us like that. Audrey should have known better," Vivian exclaimed. I was a timid rider in the early years, and remember even now, screaming as, aged two, I was put onto an ancient grey pony, grown white with age, at the Bourton-on-the-Hill church fête. My mother wisely did not persist and Polly came to us when I was four from Audrey Whitfield in Chipping Campden, mainly so that I could comb her mane and tail. My predecessor as Polly's jockey was Audrey's son Paul, much later sometime Managing Director of Christies (and of Bonhams and Sothebys).

Polly was succeeded by Shadow. An ordinary grey pony, also very old, he was now white – only iron greys keep their colour into old age. I adored him, he was my constant companion and I only wished that he could come into the house with me. He had, as have many grey ponies, the most luxuriant eyelashes, framing still alert eyes with a keen intelligence – the undoing of knots was not his only talent – and he remained with us until the end of his mortal span, when I was about eight or nine.

Tich or Drummy ('Sir Greedyson Drumstick' to give him his showing name, devised by me) came next, from Stow Fair. He was a dab-hand at shepherding, and had been bought when I was about three years old with the idea that he would grow up with me, but his acquisition was not a success. Though a very good-looking pony of around 13.2hh (a hand equals four inches, and don't even ask me the metric equivalent) he would, as the saying goes, not 'jump a stick'. I thought perhaps to show him at Moreton Show in the 13.2hh and under class, where jumping is not required, but even that was denied to us as he clearly had something wrong with him by this time: he was diagnosed with TB of the spine and had to be destroyed.

My cousin Elizabeth came to stay with us a good deal as the decade went on – though some years older than me I suppose my company improved a bit as my age advanced towards nine or ten, and she was a keen and talented rider, Caroline (her older sister) coming to this only later on. She came out hunting on Pompey, a rotund iron grey gelding, long of body and short of leg, standing around 14.hh. He was terribly obstinate, my mother once having a three-hour battle with him to get him to rein-back (step backwards)! We had bought him from General Winsor who lived near Chipping Norton and had only one leg, having lost the other while fighting in the trenches during the First World War. The General lived in a long low house which had a connecting middle corridor facing outwards on both sides. It was possible for the horses to traverse this corridor as it had two outside doors facing one another. I was much impressed by this, strongly approving of the idea that horses might even come to live in the house.

My increasing ambition had taken a bit of a bashing. I was almost ten years old by now and eager to progress. Both parents were gratified by this, and sought locally for that most precious and usually unattainable perfect child's pony – unbelievably, their and my wish was granted almost immediately in the shape of Stubbs, who had belonged to my erstwhile school friend Robin Dale in Bourton-on-the-Hill. She measured a whole hand less than Tich, and was long of body and short of leg, as are many mares, but her heart was courageous, her honesty unrivalled and she never refused a fence – for the first time in my life I began to be 'in the ribbons' at small shows, and she provided the perfect stepping-stone to larger ponies.

My parents continued the decade by adding to the horse population with a raking bay Irish hunter by the name of Kilmurray, bought from Charles Napier who lived at Broadway. He had a great blaze of white down the front of his face and he enjoyed his hunting. Anna Maria, who was half Clydesdale and a formidable jumper, completed the stable of adult horses. Ted was devoted to her – "the best hunter I've ever known" – and so great was his admiration that he would ride her also in the summer, sometimes to farm sales as far distant as Milton-under-Wychwood fifteen miles away. Hunting people rarely bothered to ride in the summer in those days although the fuel rationing during the Suez Crisis temporarily changed their ways. She was lucky not to die from an infected coronet, just above the hoof, caused by a blackthorn acquired out hunting. This produced a violent infection: her hoof actually peeled and her leg swelled into a shapeless pillar before the blackthorn was expelled. She was left with a deformed foreleg – the hair never grew again above her hoof – but her hunting abilities were unaffected.

Simon, such a gentle good horse, died at some point during the decade from a huge infestation of redworm which perforated his stomach wall and which was quite untreatable in those days – it is difficult and very expensive to treat even now. His early bouts of colic and periodic lack of wellbeing were an early indication of this.

A crop of foals, the progeny of Rhythm, arrived during our first ten years at Bourton Far Hill. The first of these, the result of her 'marriage' to Jack Slatter in our first year at the farm, was Cresta Run, so named as his paternal grandsire was Bobsleigh, who also sired Oxo, winner of the 1959 Grand National. Born on Tuesday, 21 June 1952 – '3.30pm about [unusual, as foals are more often born in the middle of the night, away from unwanted observation] – chestnut colt foal born to Rhythm.' Two days after the birth, he and his mother 'galloped a lot' and took a long time to catch – two days old and he was already showing his paces. He was a divinely handsome horse, the inspiration for all my stories of *Baron de Cur*, and from an early age showed a most distinctive and amiable character – he would lie in his box, 'singing' to himself, never getting up (as most horses do) when anyone came in, but lying quite still and allowing himself to be sat upon and climbed over. His neigh had the ring of bells about it, and his presence was commanding – he did not stand especially tall, a little under 16.2hh, but had an aquiline head decorated with an almost perfect white rosette, and ears always pricked for the next point of interest. His castration on 11 June 1953 did little to diminish his personality.

Cressie demonstrated an unparalleled boldness out hunting, jumping anything and everything without question, and Vivian even began a little (rather *outré* at the time) flatwork with him, to make him go 'from the leg' and move laterally (sideways). Thus it was that when in the winter of 1957/8 Sheila Willcox came on television to announce that she was looking for another horse to succeed her great eventer High and Mighty, Vivian immediately contacted her and she came to try Cressie and to take him for a day's hunting. She shocked everyone by coming out wearing a competition jacket with the Union Jack sewn onto the breast pocket – "How vulgar!" the stuffier hunt members exclaimed.

Sheila bought the horse, and having won Badminton Horse Trials twice in successive years on Chips (High and Mighty), in 1958 by a 47-point margin, she attempted the same feat on 'our' Cresta in 1959, the third year running. By now she had married John Waddington – the marriage did not last. She had bought Cresta less than eighteen months before and he was not quite seven years old that April. The pressure exerted on a horse in order to have reached that level in so short a time must have been almost unconscionable, the visible evidence of this being that he ground his teeth uncontrollably, which is an unforgiveable sin as it indicates tension in the dressage phase, and he had to be administered dark sticky toffee as an attempt at concealment before entering the arena. My own childish tension was exacerbated by being made to walk the cross-country course *twice!* The ground was terrible throughout the three phases as it rained almost ceaselessly – Cresta's early hunting experience with Vivian stood him in good stead as he stolidly negotiated the cross-country course, fortunately slightly modified on account of the weather.

As the show jumping phase began on the final day, the pair were lying in second place behind David Somerset (later the 11th Duke of Beaufort) and his wonderful Countryman, with less than one fence, if knocked down, between them. The jumping always takes place in reverse order, and Sheila and Cresta managed to put the pressure on by jumping clear. The same could not be said for David and Countryman, who forfeited victory with just one mistake at the third fence. 'Our' horse had won, giving Sheila that third win, but at too great a cost. He fell with Sheila at the Three-Day Event at Harewood in the autumn of that year, unable to keep up with her demands, and in her characteristically unsentimental way she sold him to Lana du Pont in America.

Dorian Williams, in *The Horseman's Year* for 1960 of which he was the editor, put it thus: "Summing up at the end of the television [broadcast], I suggested [in reply to a question asking how Sheila had managed such a feat] that it was a unique combination of horsemastership, training and determination. More, she had that singleness of purpose that enables her to treat both herself and her mount merely as instruments – machines, if you like – to be used relentlessly in furthering her aim. And, of course, she has the priceless gift of timing. She is never wrong at a fence, thus saving not only precious seconds, but also herself and her horse." I could not put it better myself, save to add that in subsequent years this relentlessness and refusal to allow the horse any discretion in what is supposed to be a partnership, thus meaning that she always had to be right, led to a number of serious falls, some ruined horses and her eventual partial then permanent disablement when she suffered a near-fatal fall at the Tidworth Three-Day Event in 1971. She retired to live in Cheltenham where I would go to share always immaculate lunches with her; she was an accomplished cook. Our friendship began in 1957 with her first visit to see Cresta. When she married, I and her two other bridesmaids wore orange organza dresses with matching gloves which I hated, constantly trying to remove them. The only bright spots were a bridesmaid's present of a pretty embroidered jewel box (later stolen in a London burglary) and a couple of nights spent alone in a double bed in our hotel – total bliss. Sheila died in 2017 aged 81.

She had always maintained that the proof of a great rider is the ability to produce many good horses to a top level, and to succeed with them – it is not enough to be successful with just one horse, which the ordinarily good rider was just lucky enough to find. It is indisputable that she produced many horses brilliantly over a period of twenty years or more, but none of them went on to succeed with anyone else – no one else could reproduce that uniquely dominant influence that they must have learned to expect. Even High and Mighty, her first and greatest partner, was not selected for an Olympic team once he had been sold on to Ted Walsh, a British rider, as women were still then not allowed to ride in the Olympic Three-Day Event. Interestingly, in later years, Vivian's Russian horse Dekabr (so named because he had been a December foal) who would go like the wind for my mother or me, simply refused to jump for her at a local show, resisting all her attempts at domination.

Cresta's fate should have taught Vivian a valuable lesson, but she went on believing that so many of her horses would achieve lasting, and similarly instant, fame, and she largely shared Sheila's methods and sentiments with regard to the training of horses possessing a strongly dominant streak herself: use your own horses for your own enjoyment, and if one of them is talented enough, take the time just as for a child, and do not keep changing the rider in the hope of a better result as she so often did. Cresta was never heard of again, our beautiful, singing dream horse. I weep as I write this sixty-five years on, and the memory of him remains bright, always.

Rhythm's second child, a bay filly foal this time, was born the day after Coronation Day on 3 June 1953 at around five in the morning. She simply had to be named Crown Fanfare in homage to the occasion and was known as Fanny. There was much TV-watching the previous day as grandparents Wilf and Mabel came to watch the ceremony – my mother had won the television by composing the winning 'jingle' on the back of a cereal packet. It stood, its tiny screen blinking at us in the corner of the small sitting-room, couched in a gargantuan wooden case. The Coronation scene as the rain poured down in London is one of my earliest memories – the rain at home was 'filthy, cold, squally' – there is nothing new about a cold English summer.

Fanny was by Gough's Auction who stood at 'Bing' Lowe's Fox Farm near Stow-on-the-Wold, where the Heythrop Hunt Point-to-Point was run at that time. She was smaller than Cresta, only around 15.2hh when fully grown, and turned out to have a tricky temperament – she was not averse to going for you in the stable, and would buck while standing still, a particular embarrassment at a meet (of the hounds), where she was quite capable of dislodging even Ted from the saddle. Eventually Vivian had had enough, and I remember well the terrible thrashing that Fanny received from her one day while shut into the enclosed space beside the Beecham building at the top of the Paddock. It seemed to go on for an eternity; at first I thought it amusing, but as it went on I became increasingly upset and ran for cover into the house in the company of Tinker. When it was over, Fanny returned to the stables, foaming with sweat and literally laced with weals from the whip. But she was cured from bad behaviour, made into a lovely mare to ride, as I found when I was a little older, though her expression told of a broken spirit and she never again performed with any élan. She became a brood mare, breeding three foals who all went on to future success – all colt foals, they inherited none of her difficulty. In retrospect it would have been kinder and wiser perhaps to have put her in foal to start with, as this often settles a temperamental mare.

Rhythm's third and last foal, by a horse called Solarial, was another much larger filly called Sundial. She was part of a commercial deal, which involved Billie Welton from Childswickham taking on both mare and foal until Rhythm could come home once Sundial was weaned.

What a hold all these creatures had on us, they were part of the very warp and weft of our lives, as our animals are now. "Do animals have souls, Mummy?" I remember asking as a precocious eight-year-old.

"I'm not sure darling," she replied, "but Auntie Violet thinks they have, if they have been greatly loved."

10

GIN AND FRENCH

'Go thy way, eat thy bread with joy, and drink thy wine with a merry heart, for God now accepteth thy works'
– Ecclesiastes.IX.7, a favourite Biblical quote of Ted's

'Let's have one for the road'
– People really did say this! Some still do.

Prohibitions against drinking were virtually unknown in my childhood. One day, I having recently started school aged four, my father remarked to my mother that the level in the port decanter had descended somewhat rapidly; he kept a 'wether eye' out for such things as he regularly had a glass or two upon returning from a day's hunting. This was a habit to be imitated.

My mother, denying all knowledge of the matter, I without a moment's hesitation piped up: "Oh, but I have a glass when I get home from school. Daddy always does after hunting."

Imagine the shock and horror such an admission would cause nowadays – it would be a matter for referral to the 'health police' of our pathetic surveillance society. My parents merely hooted with laughter and asked me why I needed port after school.

"Well, I get tired, you see," was my studied reply. "I need a bit of a boost." Such reasons as I had heard given by grown-ups. There was a gentle ticking off, and an admonishment not to help myself to that or any other decanter again. Such tactics are far more effective than today's alarmism.

Gin and French was the staple drink on the party circuit in those days, certainly at lunchtime, and especially on a Sunday after church when everyone dressed formally, the men in tweed or flannel suits and the ladies similarly besuited and hatted. Jugs of 65% gin were offered in most sociable households, with just a sniff of Vermouth and a twist of lemon added to round things off, and with a lump of ice . This rendered the assembled company voluble, and quite incapable of conducting a safe journey home across the hills as drivers would send their cars careening from one verge of the road to the other, little or no concession being made to soaking up the alcohol with any accompanying 'eats'. I never remember any resulting accidents though, the traffic being about a tenth of what it is now, and correspondingly slower.

Sherry, usually dark and highly alcoholic from long captivity in a decanter, might be offered as a gentler refreshment or if guests dropped in unexpectedly, while whisky-and-soda was the tipple for the evening as was the gin variant with tonic, a concoction containing quinine, an essential preventive in the malarial climes of Empire – its admixture with gin came later. The taste for Gin and It (Italian Vermouth/Martini) had been acquired by those serving in the Italian Campaign, fighting their way up from Sicily in the second half of the war. Other accompaniments to gin or whisky were confined more to the public bar, and cocktails comprising anything but the most basic ingredients were considered definitely 'fast', and not quite right for orthodox society. Wine was rarely drunk except on high days and holidays – it was quite simply unavailable in any quantity or in much variation. Wine from France was all that came to hand, and the rare trip abroad would furnish the only opportunity for sampling more varied origins. My darling Aunts Violet and Elsie were partial to a glass of Marsala, the eponymous sweet wine of Sicily, at some time around mid-morning, together with a slice of seed cake, thus maintaining the traditions of an earlier age. Granny drank little, and water was the usual drink with meals, or an occasional glass of bottled beer – Whitbreads IPA (Indian Pale Ale) owed its comparative lightness to being brewed for consumption in warmer climes by those of the British Army serving there. Arkells Ale (and cider) from the local brewery was sterner stuff.

Alcohol intake was supplemented economically by my father's homemade wine, produced from potatoes (rather dull), elderflower (delightfully aromatic), elderberry (fruity, but hard work to make as the berries are so small) and dandelion. This latter became the favourite as it was easy to prepare and had a highly idiosyncratic taste; it also served as a diuretic, ensuring frequent passages of urine which was regarded as a 'good thing' and thus why it is known in colloquial English as 'wet-the-bed'. As the wine matured with an addition of yeast and sugar, my father would go down to the cellar to listen to the barrels and ensure that they were starting to fizz. He never seemed to have any difficulty in hearing when doing this, and never asked for any help.

It was a point of honour with many men of our background to have little or no knowledge of wines as it was considered somewhat suspect to do much more than 'stick a pin' into the wine list when out for dinner in a hotel – there were few restaurants, as such, outside London and the large cities in the '50s. One notable exception was the Redesdale Arms in

Moreton-in-Marsh, run by John Oldrey – an early aficionado of good food and wine who did much to make an interest in such things acceptable by educating us locals. He kept a horse in the stable-yard at the back of the hotel and went hunting from there. More than once the stables served as a refuge for us when the Land Rover was snowbound at the farm and we were compelled to ride to Moreton for our essentials, as in the long winter of 1962/3.

Much the same reservations attached to dancing – it was generally 'not done' on the part of men to show much more than an aptitude for a gentle sway round the dancefloor, devoid of any rhythm or a pattern of steps. Ballroom dancing lessons, universally taught at school, were really only effective for the girls although boys were equally instructed: men who *danced too well* were suspected of loose morals. The only exception to this was in the execution of Scottish dancing, which but for the Gay Gordons was performed in a more acceptable group formation for reeling, and it was essential to know the steps, some of them complicated, in order not to wreck the dance for everyone else. During the war the officers of Highland Regiments were drilled in the complexities and skills of making the *Cabar Feidh*, 'setting' the arms in the form of an antlered Highland stag.

Social life on the bleak summit of the North Cotswolds included some memorable characters, mired in eccentricity sometimes as a result of war and its consequences, sometimes from more convoluted causes such as alcoholism. This latter was the case with Jock Manby-Colegrave, scion of an Anglo-Irish family, pre-war dashing racing driver, who sought relief from whatever black hole afflicted him in the daily dive to the bottoms of several gin bottles. He lived at Slade Farm, just the other side of Bourton Hill, with his lovely American wife Diana. She haled from Pittsburgh, and had scaled the social ladder from fairly lowly origins to become the in-house singer at the

Coconut Grove in London. Jock had met her through his co-ownership of the club with Edmundo Ros, the band leader.

"Give the girl some candy for God's sake," shouted Jock, as he swayed down the stairs at The Slade one day. Poor Diana, by now the full-time carer of an alcoholic husband, with her days as a *chanteuse* well behind her, did her best to put a brave face on the spectacle of her husband, his handsome face now blotched from drink, the moustache attempted as some kind of cover for a life gone wrong.

We had arrived for a visit, cut short despite Diana's admonishments to Jock – quite useless as I now know in the case of an alcoholic – and her entreaties that we should stay. Life must have been extraordinarily isolating for her, and her good fortune came in the shape of Jock's death very soon after from cancer of the throat, the occupational hazard of the excessive drinker.

When I was much older, and a regular attender at her house for tea, I remember asking her about her early life: "It was so sad," she explained. "I was pregnant once, soon after the war. He was a little boy, my baby, born dead."

"Couldn't you have any more?" I asked.

"No, that was it. No more children for us." Not many people knew that Diana had borne a child, and stillborn too.

She cultivated an extraordinary closeness to the young of the area, keeping a more or less open house for us all – Fiona and Glenda Hannay, Peter Asquith (a cousin of the Hinchwick Asquiths – Didi, his mother, was one of Diana's dearest friends), Robert and Mary Wharton, Susanna Gilmore, and her two sisters Victoria Wolkoff (a director for many years at Christies in South Kensington) and Natasha. The Gilmores were not local, but paid regular and protracted visits to their 'Aunt' Diana from their home at East Grinstead. Their American journalist father, Eddie, spent some years in Russia as an international correspondent after the war, meeting his Russian ballerina wife Tamara in Moscow, and marrying her while they were still 'confined to barracks' – they (or at least Tamara) were not allowed to leave for the USA, and later Britain, until after Stalin's death in 1953. He later wrote a memoir of that time, ungrammatically entitled *Me and My Russian Wife*.

Diana's kindness was boundless, and in later years she was always there to provide a listening ear to a puzzled teenager, leading her strangely incongruous life in her small farmhouse surrounded by cattle and their offspring – she insisted on keeping cattle as Jock had done when they first moved to The Slade – until she was well into her seventies, though she knew absolutely nothing about them, and relied on neighbours for help in the rearing and marketing of them.

Her parties were legendary, providing a strangely exotic milieu where the 'duke and the dustman' could mingle on a routine basis. The grandest friends from her days in London would arrive to consort with Mr Strong, the tailor from Moreton (who had a most disconcerting squint), but who appeared quite happy to mingle with the Asquiths from Hinchwick, the gates on their fifteen-hundred-acre estate all painted cream in those days, a sort of livery. Her natural talents as a hostess (and she produced delicious, slightly bohemian food from her tiny, not very clean kitchen) put everyone at their ease in those more stratified times. The drink would flow, and everyone would exclaim at the latest addition to her incomparable collage of photos, which occupied every glass-covered surface on the ground floor. Children too were welcome so that she provided me with my earliest experiences of 'high life'.

"Oh God no, not again!" Ted would exclaim when the boot was occasionally on the other foot and Diana was due to dine with us – she took no account of formal rules regarding the 'turn and turn-about' of invitations.

"It's just awful, that smoking all through dinner." Diana had the *déclassé* American habit of cutting up all the food put before her, laying her knife to one side, and then proceeding to smoke her way through the meal, even stubbing out cigarettes on the side of her plate. But she was always forgiven, with her rasping laugh from a lifetime's devotion to smoking, and her heavy make-up; she was a true life-enhancer, and for us children a window onto a world outside that we would otherwise have missed.

The main help with Diana's cattle came from her sister-in-law Pam, who lived across the road running from the top of Bourton Hill to Hinchwick, at Sezincote Warren. Despite the fact that her Plowden cousins from Plowden Hall in Shropshire (one of the few eponymously occupied houses left in England) kept in regular contact, even asking her to come and live with them, she preferred an unconventional ménage with Reggie Sherston, who for the sake of 'form' had a house some way along the Moreton-in-Marsh/Chipping Norton road at Kitebrook, but who resided almost entirely at The Warren. Reggie, apart from helping Mum with butter-making, helped to run Pam's small farm of around a hundred acres devoted mostly to a milking herd of Jersey cows – no wonder he was a dab hand with the butter. The irregular arrangement between them stemmed from the fact that Reggie, or 'The Brig' (Brigadier) as he was often known, had a wife in New Zealand whom he would not divorce on account of her mental instability. They had not lived together for many years as First World War service had brought him to England, and here he stayed. He was therefore somewhat older than Pam, and had a straggly moustache.

I was struck, as a neatness-loving child, by the bedragglement of them both; they were obvious strangers to the dentist's chair and that of the hairdresser, and as the years went on things would only grow more extreme in that quarter. The idyllic house, one of the impossibly many where Charles II is supposed to have hidden after the Battle of Worcester, revealed an almost pathological untidiness. Dogs, of whom there were several Collies, reclined on most chairs, while these same chairs disgorged huge quantities of horsehair stuffing onto the surrounding floor. The preparation and cooking of food must have been hazardous in the extreme as there was almost no space left by the mounds of unwashed dishes, and what little space there was enjoyed a covering of multiple layers of grease and grime. Neither Pam nor Reggie had children. Pam never married, and the presence of us juveniles seemed therefore welcome. The dirt proved too much for me though and I ventured into the house only rarely. The condition of Pam's van, bearing traces of high endurance and luminous blue paint, and of an indeterminate age, served to reinforce my caution. Once its doors were opened you were assailed with a smell whose origins were best left unexplored, while the interior was reinforced with a considerable growth of grass from the mud deposited by many pairs of boots, and the stuffing of the seats lay mainly on the floor as a result of Collie attentions.

The farm buildings too were similarly disordered, and it appeared something of a miracle that small Jersey cows could negotiate the mounds of manure which secured all gateways. The only neat building on the place was a wooden bungalow to the right of the farm entrance and facing the road, which Uncle Midget had built for them during the war to lend a helping hand and provide a dwelling for resident labour. This bungalow still stands.

It was Pam's step-father Frank Atherton Brown who had drawn Pam to live at The Warren. An Old Etonian, in common with a good many professional horsemen then and now, he had temporarily hung up his boots after a bad fall at Windsor while on leave from his war service as a machine gunner, which was then followed by the breaking of his spine in a race at Stratford-on-Avon; he was lucky to be able to learn to walk again, but his thoughts inevitably turned to the training of racehorses now that riding them was precluded. Married to Hilda, Pam's and Jock's Irish mother, he came upon Bourton Hill during his quest for a training establishment. Possessed of twenty-two loose boxes it seemed ideal and had served others in a similar capacity before the war. Geoffrey Shakerley at Moreton-in-Marsh was one of those who had kept his horse in training there and had galloped along the glorious Bourton Downs before he broke his back in a pre-war Grand National.

In his enchanting book *Sport from Within*, published in the year of his death, Frank wrote, 'Though the place was easy on the eye it was not so easy on the purse, and an old stager who had lived close by all his life issued the warning that all the previous trainers who had lived there had gone broke, gone mad, got killed or died of drink...' He spent several not unsuccessful years there, getting more and more overweight on his own admission, until he died in May 1952. 'Pops' as he was known is one of my earliest remembered faces.

George Steele, a professional farmer from Worcestershire (and an in-law to one of our later Joint Masters of the hounds, Nigel Stephens) succeeded Frank at Bourton Hill, and he in turn was succeeded by Claude and Peggy Scott towards the end of the decade. Claude was a cousin of the Duke of Buccleuch and had migrated south after a family row. He was fantastically amusing, a born raconteur, dry wit and had earlier nurtured an ambition to play professional piano in a band. This he still did at hunt balls and suchlike with the ease born of genuine talent. They became our good friends, Tom (the older of their two children) living until recently at Bourton Hill. His sister Katie, sadly no longer alive, was some four years older than me, but we often met to ride across the Downs together, she on her wonderful 'cresty' pony David, a stalwart out hunting, while we would all bundle into the back of Ted's Land Rover on a snowy winter's night to go and watch the latest movie wherever it was on. No one ever thought that we might get stuck, and we never did.

The Point-to-Point Tea at Spring Hill, all the 'great and the good' bidden to attend a gargantuan spread in the dining-room, was a very special affair. 'Left Vanguard in stable yard at Spring Hill. M and I to House for tea,' Mum wrote on Easter Monday 1959.

No cars were allowed anywhere near the House in later years, largely owing to security considerations, and by the end of the twentieth century Spring Hill Races, actually the North Cotswold Hunt Point-to-Point, had moved to a temporary home at Andoversford with the Cotswold Hunt, and then to a purpose-built course at Paxford near Chipping Campden donated by a generous hunt supporter.

Uncle Midget's commodious house, built before the war and overlooking Kildanes Valley and The Scrubs which bordered Bourton Far Hill, provided my parents with an early happy backdrop to their busy life. He maintained a close and practical relationship with the Lygon Arms Hotel in Broadway, having lived there while the house was being built, and using it thereafter for entertainments which might be too much for his staff – a cocktail party which he held there on a Sunday evening, 8 March 1953 being just one example, while also entertaining regularly at home, giving a champagne party one Sunday night that same March. I notice that social events on a Sunday night then were quite usual, television not having gained its weekend hold. His childless marriage to May, which had lasted some ten years while he farmed in Surrey and then in Kenya, was over and she remained in East Africa where he bought her a house in her preferred climate while he decided on a move to Gloucestershire, having tried out a number of areas and a number of good hotels on the way.

He was extremely short and somewhat pugilistic in appearance, perhaps partly owed to his involvement in fights over married women, a category which he seemed to prefer to those who were free and single. He was snobbish, humorous, a good violinist, a good horseman, a fine naturalist (one of his chief delights, and the chief reason for the situation of his new house, being its vantage point from which to watch badgers in the valley below), a good host and (at this point) a loyal member of his family who took great delight in young people. Ted and sister Joan would stay with him as children in the 1920s on his Surrey farm, riding the working horse Blackbird home from the fields and enjoying even less discipline than they did at home. Ted was his godson as well as his nephew and shared the same somewhat wry view of life, so that the move 'next door' was a happy one for both sides.

Midget's career in the Cheshire Yeomanry where he attained the rank of Captain, was undistinguished as Dick Verdin (Lieutenant-Colonel Sir Richard Verdin) attests in his excellent and highly entertaining *History of the Cheshire Yeomanry*. Thereafter, his attempts at working were confined to those of a true gentleman farmer, getting his hands dirty only at the busiest times of the year – hay and harvest. His time was largely occupied with hunting and with his many friends – John Bourne, Donald Corley (who had lived at Snowshill Hill in the early '30s before the Bournes moved there, and who was by now very crippled and lived at Far Upton Wold before the Hannays claimed the house back for their tenant farmer John Prentice), Dick Allan, Philip Ransome, 'Bickie' Milvain, Don Fisher (of the zipped hunting-boots), Val (Don's beautiful and tragic daughter who early showed alcoholic tendencies) – and holidaying and cruising in glamorous locations, such as a Cuban cruise in October 1954, or driving Katie (Granny's sister) to Budapest and other points east before the war. His hospitality was well-known, his house was well-staffed and Vivian would even sometimes act as his hostess without Ted.

His snobbishness extended to a pretence to those outside his social circle that his Captaincy was a Naval one, and therefore of a much higher order – military Captains, whether they were regular, yeomanry or wartime soldiers, do not generally designate their rank once they revert to civilian life, save in the cases of Masters of Foxhounds, racehorse trainers and those in the service of the Royal Household (Cecil Boyd-Rochfort provided an example of both these last, as Her Majesty's late trainer) where it is still *de rigueur* to announce such a lowly rank if you have it. The days of frequent military service early in adult life having largely died out, perhaps this practice will too. Moreover, Midget gave instructions to the Post Office in Moreton-in-Marsh that any business correspondence postmarked 'Manchester', from where his wealth derived, should be kept for collection so that his guests would not be able to make any untoward conjectures. This all seems ridiculous now. How dearly Midget would have loved the baronetcy, so contemptuously turned down by his father at the time of Lloyd George's 1920s munificence in handing out titles. Well, I suppose everyone must start somewhere, as members of our successive governments show on a daily basis.

Midget was almost invisible behind the wheel of his shiny green Land Rover, polished daily by Philip Rogerson, a sweet man with wavy hair and a smiling open countenance who lived with his family in one of the semi-detached houses halfway down Kildanes drive. The peaked cap could just be seen above the rim of the steering wheel so that you could be sure who was actually in the driving seat.

One of his visits to the farm lives in my memory. He had parked as men trained in the military did in those days, ready for his departure, outside our kitchen window, which faced onto a deep well bounded by a high wall and against which lay the rear wheels of his Land Rover. His visit done, he climbed behind the wheel, accompanied as usual by his devoted terrier Weasel, made to shift into first gear, put the car into reverse, and came to rest with the rear wheels now over the edge of the wall.

Mum and I were in the kitchen as this was happening: I watched, entranced that a real live grown-up could make such a mistake. Mum was more put-about: "Watch out, he's going over the edge. Stop! Stop! For God's sake, stop!" she yelled. Midget, meanwhile, remained motionless in the driver's seat, awaiting rescue. Pairs of strong shoulders were found from somewhere within the farm buildings to hoist the vehicle onto level ground. Midget drove away without even an acknowledgement or a word of thanks, just the smallest wave of the hand. '*Sang froid*', I'd say, or 'cool', or 'wicked' or some such.

As the '50s drew on Midget's affection for me and for my parents became less overt. His presence at harvest tea was missed. He was entering his seventies and was becoming much less active. By now our farm lodges at the end of the drive were completed, providing up-to-date housing for our labour, complete with wash-boilers (sort of early washing machines) and the most efficient fire-grates for heating. The lodge at the end of Kildanes drive became superfluous to our needs, and Midget was starting to need 'in-house' care. Not only did a Swiss nurse Siegenthaler, complete with plaited hair around her head, come to live in the house with him towards the end of the decade, but so too came Ursula Ramsay Patrick and her daughter Sally, some three or four years older than me, to live in the lodge. Sally and her pony Joey would often join us for our rides around the countryside, she being about the same age as Katie Scott at Bourton Hill.

Ursula's parents, by the name of Chapman, had known Midget in Cairo during the First World War – her father was a General, but he and Midget had still become fast friends. So it was that his attention became absorbed in this new 'family', who promised so much in the way of immediate company. Sally gave children's parties in Kildanes itself to which I was not invited – I was after all quite a lot younger. My parents were keen to be friendly with Ursula, and one of my first visits to London was in their company when we sallied forth on the train from Moreton-in-Marsh to see a performance of *Iolanthe* at Sadlers Wells – my father's treat.

Ursula had been divorced for some years and had been left with little money. She gave us the uncalled-for reassurance in her characteristically crisp manner: "I am very fond of Midget, very fond indeed. He's an old friend of the family, and this is nothing to do with money, nothing at all. I'm doing it all for love"…

11

"THE LITTLE GIRL WITH A KIRBY GRIP"

– Christopher Bourne, our neighbour at Snowshill Hill

A time of glory it was, of the largeness of things: a time of safe certainty that grown-ups were superior beings, always to be trusted and admired; a time of ponies' manes blowing in the wind; of Stevenson's *The Black Arrow* and riveting *Black Beauty*, read with gusto by the time I was seven; of eggs with shells decorated for Easter by my mother's smallest, tiny-tipped paint-brush; of my father's and my attempts at model-making, and of my bumbling attempts at painting the same afterwards; of games such as Grandmother's Footsteps – you had to be absolutely still as 'grandmother' looked back at you over her shoulder, while attempting to get close enough to touch her; and Castle Doors, a half-forgotten game which involved hiding with a newly found companion or companions until you had all eluded, if you could, your elected pursuer; of Guy Fawkes parties devotedly staged each 5 November by my father for family and friends, building a vast bonfire in the Rick Yard while we dressed the Guy, and then teasing us with Jumping

Jacks (long since illegal) which exploded beneath our feet before we consumed hot chocolate and doughnuts as the fire burned low; of black-treacle-laced porridge, hot for breakfast from its overnight in the Aga; of mushrooms in May, brought in from our fields of older turf by the bucket-load until my mother cried, "Ted, please stop! I just can't cope with any more!"; of nettles (often the oldest leaves rather than the young and acceptable buds so beloved of modern cuisiniers), stewed to extinction and used as a vegetable smelling of old laundry – a hangover from wartime economy; of the postman always crying "Postie!" as he dropped the mail on the table in the back porch; of Daisy at the telephone exchange in Moreton-in-Marsh, through which all calls were routed, advising us as to the availability of a call recipient: "Oh no, he won't be in, he's gone to Cheltenham. Shall I try later for you?"

My mother would summon me downstairs by banging on the kitchen ceiling with the Aga poker, accompanied by a cry of "Yogh!" in imitation of Tinker's (Beegie's) bark. She called me 'Toot' or 'Too-Too', 'Marian' only if she was cross with me, which was rare in those early years. But it was my father who I remember bathing me, his long beautiful hands like those of the supposed artist. And it was he who would read to me, in an enchanting monotone, R.M. Ballantyne's *Coral Island*, and slightly later, *Sherlock Holmes* in all his mighty intellectual application. As I began to read for myself, enthusiasms also included a marvellous wartime story of children escaping from occupied Poland, Ian Serraillier's *The Silver Sword*, an early dramatisation for television.

Small elements of farming lore were early impressed upon me: never climb a gate except at the hinge end, so that it maintains its hanging position rather than leaning heavily and inconveniently on its latch; never park a vehicle in a gateway (not that I could drive, but even so) – this always caused intense annoyance; always leave a gate as you find it, either open or shut; a hedge layer should always make necessary cuts in the branch of the hedge being laid on its south-facing side, presumably to aid healing growth; ammonite fossils set in the stones frequently picked from our stony fields were evidence of a pre-Cambrian time when the farm (well, much of Britain actually) was beneath the sea; when the weather was thunderous and I wondered at the noise, my mother would explain to me that "God is moving his furniture" and when the light of the setting sun was diffused in Blake-like rays across the horizon, God was "using his paintbrush".

I loathed dolls and never possessed any, sensing something sinister in their presence – indeed, Conan Doyle wrote one story on exactly that subject. And yet I would sometimes turn up at my mother's bedside of a morning, dressed in my party frock, as if I wanted to skip the day that lay ahead and 'cut to the chase' of true femininity. I did not actually enjoy children's parties though, disliking the mix of formality (one or two mothers, Phayre Aizlewood being one, insisted that we girls should wear gloves with our dresses) with rough competition, which involved being knocked about during games of musical chairs, and often being shouted at by the more military-minded fathers who fancied themselves as party-organisers, one Brigadier Kennedy being a particular offender. Far better was to attend some decorous grown-up gathering and listen in on intriguing or interesting conversation, some of which was definitely meant for the adult domain. Parties at Guiting Grange, hosted by Jack and Rina Kennard for their grandchildren – one was Michael Boone, my friend who caught polio as a child – absolutely filled this bill of requirements. They were far too wise, and probably too idle, to organise us too closely, and Rina (Michael's step-grandmother) draped full-length in what looked like curtain material and wearing a turban, was a true eccentric, understanding of children's real desires – to be left alone as much as possible outside the requirements of school and formal occasions.

There was some sophistication there from the beginning, expressing itself in early experimentation with nail varnish – I must have been about four – which was ill-received as its trail lay stickily on the carpet. Auntie Daphne, married to my mother's brother Henry had fascinating hands, her nails painted the richest red – "Flowers, flowers," I would murmur as I stroked her fingers. On the other hand, if I became enraged at something or someone, I would swear mightily: "Oh, blovince!" Not bad, it has a certain resonance.

Party dresses did not come often for it was still a time of austerity – sweets did not come off ration until 1954 – and Vivian would sometimes complain of the paucity of their wedding presents, 1948 seeing Britain still at its lowest ebb after the war, compounded by the preceding severe winter. I was clothed largely in 'hand-me-downs' from my older Leamington cousins, and a trip to see darling Miss Brodie who wore a plait around her head and worked at Fodens in Moreton-in-Marsh, was a highlight. She would fuss around me delightedly: "Oh yes, dear. That looks just right, and the colour is perfect!" as she clasped her hands in satisfaction. She was truly the kindest person, with an almost childlike demeanour herself and a rare gift for 'walking in another's shoes'.

Moreton contained others equally at large in my childhood world – the courtly, courteous Mr Hill whose firm is now Howards upon the opposite side of the street, and who came every week to wind all the clocks in the house, and check upon their well-being; Jack Hale the blackened farrier and blacksmith from Claytons, the agricultural engineers; Mrs Hooper of the eponymous newsagents then next door to The Black Bear pub, a grumpy woman whose chief fascination for me was that she possessed a huge goiter indicating an underactive thyroid gland, doubtless the source of her tiredness and grumpiness; Mrs Pye, a benevolent dumpy woman who kept a small lampshade-making shop up near the police station, and who wrought miracles out of the most unpromising material; Gerry Tyack, who ran the Curfew Garage in the middle of town, and whose main enthusiasm was racing cars – he had a handlebar moustache to prove it – and who later, in his retirement, curated the Wellington Flying Museum on the Bourton-on-the-Hill edge of town, his other great enthusiasm being flying: he revered my son's paternal grandfather Mike Daunt, who test-piloted the first jet in the war years; his works manager John, a gentle giant of a man with the sweetest manner; F.J. Grimes Bros, a small building firm next to the Post Office, consisting of 'Grimesey Boy', as Vivian called him, a solid and moustached beacon of rectitude, and his brother, a slimmer and darker man. He I called 'Venevery', to his face as well, as I had never heard him called specifically by name.

"What did I hear you call him?" my mother quizzed me one day.

"Venevery, Mummy. Isn't that his name?"

"Oh, darling," she was nearly exploding with laughter as I looked at her in puzzlement. Ted was laughing too.

"You know where she's got that from, don't you?" he asked.

"What, what?" I longed to know why they were laughing.

"He drinks too much, so sometimes we say he's inebriated," Ted explained. "It's a word for someone who's drunk. Anyway, I think your name is rather good."

And 'Venevery' he remained; I never knew his real name.

Broadway too was a point of my constellation. Mr Franklin, later of Franklin and Cook our doughty deliverer of weekly groceries, would toil up either Snowshill or Fish Hill in his green van, double-doored at the back, even sometimes making two trips if an item had been forgotten. He had always had grey hair so far as I was concerned, and had unending placidity and a gravelly laugh. His whole family worked in the shop, and as the '50s drew on he began to stock delicacies such as Boursin cheese and Bath Oliver biscuits, items which quickly found their way into Vivian's shopping basket. The purchase of my weekly ice cream was a ceremony enjoyed by us both: "There you are, my dear [always 'my dear']. There's another one waiting when you want it," said with a mischievous twinkle.

The weekly trip to Broadway – it assumed a weekly habit during and after the petrol rationing of Suez in 1956 – was an essential addition to the grocery delivery, and provided me with the opportunity to question my mother closely on such matters as the nature of the heavens: "Does the sky just go on and on? Do you get lost if you fly too high?" I had been watching a fairytale on TV about a flying horse.

One day there was trouble; I had been in Mr Warrens's ironmongery shop, now Small Talk opposite Lloyds Bank, where an unaccountable desire to possess a gold, (or was it silver?) bristled head to a washing-up brush had overtaken me. I emerged clutching it in my hand, no attempt at concealment. It was quickly spotted by Vivian, and I was unceremoniously hauled back into the shop 'by the ear' and made to relinquish my new best possession, and apologise, in full view of other customers. I couldn't quite understand what all the fuss was about; I had simply wanted the brush. My mother could overdo things when it came to instilling rectitude, but I never went shoplifting in teenage years when it became quite the fashion among the more 'clever' and 'daring' of my school contemporaries.

All blows would be softened by a visit to kindly Mr Arnold the wine merchant, a little way up the street towards Fish Hill. He did not deliver outside the town and we would take our fortnightly order-book, one or more pages filled out neatly in Ted's hand, so that our two or three wooden boxes might be stocked, mostly with the 'hard stuff' of gin and whisky (vodka was little drunk then, possibly not even much available) and a peculiar very dark South African sherry labelled 'Landdrost'. Vivian had a sweet tooth and generally commandeered a bottle of rum for herself. Champagne was freely available if required for a party, and became our basic ration one winter when a planned entertainment had to be cancelled and we were stranded in the snow. Mr Arnold came early to wine importation, and by the end of the decade had begun to stock a fair selection of French wines. He was ably assisted by Denis, and by his son, 'Young' Arnold. The three of them wore brown dustcoats, and I always thought of them as slightly dusty musketeers. Whatever the requirement they would do their best to fulfil it, always accompanied by "Very good, very good." At the upper end of the town, the shop went out of business earlier this century, surely not helped by the ascent up Fish Hill having been made a cul-de-sac as a consequence of Broadway's bypass. It was a haven for the Broadway wine connoisseur.

A trip to Cheltenham was much prized, as it usually involved more than one ice-cream and probably lunch at Kate's Kitchen in The Promenade. My mother's weekly trips there, to get a string of pearls re-strung, to arrange for the repair of hunting boots, to have her hair done, or to get some item of saddlery mended, were more and more an outing for me too, culminating in the purchase of my school uniform at Daniel Neale in my ninth summer before I went away as a boarder to Seven Springs House some five miles out of Cheltenham at the Cirencester/Gloucester road junction, said by some to be one of the sites of the source of the Thames.

'Turkie boy', Mr Turk the Saddler in Winchcombe Street, was one of Vivian's favourites. Unfailingly helpful and with an unsurpassed knowledge of his craft, he towered behind the counter in a white dustcoat, carrying an air of authority which must have come from fields other than saddlery. He was of the gentry, thus almost unique in his profession, and spoke with an almost tongue-tied earnestness – the customer was always right and his rubicund face shone with the desire to be of service. I think that he was actually not very well, and his temple to the horse closed quite soon after the end of the decade. Slades the Bootmaker in The Promenade did not last beyond this point either, and was used by my mother more for repair than for the actual purchase of boots. Beards the Jeweller – she never used the better-known firm of Martins – was almost next door to Slades, and from there it was only a short step to Cavendish House, the department store, carpeted in a genteel beige with a brown pattern. This was also the haunt of the dreaded Miss Clutterbuck lurking in her cream and frosted glass cubicle, black hair tightly permed, eyes a-glitter, as she wielded her scissors upon my unwilling head of hair and the tears poured down my face.

A look afterwards down the shoe department's X-Ray machine at the skeletal structure of my feet and possibly a purchase of some shoes, would do a little to take my mind off my newly shorn appearance. I cannot understand why it was necessary to X-Ray a child's feet first, and in later years the practice was discontinued as the dangers of radiation became better understood. Steeles Garage in Albion Street provided servicing for the new green Land Rover, often combined with the day's shopping.

School came early into my life; Pilgrim Cottage, just off the main road in Bourton-on-the-Hill, was my destination in the autumn of 1954. Both parents were there, courtesy of the cream Willys Jeep, to launch me on my academic career. Forlornly I climbed the steep steps to the front door that first day, with a feeling that I had been deserted by my parents and that I was being thrust into a whole new, and utterly undesirable, world from which I would try to escape at the earliest opportunity. I did not, of course, coming closest to it only on one day when I was found at the top of the hill, determined to make it the three miles home as whoever was fetching me was late. With only twelve children in the whole school, divided by age and ability and according to subject, I must have slipped away that day unnoticed, somehow evading the school count, determined to make my way home past the old man who lived at the top of the village and who spent all day sitting on the pavement outside his house in a kitchen chair watching the world go by.

Carole Summers – one of David's daughters, he from whom we had bought the farm – was my greeter on that first morning. She had a deep voice and a lovely laugh to match, sharing her father's nonchalant approach to life. Her favourite adjective was 'terribly', usually repeated, to qualify any noun. She stood at the top of the steps and being one of the seniors – some stayed until they were twelve – she took me by the hand and ushered me in with a cry of "Welcome!"

A whole new world took shape in those first weeks under the auspices of Miss Woolrich, later Nean Holder, who later married Bertie, Peter Thin's tenant at Bourton Far Hill during the war years. She was a strict disciplinarian, but she provided her pupils with a firm grounding in the 'three R's' of reading, writing and 'rithmetic – though my maths was always poor – and absorbed us in the subjects of history and geography too. Such a 'dame school' inevitably lacked the resources to be able to attend to the weaker subjects of its pupils, but it engendered a rare companionship and a precocity in the subjects that we found easy. Here began my early love of reading which I mastered within the first year.

A hot lunch was brought in every day in sealed canisters, and the school always passed its annual inspection by the local authority with flying colours. Mr Amphlett the Vicar who lived only a hundred yards away in The Chantry, a fine Georgian house, provided the only whiff of scandal: he was defrocked at some stage during my time at the school for some undisclosed misconduct, and his duties as Scripture teacher were taken on by Canon Noot, retired and living locally.

The gardens of The Chantry provided the venue for the annual school play, put on at the end of the summer term. Despite my love of party dresses I disliked dressing up in public, and my performance as Prince Robino John in some long forgotten drama proved a disaster as I stood there, mouth soundlessly opening and closing, my lines entirely eluding me. If I had to play any part I wanted it to be a female one, but being so tall for my age male roles were those allotted to me. This extended to dancing class too – at Buzz Shakerley's house, Wells Folly near Moreton-in-Marsh – so that in slightly later years I would often commit the cardinal sin of initially clasping my male partner around the waist.

Organised games were rather difficult to arrange with such small numbers, and exercise generally took the form of a nature walk up Kite's Lane out of the village, to spot wild flowers such as the pale mauve Scabious, and the charmingly named 'Eggs-and-Bacon', 'Bird's-Foot-Trefoil' and 'Ladies' Bed Straw', perfectly describing their respective appearances. Violets abounded on the March verges, and the yellow charlock came later to accompany the poppies in their invasion of the cornfields. Cowslips were commoner then than now, as were celandines, the pointier version of the now ubiquitous buttercup. The girls in the school made daisy chains from those cheeky enough to decorate Miss Woolrich's lawn, and the reflection of the buttercup beneath one's chin denoted a liking for butter. More excitingly, Mr Wood's shop at the bottom of the village provided us with illicit 'farthing chews' and sherbet lemons, bought 'under the counter'. There was a second shop then in the village, the Star Stores on the left of the road at the bottom of the hill. Now there are none, and haven't been for forty years or more.

Only in after years did we learn of Miss Woolrich's wartime experiences: she had been governess in a Dutch family when the Netherlands were invaded in 1940; too late by then to get back to England, she spent the rest of the war in increasingly awful privation, as did the whole Dutch nation, lucky not to starve to death as some did. By the war's end, many, she included, were reduced to eating tulip bulbs to stay alive. Not surprisingly she was always very thin. It is said that a similar experience was responsible for Audrey Hepburn's lifelong slenderness, too.

Social life in term-time was dictated by school and some friends now are those that were made then. Robert Wharton, later to become a 'terror of the highways' in the company of Jeremy Nabarro and Richard Clifford, was some two years older than me and given to impatience with the female of the species – even his sister Mary, one of my greatest friends (and the first to be lost, in a car-crash in Ireland at the age of eighteen) would occasionally suffer at his hands – I generally managed to 'steer clear'. Their parents farmed at Luckley near Stow-on-the-Wold – their father Harry had suffered from TB before the war began, and thus remained as a farmer for the duration of hostilities, it being a 'reserved occupation' essential to the war effort. There were two more elder brothers and an older sister in the family and their house was always full of their mother Daphne's cooking aromas and a welcoming smile. Robert and his third wife Pauline, from Australia, live there still.

Martin Elliott was a year or two younger than me. His mother's family had lived at Broadwell Manor just outside Stow and his father Joe kept an Alpine nursery, one of the most famous of its kind in the country. Martin and I were wary of one another for reasons which I cannot now recall, though he did quite justifiably berate me one day for taking a drink from the bathroom waste-pipe emptying itself into the flower-bed beside the cottage. I must have thought this a clever idea; he, not unreasonably, doubted my sanity. My mother and Joe were good friends, keen to discuss gardening at length.

Robin Dale was a little older and came to school from Manor Farm across the road. This is still part of the Batsford Estate, and Robin and Ros (his wife) are tenants of Michael Dulverton's, the son of Tony the erstwhile Master of the North Cotswold Hounds.

Robin's weak point in those days was arithmetic – for his mistakes he was most brutally rapped across the knuckles with Miss Woolrich's ruler, often reducing him to tears. I wonder if this was really the best method of instilling arithmetical expertise, and I was always glad that my mathematical inability was never quite sufficient to lead to such a painful punishment. Next to him would sit Ian Wills, Tony Dulverton's second son. He and I were friends bound together by a wry view of life, his perhaps engendered by an already deteriorating family situation and mine by all the perceptions which are early thrust upon an only child. Even now, whenever we meet, that bond is not entirely fled.

Apart from Mary Wharton, my greatest friends among the girls were few – Carole Summers was much older than me, and her sister Katherine ('Kitten') was younger, but Rosemary ('Buzz' as her mother called her) Shakerley was then, as she is still, one of my closest chums, and we early began a 'tea ceremony' in each others' houses, but this friendship was not shared between our parents – shades of the snow-plough!

That left Susie and Priscilla Saxton, the daughters of the Moreton doctor, Arthur. He drove a yellow MG, almost always open to the four winds even in the foulest weather, wore thick glasses (or were they goggles?) and was always laughing. Some of the more snobbish parents were a bit dubious about him as his family came from Frinton-on-Sea, which was not regarded as a patch on Gloucestershire, let alone the Cotswolds. He was a good doctor though, and his frivolity was kept in check by a rather serious wife, Anne. I envied Susie and Priscilla their plaits, so carefully done by their mother each morning, and was an occasional guest for tea at Bengal House in London Road, later the headquarters of the Moreton-in-Marsh Show Society. But once we had left Pilgrim Cottage I never saw them again; I think their father moved to another practice quite soon after we had left the school.

Pony Club ruled in the holidays; I rarely saw my non-riding friends except in term-time. Although not a brave rider during my first decade, I was early introduced to the Pony Club as a place of companionship and as a contrast to my gloriously book-laden solitude, otherwise interrupted only by Fiona and Glenda at Spring Hill. The organisation itself had been founded in 1929 to foster the qualities of citizenship through the medium of horsemanship and the discipline and occasional self-denial that that entails, and the North Cotswold Branch was begun only a year later during the Mastership of Major E.A. Fielden. Branches in those days were based on hunting 'countries', as they mostly still are officially, and were run by district commissioners (as outlying areas within the colonies had been), assisted by one or more secretaries. It was run on military lines then, and both the officials and the instructors came mainly from such a background. Our first DC was Brigadier W. Rankin, followed by Colonel S. Whetherby, who was succeeded by Captain C.M. Napier who was the DC when I arrived on the scene in the mid-'50s, and from whom we bought Kilmurray. Charles' tenure, interrupted by the war when Mrs 'Titch' Peacock (who as 'Titch' Rigby had for a while held the

British show-jumping record for height with 'Boy' Whitehead's horse, Scorchin) had been assisted by Mrs ('Bickie') Milvain as Secretary until 1952. It was she who took me for my Pony Club 'D' test when I was around six years old, the first proficiency test of four laid down by the Pony Club. She walked with two sticks, having had several serious accidents out hunting, but this did not stop her from instructing the junior ride, another military term, meaning a class or form, nor from awarding me and my beloved Shadow our first-ever ribbon, a prize for the ride's best turned-out pony and rider.

It was at this point that I managed to discard the degrading green felt saddle, with its equally humbling attachments of crupper (to keep the saddle straight on a fat pony's back by means of attachment to the tail) and safety stirrup irons with detachable rubber sides to them, which freed the foot if necessary when falling off. During the days of Polly, this hated saddle was her compulsory wear, so that I might stick to the felt; now it was cast away in favour of more grown-up attire, only later to be used by Pompey the fat, grey and very stubborn cob, whose roundness made it hard for him to wear anything else.

Johnnie Pearson was a close neighbour of Charles Napier's in Broadway's Springfield Lane. He was quite old, too old to have served in the war, and must have been a veteran of the '14–'18 conflict. He was a sweet, mild-mannered man and unusual in that he instructed us younger ones, ladies generally being assigned this task. Beryl Warren too was one of our mentors and she, now in her nineties, guides so many of us still on hunting matters with her indispensable wisdom.

As I grew rather taller and older, and Shadow was no more I found myself in a more demanding environment under the tutelage of Major Rob Fanshawe, brother to Dick who had been our Master of Hounds at the beginning of the decade, and as different from him as chalk from cheese. Entirely devoid of charm or any traces of humanity, he 'took no prisoners', and we were expected to conform and to obey the very letter of the law. The whole lesson, probably two hours in length, was conducted as if on military manoeuvres. "Leading file [a single rider leading the column – as perhaps in Afghanistan] canter to the rear of the ride," he would bark at the leader as we trotted in a circle around him. If you were on a lazy pony, unwilling to proceed without the surrounding comfort of his companions, this exercise could be sheer torture as you kicked and strove to get even one canter stride (probably on the wrong lead – the pony putting the outside, instead of the inside, fore and hind legs to the ground first) before breathlessly and somewhat shamefacedly gaining the welcome sight of the rear pony's backside. Major Fanshawe never commented, never attempted any communication with us outside the matter in hand, all commands were delivered in stentorian tones as he surveyed us, moustache bristling and blue eyes glaring from his pugnacious face. I was definitely a little afraid of him as I suppose most of us were, but he taught us to persevere, even with the most unpromising ponies, and to ride accurately and with awareness, an inestimable benefit when it comes to riding dressage. At the end of a morning's hard work, invariably on a boiling hot day, our final instruction would be the cavalry order, "Make much of your horses," obeyed by us with much relief, and perhaps the tiniest bit of satisfaction that the lazy pony cantered just that little bit more readily than before.

    Times have changed mightily, with health and safety and all that it encompasses coming much more between instructor and pupil than any shouted direction might have done; it is no longer permitted to touch a child's leg, so that he or she might improve its position, without saying what you are going to do first. The child can then refuse to be touched, in case of sexual intent! So much for the pursuit of 'improved communication' that we are all supposed to want so much. I cannot recall one incident of a dubious nature during all my fifteen years in the Pony Club, or later on when I myself rose to the rank of occasional instructor.

Pony Club days, the height of which came with the Three- (later Four-) Day Rally at Spring Hill in July or August, were not all hard work. There was plenty of opportunity for bad behaviour and mischief, frequently led by 'Midge' Evetts, grandson of 'Pug' Ismay, Churchill's Chief-of-Staff throughout the war. 'Midge' (John), though he grew to be a tall man, took his time about it, not really growing at all between the ages of seven and fifteen. He it was who pressed a select gang of us one hot lunchtime, to free the ponies tied to the iron railings surrounding the park so that they might, to our great joy, career out of sight, stirrups and halter-ropes flying. Adult anger was great which only increased our mirth, and only after much close questioning was the identity of our inspiration revealed.

Some of our number went on to greater equestrian feats: Nigel Tabor, a renowned trainer of three-day-eventers and their riders, and who himself achieved seventh place at Burghley Horse Trials one year, began Pony Club life on one of the smallest ponies ever seen in our branch, a strawberry roan named Holly; Richard Clifford (of Bourton Far Hill Lodge fame) had a successful career in Pony Club Horse Trials (now more commonly known as eventing) on a wonderful chestnut cob named Briton, and went on to play polo for the army, and to train a stepson who has been successful in the same discipline; Niccy Gretton (née Tollit), whose earlier triumphs were achieved on Richard Clifford's former mount, Peter Pan, became a great show rider, and one of her sons Tommy inherited the farm where he now runs a training yard, the other Edward works in racing administration; Patrick McCanlis rode round Cheltenham in the Foxhunters' Amateur Chase; George Hyatt and Tishy Evetts (Midge's sister) both achieved fame in the point-to-pointing and chasing world – George as a jockey, and also as an amateur huntsman (and therefore Master) of a number of packs of hounds in England, Ireland and Canada, and Tishy as a trainer and bloodstock agent with her late husband David Smyly: they later moved to France and the Loire Valley for some years. I for my part did my best in a variety of equestrian disciplines, but my greatest claim to fame was probably appearing on television in 1957 as I led Cresta Run (later Airs and Graces) down the ramp of his horsebox on his arrival at his new home in Lancashire as Sheila Willcox's future (1959) Badminton Horse Trials winner.

During those first busy years there were few holidays, though Ted and Vivian did spend ten days at Windermere in the summer of 1952. They took me away with them for the first time when I was four, to their favourite haunt of Wales; Rhayadr (whose reservoir had been created early in the twentieth century), Bedd-Gellert, Bettws-y-Coed and Llanberis (all wonderfully portrayed in watercolour by the Birmingham artist David Cox, a fine collection of whose work is in the Birmingham City Art Gallery) were favourite destinations dictated largely by their Myriapodological possibilities. We stayed at the Pen-y-Gwryd Hotel in Llandudno on that beautiful north coast looking across to the Wirral Peninsula with Birkenhead at its tip; close therefore to Ted's beloved Cheshire, and more importantly a happy hunting ground for centipedes. I slept in a small bed in a corner of their bedroom, and my stay was marred by two mishaps exacerbated by wretched weather.

The day was stormy, and presented the opportunity for a dramatic walk along the beach. It was the first time that I had seen the sea with its hypnotic rhythm, and its tide, white-rimmed and inviting at the undulating edge, definitely worth exploration and pursuit as it retreated to the main body of water. Before I knew it my feet were caught in the undertow, I had toppled over, and a surge of water took my small body in its great hand, sucking it away from the beach. I was entirely out of control for the first time in my small span of memory, and as a wave engulfed my face I knew too, for the first time, true terror. There was nothing to be done but scream and struggle as the great hand took no notice at all. My father was there though, in what must have been a split second but felt like an eternity. He grabbed me by the scruff of the neck, hauling me beachwards, soaked and still too frightened to feel much relief.

The hotel staff were kind and I was fitted out with borrowed clothes, unpleasing to my vanity – I seem to recall a lot of brown scratchy wool. This was to enable us to continue this hateful day with a trip up Mount Snowdon on the legendary rack-and-pinion train, which could cope with the steep gradient. I remember seeing nothing at all as we ascended, save for steamed-up windows streaming with outside rain. Moreover, the woolly clothes were uncomfortable and unbecoming, and I wept in protest all the way. My poor parents must have wondered where they had gone wrong: the steeliness of their resolve to do all that had been planned for the day ensured a rocky ride.

Later holidays were spent at Eastbourne staying in the Cavendish Hotel, where my grandparents eventually went to live in their final years. Great was the excitement as the Vanguard – we had graduated to an estate car by now – was packed to the gunnels the previous day with things that we would never need, so that we might leave at four the following morning. An assortment of Ordnance Survey Maps covering every conceivable deviation along the way would accompany us, Ted being keen to vary the trip by taking unexpected short cuts: "Wait a bit," he would say, sucking on his pipe, as it turned out that we had gone wrong again, frustration mounting as we longed only to reach our destination.

The purchase of a car had been fraught with problems, the £700 price-tag having already presented some difficulty.

"What's that space below the dashboard for?" my father had inquired.

"Well, you might like a radio, Dr Eason. They're all the rage now, you know. Keep you company on a long journey, and there are such interesting programmes nowadays."

"I've been on more long journeys than you've had hot dinners," he sturdily replied. "And anyway, I can't hear the damned radio when it's in the same room, let alone when an engine's running. Good God, what's the world coming to?"

Disappointed on this front, the salesman had attempted a few other 'extras': the heater had been a bone of contention between Ted and Vivian – she found the cold trying, probably because of her tropical birthplace, and won a concession on this front, though he persisted in his contention that it was a 'decadent' requirement. His resistance to fog-lights proved more successful (I'm not sure how effective they are, even now), and also to floormats, resulting in the Vanguard's rapid acquisition of an ash floor as already described. Indicators which flipped out horizontally from their home behind the two front doors of the car were, however, regarded as essential – hand signals are not much visible at night. The surprise to a modern reader is how many (now) perfectly normal fixtures and fittings were then regarded as extra, and accordingly subject to extra charge. And what would Ted have said to air-conditioning? Let alone the sat nav. "I found my way back from Burma…"

The trip to the south coast in those days took around five hours, and was best undertaken during the early hours before much traffic was about, so that a hearty breakfast could be consumed upon arrival at the Cavendish Hotel where we always stayed. Joan and Griff and my cousins Margaret and Wendy together with the grandparents, shared these holidays with us – days of bliss spent beachcombing and shell-collecting, and of course, giving Ted the chance to explore the fauna and flora, and my mother a much-needed chance to relax and read as she found that she and Joan got on rather well after all.

One wet day there afforded me my first visit to the cinema at the age of seven; we saw *Genevieve* starring Kenneth More and Kay Kendall. 'The pictures' were frequently attended after that, mostly in Moreton where the US had an air base – the Fire Service Training College has since found its home there – which provided a reliable clientèle for the films shown in what is now the back part of the Manor House Hotel. *The Pathé News Reel* was an essential prelude to every film programme, as was the National Anthem (for which we always stood, my father 'at attention') at its end. Otherwise, we went either to the Clifton in the High Street or the Regal in Bridge Street, both in Evesham, to Chipping Norton or more occasionally, to Cheltenham. *The Time Machine* starring Rod Taylor I remember as one half of an excellent double bill – almost always a double bill in those days; some of the 'B' Movies then weren't half bad– and on another occasion I gave much amusement to David and Eve Summers as we watched *Davy Crockett* in Moreton's 'flea-pit', and I made the childishly knowledgeable comment that "Crockett's horse has a very ewe-neck."

Sidmouth in Devon, prettier and smaller than Eastbourne, enjoyed our attentions one summer just for a change, as did Honiton and the beaches of Minehead (a small book, *The Folk Tales of Devon* became a consuming interest for a while) but our family who lived in and around Eastbourne proved the greater draw. Old Auntie Edith as she was known, was married to Fred Ecroyd – he stayed in bed for much of his life, and successfully played the stock market though dying relatively young, so I do not remember him at all.

"Why do you always wear that hat, Auntie Edith?" I boldly enquired one day of Grandpa's sister, as we sat in her lovely garden in The Meads, a charming residential area of Eastbourne much favoured by our relations.

Those within earshot looked embarrassed and a little shocked that one so young could be so direct, perhaps impertinent, as the young are.

Auntie Edith's intelligence and humour did not desert her: "My hair will fall out otherwise, and you wouldn't want to see that, would you?" she said in that Lancashire burr of hers.

"No, I suppose not," I answered, a bit doubtfully.

It was the truth though – her small, black beret concealed a sad lack of hair; as she grew old and I would visit her in her old people's home the beret had been replaced by a toupée, always a little askew. I never quite dared to straighten it for her as she tugged with one hand in an attempt to set it right.

Edith had two daughters and they in turn had a total of five children, who all called her 'Mops'; only one of them was a boy, my second cousin Antony, who remains childless; boys only came again with the succeeding generation.

My first trip to London was made when I was around seven years old, the parents deciding that it was about time that I saw 'the sights'. Although it was possible in those years to travel from Trooper's Lodge Garage, on the Broadway to Stow-on-the-Wold road, by coach to the capital as others frequently did, we went on the train from Moreton-in-Marsh, the Great Western line (or 'God's Wonderful Railway') employing the finest steam locomotives – British commercial steam trains ceased to run in Britain after 1965, only later resuming in the shape of an engine built at York, which enjoyed its launch at the beginning of 2009. Other steam engines now ply the Wareham line in Dorset, the West Somerset Railway, the Ffestiniog Railway, the North Yorkshire Moors, the Isle of Man and the Great Central Railway (the only double track steam railway operating in the UK) amongst others. Much of the railway between Cheltenham and Stratford-upon-Avon has been voluntarily restored for steam use, thus potentially linking the two racecourses.

They were dirty of course, and no doubt because of their use of coal, the stations themselves, including the London termini, were floored with cinders but the excitement of climbing aboard one of these living, breathing monsters can never be equalled by riding the androgynously clean diesel or electric engines. The carriages were decorated with vivid posters by such fine artists as Harold Langley, Samuel Lamorna Birch, Stanhope Forbes and Harold Knight, lauding the touristic highlights of whichever region one was travelling in.

We stayed in an establishment in Baker Street, Adam Rondale House, close to 21b, the abode of Sherlock Holmes. Though I was still a little young to make his acquaintance, the parents were not going to pass up the opportunity to pay his house a visit. Did he really exist? You would have thought so, and many do now. The Wallace Collection too was close by, though the glory of its interiors and its contents somewhat passed me by, save for the Landseer in the hall of the mare and foal reclining on a carpet within their Arab master's tent. Dickens' House – real this time – in Doughty Street displayed absolute authenticity, as if he had only just left his desk the moment before. The Tower of London filled me with a nameless dread which I quickly managed to read up on when I got home. But my greatest terror was reserved for the Underground – too scared to embark on the down escalator, and having lost contact with the hands of both parents, my father had to 'hot-foot it' back to me uphill, from further down the moving staircase!

My parents had a good many friends in London, and my father quite frequently went up to go visiting, and to do research in the Natural History Museum. My first taste of high life was tea in the Dorchester with some American friends, the MacGills from Canada – he was a scientific colleague of my father's. My main memories of the occasion were of terror in case I knocked over the cake-stand or spilt my tea – by then I had moved on from my staple of hot water at teatime – and complete wonder at the ornate decoration of the hotel's reception areas, a positive fairyland.

London was still a dirty place, despite the passage of the Clean Air Act the previous year: I remember a real yellow 'pea-souper' (fog) one evening, in which my father loomed beside me in the act of paying off a taxi – anything further away than perhaps five yards was a blur – while my mother hissed angrily at him: "What about the tip, Ted? You really are the limit."

The taxi-driver's ire was clear for us to see and hear: "Nice knowin' yer, Gov. Don't bother gettin' in my cab again, will yer?"

Was my father really that deaf? I doubt it. A bit of Eason parsimony just couldn't be resisted.

An only child tends to get packed off to stay with relatives on a fairly regular basis. My routine ports of call were my grandparents at Radway and 'E +2' (and Grandpa Haynes of course) at Leamington Spa. Radway was loved for its garden, bounded by cinder paths, never seen now as ash is a rare by-product within today's home, and even now the cause of a scar where I once fell over and some ash lay forever embedded as the resulting wound healed. If my cousins were not visiting at the same time, Jane Starkey was called into play; this was not enjoyable – she was six months younger but far too bossy, and my defensive walls would quickly go up. Our games of croquet were not a success. The times that I loved best were when I was on my own with Granny, and less frequently Grandpa, and could discuss things with them which mattered to me. It was from Granny that I learned, in a practical demonstration, that even the tightest-fitting, seemingly impossible-to-remove ring can eventually be coaxed from the finger with the aid of soap and a little water. 'Grandparents have time', we hear so many children say when they have reached the age of enquiry. Long winter afternoons spent in the snug facing onto the verandah and the rolling garden beyond were bliss, especially with a book and the strike of the library clock to counteract Granny's intermittent comforting chatter.

And the leather-chaired library was a place of enchantment, its leather-bordered shelves filled with heroic accounts: Sven Hedin's *Overland to India* (he was Swedish so it wasn't only the British who were great explorers), Scott's *Last Expedition*, Amundsen's (Norwegian) *The South Pole* (he being the only one to reach it before the First World War), Ernest Shackleton's *The Heart of the Antarctic*, Apsley Cherry-Garrard's *The Worst Journey in the World* (he was the doctor in Scott's *Last Expedition*). All of these had the added significance of knowing Dad's friend and Titus Oates' (*I may be gone some time*) nephew Ted. The books were heavy for young hands, but their contents revealed whole worlds undreamed of.

Soon the gong would sound for dinner – we grandchildren were expected to change into a dress for this as we grew older. 'Healthy' foods were the norm; Granny's adherence to the tenets of *Radiant Health* made sure of this, junket (even with chocolate) being particularly disgusting – slimy and cold and vaguely sour, betraying its milky origins. There was no need to worry at Hemp Close about an onset of acidosis, a juvenile reaction to fatty foods which involves nausea and a temperature, and which I suffered from in early childhood. Poor Grandpa suffered wordlessly under this regime until the Cavendish Hotel offered an escape much later on.

Otherwise it was an easy-going household, and I recall committing only one misdemeanour which earned anything approaching wrath. As I lay on the bed in 'Mr Ted's (my father's) Room' for the compulsory afternoon's rest one day, giving the grown-ups a much-needed break, I grew bored, a blue biro came to hand, and I surveyed the blank white wall which stood beside me. It presented an ideal surface for the depiction of a few horses, my main subject when it came to artistic endeavour. Before I knew it, the entire wall was covered in horse's heads, done in Egyptian profile, and rather impressive to my mind. Granny disagreed and let me know it. I was confined for the rest of the day, and probably fed junket for supper as a punishment. Biro being indelible, the wall – and probably the whole room – had to be repainted.

Sites of exploration included the loft above the wooden garage behind the house, where my mother found several quite decorative oil-paintings in an advanced state of decay, to be rescued just in time, and the back parts of the house, floored in muted shades of linoleum – now having made a comeback, being of organic composition. These back parts of the house, as the servants' quarters, were no longer in use, the Mainwarings having their own cottage in the stable yard. The empty rooms and the unused staircase provided a haven of mystery and silence which I could people with the imaginary characters of childhood, but one character who was non-imaginary loomed over all – that of Mrs Logsdail. Mrs Logsdail and her family had come to live at Hemp Close as wartime evacuees from London. Theirs was not a happy experience as Mrs Logsdail conceived a violent antipathy towards rural living and towards her immediate neighbours, eventually refusing even to leave the house. Her presence was a malevolent one, not alleviated by her constant proximity, and Granny lost several valuable items during her stay including my father's Hornby train set, which Mrs Logsdail was suspected of having cunningly secreted piece by piece. My father's homecoming from India was much marred by this and by Granny's thoughtless disposal of all his medical journals (funny how so many parents do this to their children).

Mrs Raw kept the Post Office Stores in Radway (now shopless for many years) where sweets, only 'healthy' ones such as treacle toffee permitted of course, could be bought. Mrs Timmins who lived at the far end of the village possessed a state-of-the-art knitting machine which took up most of her front room, and from which she was said to make a fair living having been left to shift for herself after her husband's demise or departure, I forget which. But the greatest source of entertainment, at least when it snowed, was a ride in Armorel Cary's sleigh, wrapped in thick rugs Russian-fashion, and drawn by her brisk bay pony Lollo, who I could swear wore bells on his bridle, just to make things perfect.

Armorel was a scion of Lucius Cary's family – she was unmarried. He was a Royalist commander at the Battle of Edgehill, fought on the hillside just above the village in 1642, and was killed the following year at the Battle of Newbury. If you visit Great Tew in Oxfordshire, where he lived the greater part of his life, the village pub bears the name The Falkland Arms: he was the 2nd Viscount Falkland.

Radway still carried a great awareness of the Civil War and the part which it had played at the time together with neighbouring Kineton. It was said that if you rode or walked at night up King John's Lane, on the left as you departed the village heading towards the main Banbury Road, you could often hear the clash of arms from those momentous days and even see shadows in the sky. I never quite dared to look.

Until my grandparents left Radway when I was in my early twenties, the Mainwarings deciding that their time for retirement to their family in Cheshire had come, every Christmas lunch was taken at Hemp Close. There would generally be nine of us –

the grandparents, Ted, Joan and their respective families. More distant relations sometimes joined us in the much-too-small dining-room with its tobacco-coloured carpet, including John Hashim and his family one year, all the way from Suffolk. It was an uncomfortable business, as we sat upon straight-backed, rush-seated country chairs, while Grandpa carved wafer-thin slices of turkey, so that some might be saved for the next day. Luncheon cake was amply supplied at the end of the repast to fill in the empty corners once we children had had a chance to extract some silver sixpences from the Christmas pudding.

We drank champagne from an early age (it was generally regarded as a 'pick-me-up' for the ailing at any time of life, and most certainly for my father during his days of childhood illness), toasting Her Majesty's health in response to Grandpa's "The Queen, God bless her." Absent friends too were remembered, carrying a weight of meaning for those older, who had all lost friends, not just from natural causes, but in the time of war. Throughout all this, Mrs Mainwaring – red-haired and voluble in 'Lancashire' – would tirelessly serve us, having cooked single-handed from early that morning, always with unfailing good nature. She and Bob would have their lunch on Boxing Day. She never stopped working, the whole house smelling always of wood polish and clean carpets, and fresh-cut flowers in summer.

After lunch, the window-seats in the library would quickly be denuded of their piles of presents, so carefully laid out by Grannny and so carefully chosen. Only some years afterwards did I realise that not everyone enjoyed such a happy family time on Christmas Day.

Christmas fare would continue with cake and more cake at Dunraven in Lansdowne Circus in Leamington, where Auntie Evelyn had no qualms about producing the richest and fattiest of foods for our delight, the four of them remaining remarkably slim nonetheless. We would arrive in time for tea, Ted's teeth clenched on his pipe in anticipation of a monologue from Grandpa Haynes on composting or Malaya.

"Come on in, come on in!" Auntie Evelyn would exclaim, as if we might otherwise take wing and fly away. Divested of our outer clothing, tea would be taken around the large table in the dining-room, the wall above the fireplace embellished with a print of William Blake's Canterbury Pilgrims, filled with dancing horses caparisoned as only the Victorians could imagine. Perhaps the thin slices of turkey at lunch were a blessing after all as the demands of Christmas cake, chocolate cake, sponge cake and a multiplicity of sandwiches made their demands on our tummies. These were a joint production between Auntie Evelyn and her 'daily', Mrs Johns, who produced miracles from a galley kitchen next to the dining-room, still at this time equipped with manufactured gas as its source of cooking power, filthy because of its coal-fired origins. Afterwards, we would sit in the pretty drawing-room, facing onto the Circus, brightly lit for Christmastide, and I would watch the flames behind the doors of the blue ceramic stove while Auntie Evelyn, a petite version of my mother, even her voice so similar, would wisely leave me to my thoughts.

"Thank God that's over for another year," Ted would exclaim as we journeyed homeward. "Your father was on again about compost. He really is the most God-awful bore." Vivian found it hard to disagree. The hum of grown-up conversation would comfortingly continue as I dozed content in the back of the car, often not getting home much before 8.30 that night.

Grandpa Haynes had at least one redeeming feature; he did provide a home for 'E+2' after her miserable divorce from a distant cousin Wilfrid Haynes, and Caroline and Elizabeth found childhood fascination in his tales of his long time in Malaya. He combined the roles of father and grandfather, and his importance in their lives was inestimable. By the time I could remember him though, he was quite crippled, walking on two sticks, which probably did not improve his temper as he seemed never to be in good sorts and we were told not to do anything which might irritate him. It followed that there was no opportunity to establish any relationship with him, and his death when I was thirteen went sadly unacknowledged by me.

Dunraven, a pretty Regency House, dwelt at the top of Lansdowne Circus, a 'horseshoe' of similar houses in the best part of town, built at a time when Leamington was actively earning the appellation of Spa, and attracting those who sought benefit from the spring waters at the Pump Rooms. A small front garden gave onto the encircling interior road, whose other side was occupied by the communal gardens for the Circus, extensively used by resident children. I always remember one Good Friday spent mostly in those gardens, with a picnic lunch and the strict instruction that we should be quiet on such a holy and such a sad day. The house was built on three floors, and must have had around five bedrooms. Mine wore darkly flowered wallpaper and faced to the back of the house, from where the daily horse-drawn milk round could happily be observed.

It was always a joy going to stay there; Caroline and Elizabeth were sufficiently older than me that as the decade went on we three could go out on our own, sampling the delights of town life which I loved from the beginning; I declared early on that I really wanted to go and live in Coventry. The Lights of Leamington were a great attraction – The Jephson Gardens were lit with fairy lights depicting scenes from children's stories for two weeks every year, an occasion not to be missed. Sometimes the three cats, Powderpuff (a rather ancient fluffy white), Binkie and Cosy (two tabbies from Bourton Far Hill) would accompany us on collars and leads, which were specially elasticated in case they got stuck up a tree. Besides, the cellar at Dunraven was the hiding place for a typewriter, which I used to produce a typescript of jumbled letters even before I could read or write properly. Auntie Evelyn was endlessly tolerant of my eccentricities and enthusiasms, and provided us all with so much affection and understanding that even now I feel blessed.

Aunties Violet and Elsie were lodestars in Mum's life – they were, in fact, cousins at one or two removes. They both lived in Chipping Campden, Elsie at Barrel's Pitch, a wooden bungalow, appropriately black, on the Stratford road leading out of the town; Violet at Flag Close, up a turning opposite the Eight Bells and closer to the centre, where Mum lived when she met my father. Elsie had been married in the distant past, but was childless, devoting herself to good works. She must have been heading for her eighties by the time I remember her, tiny and round, white hair in a bun, and with the most divine puffy cheeks covered in face powder, which I adored kissing. She did not drive, unlike Violet, whose grey, bee-shaped Morris Minor came frequently up our drive, and was more than once pressed into service for travel to Leamington or Radway, and for carrying me about. She was a bold driver, having driven ambulances in Flanders during the First World War, unlike Granny, who I remember surprising herself once on the Fosse Way when the speedometer hit fifty. I was overjoyed at this uncustomary daring:

"Granny, you're doing fifty!" I cried.

"Oh, I never realised the car could go so fast," she artlessly replied.

How unnerving it must have been for Grandpa when he travelled with her to come and see us, for some reason stuffed into the impossibly small back seat of her grey Austin as she shot off up the drive towards home amid a spray of gravel and spinning wheels. But at least they did not linger once they had bade farewell. Auntie Evelyn would sometimes carry on a further quite long conversation after saying goodbye, standing in our often windy open front doorway until we wondered whether we shouldn't ask her in again.

"Why are you making that hissing sound, Auntie Violet?" I quizzed one day, as we drove slowly up the bank from Smallthorns Cottage, just short of the farm drive. She was leaning forward at the same time, in an attitude of urgency.

"It helps the car, dear; she needs encouragement." Cars were always 'she'.

The greater part of Violet's life had been spent using horse-drawn transport – hissing and leaning forward would have been entirely proper help to give the pony between the shafts of the trap.

She too was childless and never married, but she had a profound understanding of the young, often having my cousin Caroline to stay for a week or more and treating her like the daughter she had never had. Her house, softly gaslit and possessed of a tiny green spinet – a sort of early piano – was a fairyland. She had protruding teeth and a ready laugh, and wore large pieces of jewellery: the eating of soup was a risky business for her as her heavy bracelets, laden with charms, became vehicles for soup to leave its mark on clothing, table and floor. Dad would profess himself quite enthralled by the whole performance and I would often catch his eye, exchanging a wink and a grin. She was the support to my mother which Granny had never been, for reasons of absence, and later on, ill health and depression culminating in her early death. Violet had style, her clothes were colourful and her grey hair was always caught by many tortoiseshell combs to lie high on her head – she had many friends and a devoted family.

One of the Christmas highlights was the journey to Spring Hill with a present for Basford, and then on to Campden with my mother each Christmas Eve, bearing a basket of gifts for Violet and Elsie, and for Betty (Tunbridge) and Marjorie

(Haynes) also – two more older cousins who were sisters. Visits to Betty's home, Clifton House in the High Street, were a joy to me, not only for the excellent tea which was always provided but because of the cuckoo clock in the hall with its entrancing mechanism and realistic bird-sound. In the end, I persuaded my parents that we should have one at home.

Chipping Campden was, and still is, not only a beautiful town (fortunate that the main road avoids it) but a magnet for interesting people who come to live there. One of these was Gladys Owen, a sculptress of no mean talent, who was commissioned to do a life-size portrait bust of me when I was about four. Despite her ability, the result was not happy – my gilded face looked too old, and if I had had my way, the head would have been hidden away from the outset. Children are notoriously difficult to portray, as their features are relatively unfixed, but Dorothy Colles had more success, and her portrait of me enjoyed the honour of appearing on the cover of her book, *Portraying Children*.

I remember sitting for it over a mid-June weekend in 1954, growing more restless by the minute, only kept in check through the good offices of the wireless. Vivian's diary does not mention this, although on the second day 'Marian gave sittings most of the morning, and one after lunch too!' The result pleased her and everyone else though: 'It is a *lovely* painting.'

The decade wore on in a mostly happy way until the end, in 1959, when double blows befell me. The thought of being sent to boarding school was a disturbing one, but I was left in no doubt that this was my destiny, and that "it will do you good to get away from home. You must not get too Mummy-ish."

Oh, the perils of being an only child. The parents were right, but I was ill-equipped for such an adventure; the thought of leaving the horses and the dogs, the farm, and most of all my parents, and of having to make new friends which I found difficult, was terrifying. Besides, I was not in the best of health, being still beset with earache and catarrh whenever I caught a cold. I wept, I complained, I promised to run away back home – none of these ploys had the slightest effect. The day approached implacably, and the journey to Seven Springs House outside Cheltenham one day in September seemed like the journey to the very mouth of hell. My cousin Lizzie came with us, making a subdued little party of four as we lunched in Andoversford on the way.

What an enormous entrance hall, with such echoing walls and clattering wooden floors. The sight that greeted me as I walked through the front door on that first day came close to overwhelming me. The crowds of people, of children like me but not a bit like me, were bewildering. I could not believe that, in one or two minutes, my parents, my father *and* my mother, would leave me in this strange and stranger's land. But leave me they did. I was numb with misery and fear – I was tall for my age, I had bad breath from being unwell and I was teased and bullied mercilessly from the outset. One of my best friends at Pilgrim Cottage, who like me was in her first year at the new school, excluded me from her company, telling me that I must not mind that I was not invited to her tenth birthday party but unfortunately there was no room for me.

Salvation came in the form of worsening sinuses and blocked ears three weeks into that first term. I was obviously in need of medical attention and was taken in to the Children's Hospital then existing in Cheltenham, having first spent a week or so at home, giving me plenty of time to pack *masses* of books for my unspecified stay. My darling father came every single day for two weeks to read to me and to bring me a constant further supply of books, my mother too.

One of the nurses took to hitting me whenever I cried – the syringing of sinuses was extremely painful, especially at the

The Deaf Doctor

outset. For once, I did not conceal what was happening to me – tear-stained letters from school never particularised my misery, merely pleading that I should be allowed to come home. But this maltreatment was different – it came from a grown-up, and one who was charged with looking after me when I was ill. I felt disgust and fury at her and with no shame on my part, I told my father when he came to see me.

"You mean she actually hits you? You really mean that?" his face white with fury.

I nodded vigorously: "She swears at me too. She calls me 'a bloody little girl'."

Without a word, he got up from his chair and left me with my mother.

"Don't worry, darling. He's a doctor. He'll know what to do," she comforted me.

He knew all right: Matron was told and I never saw the nurse again. What happened to her I know not. Children who complain of abuse should *always* be believed; they almost never make things up.

January 1960 saw me turn ten years old. The birthday was celebrated with a poor day's hunting from a meet at Temple Guiting House, where Mrs Hornby lived, 'owing to Liz [cousin] losing her stirrups,' while Ted went 'into Evesham – bought cakes and M's *Encyclopaedia for Horsemen*!' Even now, a treasured reference work. Nine days later I was back at school for my second term, with a final clean bill of health, but 'poor M very nervous', only a little ameliorated by a visit to the cinema in Cheltenham beforehand, to see Hitchcock's *North by North-West* – I never did like Cary Grant much.

The first year of boarding continued unhappily. Teased not only by my contemporaries who nicknamed me 'Lofty' – "can you hear me from up there?" – but also frightened of some of the staff, and most of all of [Miss] Hood, the witchlike matron who shut us into cupboards all night for talking after lights out. I took refuge in my work and in being allowed to take riding lessons from Tom Pitman, a retired huntsman who looked after the seven or eight ponies at the school. Badger, a small grey roan with a docked tail was too small for me to ride, as was Rocket, similarly docked – this practice had been made illegal by the Docking and Nicking Act 1949, docking being used mostly for harness horses by then so that tails were not tangled in the traces, but leaving horses unable to swish the flies from each other when out at summer grass. The larger chestnut ponies, Belinda and Bagatelle, were my usual partners, and Biscuit too, a delightful bay with the tell-tale Exmoor 'mealy' muzzle, possessed even by some full-size horses such as Mary Gordon-Watson's champion three-day-eventer Cornishman. Tom's wooden tack-room was a horsey heaven for those of us who rode, its floor stacked high with old copies of *Horse and Hound* going back to the First World War, published as simple monochrome newsprint then of course.

By my second year things began to improve as I learned the unfortunate truth that it can pay to 'turn poacher' – in other words, to become a bit of a bully oneself. It was a hard world then and you sank or swam, the survival instinct kicking in. I was fortified with regular letters from home and accompanying supplies of illegal tuck which I hid in the woods and which were useful for trading purposes; and the weekly dispatch of *Tiger*, a comic for boys featuring Pride of the 27th (a soldier in the Afghan Wars), Jet-Ace Logan and Rock-Ace Rogan enjoying adventures in space including a visit to the sun, I having early spurned the delights of *Robin* and similar girls' comics. The school declared *Tiger* to be unsuitable reading but its dispatch continued.

I made my first true new friend at prep school only in my second year, the closest that I ever had to a sister – Louise

Walker – whose first cousin, Michael Daunt, I later married, the father of my son.

Years later my mother told me: "Daddy wept as he left you that first day at school," and that on that first night they had gone to bed "feeling very sad and depressed."

12

OF MYRIAPODA AND MEDICINE

'To see a world in a grain of sand
And a heaven in a wild flower'
– William Blake (1757–1827)

Ted's ruling passion was always natural history, more than medicine (the practice of which he found interesting and intellectually satisfying) or farming (which was a desirable physical challenge at times, and which united him with the landscape, though he might not have expressed it so) or horses (about which he knew a great deal, but which he regarded more as utilities than treasured pets) – "Why the hell can't I ride the horse? Just because he's competing somewhere doesn't mean he's made of porcelain." He found Vivian's disdain for his (often superior) equestrian knowledge very annoying.

Childhood laboratories at home (common then, when chemicals were easily purchased at the local chemist's) and keen collection of specimens of flowers and insects when out walking were the early preparation for his writing what would become his major work, *Centipedes of the British Isles* published

The Deaf Doctor

by Frederick Warne (Beatrix Potter's publishers) in 1964. This remains the standard work on the subject, and perhaps a hundred copies a year, now published on disc, are still sold throughout the world, mostly to universities and institutions.

Myriapoda is the general term for centipedes (carnivorous) and millipedes (herbivorous), members of the division of the animal kingdom called *Arthropoda*, or segmented animals, such as crabs and lobsters, whose encased outer bodies form the skeleton from which the muscles within proceed, and as their particular name suggests, possessed of many legs. Centipedes are further defined as *Chilopoda* and those in warmer climes are quite capable of giving an unpleasant bite, though they are not venomous. The African *Shongololo,* to give him his Zulu name, is an especially spectacular variety – some eighteen inches long, he bears a black articulated shell so that when threatened he can curl into a tight spiral, posing inertly.

Diaries for the early years at Bourton Far Hill constantly refer to 'Ted *Myriapod*-ing… Ted to Oxford all day' (sometimes in the Jeep) where he would read in the Bodleian, or 'Ted to London for two days' where he would research in the Natural History Museum at South Kensington, part of the British Museum. Although an amateur, as opposed to an academic in full-time study, he was widely respected and admitted to any academic institution as required, having already published a number of papers on the subject.

The assiduity of his studies, which culminated in some years of preparation for his book, would bring forth resentful cries from Vivian: "Why can't you spend more time on the farm? The whole place is going to pot. Look at the state of it!"

She was at the sharp end of any neglect as gates began to need re-hanging, wire spooled onto the ground as sheep freed it from its moorings, and machinery began to descend into dilapidation, all this bringing with it inevitable emergencies as things went wrong. By the end of the decade, as labour costs began to rise and farming was becoming increasingly monocultural, Ted had decided to 'dog-and-stick' it, doing any necessary day-to-day work himself with contractors brought in, and later share-farmers including Robert Wharton, to carry out any larger operations.

All this left more time for study, both practical and academic, culminating in his election as a Fellow of the Linnaean Society, situated on the lefthand side of the archway leading into Burlington House in Piccadilly and onto a courtyard with the Royal Academy opposite. The rest of the courtyard is occupied by various other academic societies: the antiquaries, the astronomers, that of chemistry, the geological (on the right-hand side of the gateway), all of them born of the Age of Enlightenment in the later eighteenth century when practitioners, such as my father would have been then, were all still amateur and nearly all 'gentlemen of leisure'. In 1980 he also received the annual Stamford Raffles Award for amateur research from the Royal Zoological Society. This was when I sat next to Lord (Solly) Zuckerman, he of organophosphate infamy, at lunch.

The Linnaean Society was founded in 1788, obtaining a royal charter in 1802, and was named after the Swedish botanist, Carl Linnaeus (1707–78), the father of botanical classification and by extension, of the classification of fauna too. Taxonomy, or the classification of physical features in order to distinguish and identify a species, was the absolute basis of my father's researches, and led to the naming of a previously unknown centipede identified by him as *Lithobius Easoniae*. He was also a chief supporter of the Fauna Preservation Society, for which he wrote a number of papers.

My father's work in the field of *Myriapodology* stemmed not just from a natural interest in the insect world but from active encouragement while he was at school at Malvern from Theodore Savory, who taught there for thirty years. Savory was no slouch himself in the authorial line, writing several books on the *Arachnida* (spiders) as well as others, including *The World of Small Animals*. Published in 1955, this book demonstrated its author's long-held ambition to encourage his pupils in the enjoyment of their studies by looking more closely at 'one of the less popular orders or families of small invertebrates', encouragement from which my father profited hugely. He dedicated his book to Savory, who was deeply touched.

> 'I particularly appreciate it because so much of a schoolmaster's work produces results which he never sees or hears of – unlike a doctor!... By now, 11.30pm, I have really read properly the introductory chapters and the final ones... It is good; no doubt about that: it is admirably written, the balance between the scientific and the popular is well held, the illustrations are splendid (I wish I could draw like that!) The book... is sure to add a few chilopodologists (is that what you are?) [actually, he's right] to the fold... I have so intensely admired Sidnie Manton for so many years, though I only met her once, that I almost rejoice sharing a part of a book with her... Well, you have done a fine piece of work, and I end with my heartfelt congratulations and gratitude...
>
> Yours always,
> Theodore Savory.

Charles Darwin was inevitably a great guide and inspiration to Ted. He too did not ignore the small earth-dwelling animals as suitable subjects for books; his last was on *The Formation of Mould Through the Action of Worms*, and in it he described them as 'lowly, organised creatures, yes, creatures, as in creation.' Jean Baptiste Lamarck (1744–1829), the French biologist, educated at the Jesuit College of Amiens (the great scientist Theilhard de Chardin in the twentieth century continued as a Jesuit priest throughout his life), also interested him. Lamarck is described as an 'evolutionist' in my *Chambers Encyclopaedia* (1908), but the ensuing century has seen him much reviled and almost totally rejected for his theories on physical characteristics that could alter and also be acquired in a short time-span, all according to the changing environment. In fact, he expressed the theory of natural selection in his *Philosophie Zoologique*, and was much interested in the work of Buffon, being a member with him of the post-Revolutionary *Jardin des Plantes* (now Paris's zoo in the rue Buffon) which was founded by members of the French Academy and Garde de l'Herbier du Jardin du Roi. He was also interested in the work of Dr Erasmus Darwin, Charles' grandfather, whose poem, 'Loves of the Plants' had been translated into French in 1799.

Darwin expounded his long-gestated theory of natural selection, which supported what is now generally accepted as the fact of evolution, in a presentation to the Linnaean Society on 1 July 1858, having been spurred into action by the contents of a memoir sent to him from the Malay Archipelago by Alfred Russel Wallace (the eminent explorer), and which expressed the essential points of Darwin's own theory, later published as *Origin of Species*. He was encouraged in this by the geologist Sir Charles Lyell and the botanist and naturalist Sir Joseph Hooker (son of Sir William, also a celebrated botanist), at the same time reading a paper of Wallace's.

After nearly two centuries of obscurity Lamarck is again being considered for the work that he did. I feel that my father and I have some tiny affinity with him: his daughter took down his dictation of the final volume of *Histoire des Animaux sans Vertèbres*, as I typed some of the papers which my father wrote after the publication of *Centipedes of the British Isles*.

'But why centipedes?' I can hear the reader ask. They are not widely visible, they are (some might say) not the most attractive of creatures, and as such, they come pretty much below spiders and beetles and suchlike. Exactly for those reasons, my father chose them as his area of study in accordance with Theodore Savory's ideas. He was one of the earliest commentators on their distribution, done on a county-by-county basis, work hitherto on this being incomplete. They are numerous, one of the commonest animals on the planet, with more than one hundred to a square metre of such varied ground as woodland, grassland and arable, and are easily discoverable, residing under stones and in rotten wood. There are plenty to choose from – forty-four distinct species divided into four orders.

How many legs has a centipede? This is by far the commonest question. The most frequently encountered are the *Lithobiomorpha* which have fifteen pairs of legs and are brown and active – there are seventeen species divided into two families, the other (the *Lithobiidae*) being divided into two subfamilies – while the *Scolopendromorpha*, which occur also in the tropics, have twenty-one, and besides being blind are small and active and of a pale brown colour, consisting of only one genus known as *Cryptops*. The long and slender *Geophilomorpha*, also known as 'legged worms', always have more than thirty-five pairs and may have as many as a 101; the females are often larger than the males with more legs, and they range in colour from reddish brown to pale yellow, aspiring to phosphorescence in the autumn or when disturbed or stimulated; they have a worldwide distribution and are well represented in the British Isles. The *Scutigeromorpha*, which on Ted's own admission has only the slenderest of claims to be included in the British fauna, being distributed chiefly in the tropics, has one species which is established in the Channel Islands and is occasionally found in Britain. They have fifteen pairs of legs like the *Lithobiomorpha*, but are in all other respects different, as quoted in Ted's book:

'... Being of stout form [with] prominent eyes and dorsal stigmata [markings along the back] suit[ing] them for a quite different mode of life from other centipedes... they are not confined to dark, damp crevices, but seek open situations where their enormously elongate legs and antennae, together with other highly developed sense organs and a more efficient respiratory system, make them extremely quick and agile both in capturing prey and escaping enemies.'

Although I showed little aptitude for the sciences, I would gaze transfixed down the microscope as one of these creatures lay on a slide ready for examination, its magnification revealing a myriad colours and unexpected shapes. There was a distinct visual, almost devotional, satisfaction to this study and my father, though no artist in the accepted sense, did all the anatomical drawings for his book relying on Cambridge's Dr Sidnie Manton only for the few photos. He was never happier than when in his study, at his microscope or with sharp-nibbed pen in hand for writing or drawing, content that my mother was somewhere in the house but that his work should be uninterrupted. She, naturally, did not entirely share this contentment and felt that her own need for companionship went largely unregarded. For any endeavour to be successful some degree of selfishness is necessary. His roll-top desk would await attention, sometimes for weeks, groaning under the weight of unopened mail while he meticulously drew or wrote detailed notes of his studies, as every serious natural scientist must, on a tiny collapsible wooden flap looking out onto the garden.

Many colleagues visited the farm in connection with *Myriapoda*, and many more corresponded with Ted from around the world. Frequent packages would arrive from all four corners of the globe, containing specimens in need of identification. Although he travelled little, inhibited by his deafness, his opinion on such far-flung matters was widely sought. In later years a triennial myriapodological convention was held, either in Europe or America, which he always attended, in the company of his great friend and Manchester University colleague, Gordon Blower, a generous reviewer of his book and the author of the only preceding work associated with the subject, *British Millipedes*, which was published in 1958 as part of *The Synopses of British Fauna*. I too accompanied him once to a Paris convention, playing the part of a rather incompetent interpreter, together with my son William.

Other friends in this circle included John Lewis late of Khartoum University where he taught for many years, Klaus and Hoffmann both from Germany, Ralph Crabill late of the Smithsonian Institution in Washington (who shared all Ted's rather dystopian views on modern culture and mass-politics, and had a face of unremitting and most charming gloom) and Matic, a tiny Rumanian whom his Communist masters allowed to travel and even to stay at Bourton Far Hill because of his eminence in his field. He left an umbrella behind once which was in need of mending, but sadly no English repairer could undertake the task as the pattern was different from that of an English umbrella; my later attempts to get it repaired in Prague met with failure too. Beron was another Eastern European colleague, from Bulgaria – after the fall of Communism he took a post in the new democratic government there.

Retaining an interest in medicine was all of a piece with the studies already described. As Ted said in a letter to the British Medical Journal of 13 April 1963:

> Medicine is essentially a practical art... Harvey lived in an age when medicine, natural history, and many other branches of learning went hand in hand more often than they do nowadays. Linnaeus was a doctor of medicine [initially] and in more modern times Huxley was medically qualified.

And there you have it – a continuation of the ideals of the Renaissance, the nurturing of 'the whole man', one who saw unity in all high human endeavour. These ideals and ideas were fast losing ground even then, as popular demand and mass culture, aided by a rapidly advancing technology – and now, of course, impossibly speedy 'information highways' – started the journey towards a debased and stultifying egalitarian culture, catering for and encouraging the 'lowest common denominator', as Vivian so accurately described it with relish.

Ted must instinctively have felt the onset of this process for he, along with a great many doctors, opposed the founding of the National Health Service. No one, least of all he, thought that medical provision was entirely satisfactory before 1948. Provision was patchy (what's new?) and hospitals themselves were often in a poor state, deprived as they were of revenue after a recently fought and catastrophically expensive war – the Americans profited from the conflict, which effectively ended the Depression which had lasted throughout the 1930s, but Britain experienced a very different outcome: virtually bankrupted by our necessary wartime borrowings from the US, our public finances were dire, not helped by one of the severest winters (in 1947/8) in living memory. We only completed our repayments to the US of this wartime debt at the end of 2007.

Public health, rather good during the war when people had been compelled to eat only the essentials, was already a cause for concern as there were no longer the disciplines and supervisions of service and institutional life which had been the wartime experience for many. There was a general feeling that the populace was 'owed' something for all that it had suffered, hence the election of Attlee's Labour Government in 1945 which promised to nationalise public utilities and to nationalise healthcare too. Nye Bevan's plans for the Health Service were huge, gargantuan really, later replicated in Gordon Brown's continuing focus throughout his time in office on all medical care being 'free at the point of delivery'. The healthcare debate has since only raged the more fiercely, and I can't help thinking that if Ted had been alive today there might have been an element of 'I told you so…'

What a fine idea, but as with so many fine ideas, the devil is in the detail, and the devil was soon quickly revealed in a burgeoning 'rights culture', a determination that Ted saw only too often during his medical practice, to have as many prescriptions as possible, as many treatments as possible, because 'after all, we've paid for it haven't we?' As the perception grew that all medicine was 'free' (at the point of delivery anyway) so it and its practitioners appeared to become less respected and less valued: it is a truism to say that we only value properly those things for which we have, in our turn, given value, some 'consideration'. Ernest Beveridge's strictures against 'idleness' as he worked to found the Welfare State – as he saw it, the highest moral enterprise, to be used for the alleviation of genuine need – fairly quickly became forgotten as the inevitable happened: a highly idealistic system was quickly abused by the dishonest and the lazy to the prejudice of the greater part of the populace, the wealth-producing class (badly managed though much business was then) being a 'sitting duck' to be milked for revenue by our socialist governors (wilfully ignorant of the lifeblood, and the creative impulse, which commerce contributes to the economy), and most especially (as now) those working hard for low wages but still paying tax, trapped in the then new PAYE (Pay as you Earn) system which all employers were now compelled to administer. My mother sometimes complained as she did the farm wages, "We're nothing but unpaid tax collectors!"

Only now, as billions have been indiscriminately sprayed at an unreformed health service, is any serious worry expressed as to how this 'Moloch' should be contained. And the rapid developments in all fields of medicine make the stated aim of meeting all needs more or less impossible. These, coupled with the needs of an ageing population will, in the end, lead to some kind of reform – perhaps not even a good kind; we are already seeing creeping 'ageism' in the treatment of those aged much over seventy.

These difficulties were no more than 'a cloud no bigger than a man's hand' during my father's doctoring days, but they are all now there for all to see, and some sort of compulsory insurance payment, except from those who are most in need, may well in the end come to replace the golden calf of universal free provision. If coupled with a deficient education system, this will lead us ever further down the path to ruin.

"Pecks and sniffs," my father would say. "They're the best way."

He was referring to the measures used by pharmacists, in those days a fairly complicated ladder of progression which mostly ensured that the correct dosage was given.

"Decimalisation? Stupid idea. You've only got to get the point in the wrong place, and you've probably killed the patient! Or you're wondering why the medicine isn't working!"

Well, our ceaseless quest for making things easier has led to plenty of error on the part of tired and over-pressed staff, though this is in no way a criticism of those at the sharp end, more an observation of the profound unwisdom of so many decisions taken from on high.

Ted's medical work finished in the mid-1950s when he ceased to perform locum duty – for a fortnight at a time – at Gloucester Hospital, though he continued to subscribe to the *British Medical Journal*, and to correspond, for many years after that.

"I wish I believed more than I do," he lamented towards the end of his life. From a youthful thoughtlessness, as with most people, he had gradually inclined towards some consideration of things unseen but I don't think he ever got very far with it. Logical Positivism would have been his philosophical creed for most of his life if he had been asked, a belief only in what can be seen. *The Life of Darwin* and his *Origin of Species* were his bedrock, and any correspondence, or lack of it, that these beliefs might share with religion were mostly ignored. The Lamarckian belief described above, that radically differing physical characteristics could be passed on in a matter of a few generations did not convince him. For my part, I can see no conflict between the theory of evolution and the creation myths. The former is evidence of God's supreme wisdom and dexterity, while the latter serves as a wonderful figurative illustration, and has been proven to be not so far off the mark in the order of its telling in the *Book of Genesis*.

Averroes (1126–98), born in Cordova in Spain during the long flowering of Moorish civilisation, was the great Arab philosopher and expositor of Aristotle; he maintained that it was quite possible to hold two seemingly opposing beliefs simultaneously, and so I think it is with the dilemma of 'God or no God' if we look at the different tellings of the story of the world's creation. The intellectual inflexibility of blind atheism, as demonstrated so vividly by Richard Dawkins, leads us into a dead end, extinguishing the spirit of enquiry. Nothing is certain – God has seen to that – thus ensuring that we are kept on our toes.

A seemingly unlikely commentator, in the form of Frank Brown, encountered earlier in this book, sums it up rather well: having broke his spine in a racing fall, he;

> '...Did some pretty strenuous thinking during my convalescence... it is plain stupid to become an atheist, because no one can prove that there is no God... on the other hand there is a case for the agnostic because it is equally impossible to prove the existence of God [nowadays, some scientists are

beginning to disagree with this]... [the third way] was to study the teaching of Christ, as the Commandments certainly do make sense... the Bible story may seem a bit fantastic, but then the whole of creation is fantastic to our limited comprehension... We see life all around us in the beasts, birds, fishes, trees, etc every day, but no scientist has yet been able to explain the mystery of the spark of life [though they are getting increasingly close]. The sun, moon and stars are always in their right places at the right time, without human beings having to do anything about it, so there must be some force which governs the orderly routine of nature to perfection... We are told that faith can move mountains, but most of us have not enough faith to push a fresh-dug mole-hill over... If religion is necessary to complete the outfit of an individual, it is obviously necessary for a nation, which is simply a collection of individuals... the majority of the rulers of the earth, and quite a few of their subjects, think that they are big enough men to stand on their own feet without the aid of religion... [and even] find it necessary to kill religion because they fear it as a rival... [but] nothing human is inevitable as long as enough people can be found to oppose it.'

Frank was writing as a Catholic, only six or seven years after the end of the Second World War, but little has really changed in the affairs of men – I would only add that true religion is still used as a cloak for unwisdom and misdeeds. It was little use Gordon Brown preaching about 'values' as a 'son of the manse' when his policies so plainly belied his words, not out of any inherent defective character but by way of that old deceiver, good intention.

St Augustine said that we are placed somewhere between the beasts and the angels. We can freely choose which of these companies to join.

APPENDIX I

BURMA 1942 RETREAT

A Doctor's Retreat from Burma
Burma Star Association, From the *Dekho!*
V.J. 50 Magazine of Winter 1995/6

In response to David Gooderson's request for information on the retreat through the Hukawng Valley, E. H. Eason sent this interesting detail of his career and his experiences of the retreat from Burma.

Much of what I have to say is almost certainly irrelevant but to give you some idea of the impact the whole thing made on me, a bit about myself as a soldier. I began as a cavalry subaltern in the Cheshire Yeomanry (Territorial Army) two years before the war, was declared unfit for service overseas when my regiment went to Palestine at the end of 1939, and was posted to the Cavalry Depot at Colchester. This meant a desk-bound job for the duration, which seemed rather pointless, and as I was an advanced medical student I managed to get leave, qualified as a doctor in 1940, transferred to the R.A.M.C. and was declared fit because they were very short of doctors. I went to India and thence to Burma just before Pearl Harbour as a General Duties Officer (G.D.O.) in an Indian Field Ambulance. After a short stint at the front in Lower Burma early in 1942 I was invalided to the base at Maymyo owing to deafness and put in charge of No.2 Burma Field Laboratory as I was good at microscope work — diagnosing malaria, dysentery, V.D., etc. where deafness was less of a handicap. When the enemy swept northwards I took to the field with my unit which was attached to a Casualty Clearing Station (C.C.S.).

When the order came to run for it we were somewhere on the railway north of Mandalay. We trained up to Mogaung and our patients — unfit people, those over 40 and women (nurses, etc.) went on to the rail-head at Myitkyina and were flown back to India. The rest of us walked. Our party was in the charge of a British Indian Medical Service (I.M.S.) major who was an old Burma hand, knew the country and the Chin language, and had been doing thyroid deficiency among the Chins before the war. The rest of the party consisted of two other British officers (I.M.S. and R.A.M.C.), both of whom I had known at Maymyo, myself, about six Indian or Goanese King's Commissioned Officer (K.C.Os.) — all either I.M.S. or A.B.R.O. and all doctors (I seem to remember that one was a dentist) an I.M.D. conductor whom I knew well, a British infantry sergeant with some rudimentary knowledge of life in the jungle, a number of British Other Ranks (B.O.Rs.) — all, I think, R.A.M.C. — and quite a few Indian other Ranks (I.O.Rs). who must have been I.H.C. I cannot remember how this party came to be made up because it didn't include all the personnel of the C.C.S. but did include some I had never met before. The members of my field laboratory consisted of me, a jemadar I.M.D., two B.O.Rs. and a sweeper (I.H.C.). I had given my jemadar leave to buzz off and join his family, who had been living with him in Burma, about a week earlier, and one of my B.O.Rs. was Anglo-Burmese and, quite understandably, had deserted, taken off his uniform and mingled with the crowd, as he had no wish to leave his home in Burma and without his uniform would have been seen by the Japanese as an ordinary Burmese civilian. My other B.O.R. was Anglo-Indian and was with our party, but I can't remember what happened to my sweeper — he was probably with our party.

Before starting our walk from Mogaung we destroyed anything that might have been useful to the enemy. I threw my microscope etc. into a nearby lake but retained the 'oil-immersion lens', an especially expensive but small article which I gave to one of the B.O.R.'s. The officers who hadn't got standard issue service revolvers equipped themselves with side-arms from a pile left behind from the Indian Civil Service (I.C.S.) and Public Works Department (P.W.D.) people, and I took a .38 Browning pistol.

Our journey was in three distinct legs, and I will describe them separately. I am fairly sure of the distances but can only guess at their duration so am not sure of the miles covered each day. From Mogaung to Klwegyi, about seventy miles, was easy going through country inhabited by the Chins, and for part of the way we were able to hire bullock-carts. It must have taken about five days. We had plenty of rice and bought chickens, eggs, limes, melons, etc. from the villagers, which had to be paid for in silver rupees as they wouldn't accept paper money. The chief problem was water as streams and springs were not very frequent and not everyone had standard issue water-bottles, only odd improvised containers. We had means of chlorinating the water and had to make it last. Normally Indians rinse out their mouths with the first swig and then spit it out but this habit was strictly forbidden, and when one did it out of habit he was tied to a tree and whipped, not very hard, but to make him look a fool in front of the others, and it didn't happen again.

No attempt was made to march in any formation but two B.O.R.'s acted as rear guards to make sure there were no stragglers, and two as advance guards in case we ran into the enemy and to police any river upstream to stop the Indians defecating in the river — normally a very worthy habit as they washed their bottoms at the same time, but not when we were filling our water-containers downstream. I had a brief bath in a slow flowing river (or [sic] canal) and came out festooned with leeches. The chaps gathered round them by touching their tails with lighted cigarettes which made them let go — we still had cigarettes at this early stage. Klwegyi was on a tributary of the Uyu Chaung and here we managed to get sampans for the next leg of the journey. Downstream to the confluence with the Uyu about two miles north of Schedwin and thence down to where the Uyu joins the Chindwin at Homalin was about eighty miles, but easy going apart from a bit of rowing at which we took turns. This must have taken two or three days, and somewhere along the line we must have split up because I cannot remember any I.O.R. or all the Indian K.C.Os. in the sampans. They have taken a different route as there were several alternatives. One of our aeroplanes dropped a package (presumably food) but it fell some way from the river bank and we left it as we had plenty of rice. A few miles short of Homalin we heard shooting. This might have been the enemy who were advancing northwards, so we parked on the river bank and the major and one other went on by themselves to investigate, telling me (the senior officer left) that if they were not back in an hour I was to lead the party back to India as best I could. I realised that this would have been virtually impossible with no map, only a compass, through dense and trackless jungle and not knowing when I was likely to hit on a track or meet the enemy. It was pretty unnerving to say the least as I would, almost inevitably, have been responsible for the deaths of all my men as well as myself. However, I assumed a nonchalant air and to my immense relief the major returned inside an hour. The shooting was the Bombay and Burma Trading Co. shooting their elephants so that they wouldn't fall into enemy hands. So we all re-embarked, went on to Homalin and started the eighty-odd-mile trip to Imphal in Manipur State (India).

This was the worst part because, although the path was easy to follow it went across mountains and very steep ravines. As we had to carry our rice, water and a few essentials, everything not essential and weighing more than a few ounces had to be jettisoned, and I threw away a pair of spurs which I had since my Yeomanry days and which must now be at the bottom of the Chindwin. We did about ten miles a day to keep pace with the slowest, starting before dawn, and each evening the major asked all the men whether they could do the same again and they all could (just). By this time we felt fairly safe from the enemy but there was a temptation among the younger and fitter to hurry on ahead to get back to the safety of India quickly. One of the advance guards did just that and I believe was court-marshalled for desertion. There were quite a few civilians, mostly Indian women, escaping from the Japanese along part of our mute, all in poor condition with children. This was the most harrowing aspect of the whole thing as our job was to get ourselves back and not to get bogged down with civilians. In a moment of weakness I gave one of them a drink from my water-bottle which I ought not to have done. Some were dying of cholera and/or typhoid, which none of the soldiery got because they had been vaccinated. At one point we were overtaken by a party of Burma Military Police, all Sikhs without an officer and each with a horse. There must have been a ferry at some point across the Chindwin as it would have been very difficult to swim the horses across. I swam my horses and mules across the Ye river in the early stages of the campaign, and that was difficult enough despite the fact that the Ye was a mere trickle compared with the Chindwin. These Sikhs had their horses loaded with all their worldly possessions, but we needed the horses for our sick and a few stragglers left behind by earlier parties, who had collapsed. All one could do was to dispossess the Sikhs of their horses, often very forcibly, unhook their possessions and jettison them and replace them with a sick man. I remember one such man, a Kings Own Yorkshire Light Infantryman, who disliked horses so much that he would rather be left to die than to ride: I overruled him, he did ride and he survived!

A colourful incident occurred when we camped by a Naga village. The Nagas were much less civilised than the Chins, and their practice was to shoot one of their pigs when wanted for the pot. We bought a pig and one of our B.O.R.'s who was armed with a rifle, shot it, much to the amazement of the Nagas. The weapon they used for this job was a rather defective rifle which, when fired, sent half the charge backwards and half forwards, so that the marksman had to move his head smartly to one side before pulling the trigger. They couldn't believe their eyes when our chap didn't get his head blown off. Although thirst was worse than hunger on the first leg of our walk, they were both equally bad on the last leg. Although all available food was generally shared out equally, there tended to be a suspicion that some greedy people got more than their fair share. Apart from the pig we existed on rice, which became so nauseating that we hardly ate anything. Severe hunger alters one's personality and I can understand how stranded explorers come to kill each other.

The sergeant had somehow acquired a few dried plums the size of very small grapes. Although he did pass a few around he ate most of them himself (and I don't blame him). I was so hungry that if it had not been for our ingrained discipline I might have attacked him and eaten the lot. I am grateful for this experience which not many people have had, as it gives an insight into my nature.

When we got to Imphal, where there was a military establishment, we were given a hero's welcome despite the fact that all we had really done was to run away. We gorged on biscuits and bully and made ourselves quite ill, as by that time most of us had malaria. It took many days and numerous large doses of Epsom salt to get our guts working again. End of story!

The success of our escape was largely due to the major (Raymond) who was a good leader and organiser. On the whole we were a happy crowd with a minimum of jealousy and disagreement, but we were lucky to get across the Chindwin in time to escape the enemy and lucky that the monsoon was just over, which made travelling easier.

I hope you have time to read all this. I have enjoyed writing it as it is the first time I have set my mind to remembering it all and putting it down on paper!

GLOSSARY TO BURMA 1942 RETREAT

A.B.R.O	Army Base Repair Organisation
B.O.Rs.	British Other Ranks (ie Not Commissioned)
C.C.S.	Casualty Clearing Station
Chins	One of the warlike ethnic groups of Myanmar District, Burma
G.D.O.	General Duties Officer; more correctly a
G.D.M.O.	a non-specialist
G.D.M.O.	General Duties Medical Officer
I.H.C.	Indian Hospital Corps (sweepers in this context)
I.M.D.	Indian Medical Department
I.M.S.	Indian Medical Service, a medical organisation with some civilian responsibilities
I.C.S.	Indian Civil Service
I.O.Rs.	Indian Other Ranks
Jemadar	Infantry Junior Viceroy Commissioned Officer (in the Cavalry, a Rissaldar), but often already a senior soldier by virtue of long service
K.C.O.	King's Commissioned Officer (as distinct from Viceroy Commissioned Officer)
Nagas	Independent warlike tribesmen who inhabited the N.E. Indian/Burmese border, and who disliked the Japanese intensely
P.W.D.	Public Works Department
R.A.M.C.	Royal Army Medical Corps
T.A.	Territorial Army

APPENDIX II

THE AUTHOR'S LETTER TO THE DAILY TELEGRAPH

Published August 2023
Thefts from the British Museum

Sir,

Discussion of resignations at the British Museum (26 August) as a result of the discovery of thefts of uncatalogued artefacts puts me in mind of my late father's research visits to the Natural History Museum (part of the British Museum) fifty or more years ago. He was an amateur Myriapodologist (centipedes and millipedes) but with an international reputation, leading to his being awarded the Stamford Raffles Amateur Research Prize by the Royal Zoological Society in 1980. His free run, behind the scenes as it were, resulted in a number of guided tours allowing sight of material brought back by Darwin's Beagle expedition.

Most of the material was uncatalogued as the Museum has quite simply always lacked the staff and the time to devote to such a quantity of material. Perhaps things are now improving, but it is easy to imagine how such a situation can develop in any department where the quantity of items simply becomes too much to deal with, and then more comes in...

Security of the collections is one thing, lack of itemisation is quite another. The BBC has a tendency to make it sound as if the Museum itself has committed the thefts rather than individuals, which is far from a true picture.

When my father died a decision had to be made as to where his notebooks and specimens should be housed for posterity. A Swedish colleague and friend of ours, working at the Oxford University Natural History Museum at the time, advised against bequeathing the material to London for the above reasons. The Oxford Museum took two years to complete a very fine job of conserving the notebooks and placing the specimens in fresh solution so that they would not dry out.

I very much doubt that the current row affects the ability of the British Museum to care for the vast majority of its collection.

Marian Waters
Pebworth
Warwickshire

INDEX

Aizlewood 106, 199, 239
Arkells (Donnington Brewery) 120
Arnolds of Broadway (wine merchants) 242
Attlee, Clement 52, 63
Augustine, Saint 285
Averroes (philosopher 284
Badminton Horse Trials 98-99, 218-219
Barnby Bendalls (removers) 92
Bennett 44
Berkeley Hunt 184-185
Bilton Grange, Rugby 3
Blower, Gordon 280
Boone, Michael 6, 239
Bourne xiv, 123, 178, 237
Bourton Hill 88, 120, 122, 231
Bowles, 'Binks' 81, 100, 103, 106, 110, 111
Brown, Antony 257
Brown, Frank Atherton 84, 230-231, 294-285
Canney, Ronald 23, 56, 67
Carey, Armorel 262
Carey, Lucius, 2nd Viscount Falkland 262
Cavendish House (Cheltenham) 91, 244
Claytons of Moreton-in-Marsh (agricultural engineers) 115

Clifford xi, xii, 196-197, 247, 252
Colegrave, Manby 226-231
Coles 194-195
Colles, Dorothy (artist) 268
COPE 68
Coventry, Earls of 158, 184-185, 188
Crotty, Joan 66
Curfew Garage (Moreton-in-Marsh) 241
Dale, Robin 216, 248
Daniel Neale of Cheltenham (outfitters) 243
Darby, Cyril 61, 166
Daresbury, Lord (4th Baron) 27
DARWIN 276-277
Daunt Snr, Michael 73, 241
Davies 9, 29-57, 70, 116, 117, 256, 263
de Havilland Miss 200
Douglas-Home 177, 161
*Dulverton 182-184, 248
Dummer Beagles 181
Eason xix-xxvi, 13, 15-20, 35, 44-57, 64, 70-71, 82, 87, 97, 99, 104, 110-111, 113, 115, 122, 232-236, 259-263, 273-284, 286-292
Ecroyd 45, 56, 101, 256-257
Elliott 247-248

Evetts 252
F.A.N.Y. (Field Ambulance Nursing Yeomanry) 49, 64, 88, 171
Fanshawe 182-184, 250-251
Fisher 87, 195
Fitzhardinge, Lord 184
Franklin and Cook of Broadway (grocers) 241-242
Gandhi, Mahatma 51
Gilmore 163-164, 227-228
Goebbels, Josef 29
Goering, Hermann 29
Grand National 97, 217
Green, Malcolm xiii
Greenall (Lord Daresbury) 22
Greenwood, John MFH 195
GREGG (of Styal, Cheshire) xxiii
Grimes, F.J. of Moreton-in-Marsh (builders) 241
Haines, Arthur Lett (artist) 130
Hannay 101, 107, 155-178, 197-198, 227, 249
Harrison 199
Harts of Chipping Campden (silversmiths) 105
Hashim xix, xxiii, 45, 263
Hay xxiv, 12-16, 56, 67, 123
Hay of Broadway (electricians) 93
Haynes 60-64, 90, 98, 99, 104, 108, 112, 122, 215, 222, 225, 240, 263-266, 267-268
Heightington, Worcestershire 70

Hills of Moreton-in-Marsh (jewellers and watchmakers) 240
Hinchwick (Pilkington and Asquith) 100, 120, 227, 228
Hitler, Adolf 31, 61
Holder 89, 100, 245
Holland-Martin, Tim xiv, 198
Holt, Katie (Ted's aunt) 38, 122,
Hooker, Sir Joseph 277
Hooker, Sir William 277
Horsfall, Maeve 137-138,
Houghton, Dr Colin (Broadway) 95, 100, 115, 120
Huxley, Julian 280
Hyatt, George 252-253
Ismay, 'Pug' (1st Baron) 252
Johnsey's Coal (Moreton-in-Marsh) 91
Juckes, Dr Mick (Broadway) 95
Kate's Kitchen, Cheltenham 243
Kennard 239-240
Kildanes 82-83, 87-88, 89, 94, 107, 108, 110, 111
King, Doctor MFH 26
Kleinwort 88, 103, 107, 110, 115
Kursiji, Colonel Sir Ransiji 46
Lamarck, Jean-Baptiste 277
Lancashire Witches xx
Leadley-Brown, Roger 65, 196
Lewis, Wyndham (artist) 101
Linnaean Society 275
Listers of Evesham (agricultural engineers) 97, 105, 109
Lowe, 'Bing' 221
Lyell, Sir Charles (geologist) 277

McCanlis, Patrick 252
Malvern College 6-7
Mann, Jock 201
Manton, Dr Sidnie 276, 279
Marland 65-66, 73, 76, 90, 100, 112, 114, 123
Milvain, 'Bickie' 250
Minckwitz 61
Morris (Cedric, artist) 91, 130-131
Mosley 21
Mountbatten, Lord Louis 52
Mr Spooner's Harriers 26
Nabarro xi-xiv, 247
Napier, Major Charles 216, 249, 250
National Health Service 281-283
Oates, Ted (nephew and heir of Titus Oates who died on Scott's Last Expedition) xxiii
Oldrey, John 225-226
Owen, Gladys (sculptor) 268
Pearson, Johnnie 250
Peel 188-189
Piccadilly Hunt Club 54-55
Pilgrim Cottage, Bourton-on-the-Hill (Marian's primary school) 122, 244-247
Pilkington 100
Polish Camp (at Spring Hill) 174-175
Pony Club 249-253
Pringle 24, 67, 101
Ramsay Patrick 235-236
Redesdale, Lord 192
Redfern, John 202

Renfrew, Archie (Broadway vet) 112
Ritchie and Eason xix
Robinson (Ted's housemaster at Malvern) 7
Rushout, Algernon MFH 185
Rycroft, Sir Newton (7th Bart) 182
Ryder, Dudley (later the 7th Earl of Harrowby) 67-68, 100, 122
Savory, Theodore (Ted's biology master at Malvern) 275-276
Sayce, Peter 23
Saxton 248-249
Scott, Montagu Douglas 231-232
Selly Oak Hospital 70-72
Seven Springs House (Marian's prep school) 268-272
Sezincote 88
Sezincote Warren 120, 229-230
Shakerley 72, 231, 248
Shekell, Tom 184-185
Sherston, Brigadier Reggie 120, 122, 229-230
Slades of Cheltenham (bootmakers) 244
Slatter 90, 109
Smalley, Chris 18-19, 29-30, 35, 37, 42, 44, 49, 50
Smith, Hector 104,
Snowshill Hill 117, 123, 178
Somerset, David (later the 11th Duke of Beaufort) 218-219
Spring Hill 84, 96, 118, 120, 155-178

Starkey 201
Steele, George 122, 231
Steels of Cheltenham (garage) 118, 244
Stone, Paul (Broadway vet) 119-120
Strongs the Tailors (Moreton-in-Marsh) 117, 228
Studd, Colin xi
Summers 82, 89, 104, 106, 245, 248
Swinton, General Sir Ernest 64
Tabor, Nigel 252
Tayler and Fletcher (auctioneers and land agents) 82, 105, 106
Tetcott Foxhounds 26
Thalmann 69
Thin, Peter 89
Tollit 199, 252
Tulloch, Rosemary ('Bunty') 21
Turk, George of Cheltenham (saddler) 243-244
Wadsworth, Edward (artist) 101
Walker, Louise 271
Wallace, Alfred Russel (explorer and scientist) 277
War Agricultural Board ('War Ag') xvi
Warren, Beryl 250
Warrens of Broadway (ironmongers) 242
Welton 109, 120, 201, 222
West Midland Farmers (seed and feed merchants) 127
Wharton xi, 227, 247, 248
Whitfeild 214-215
Willcox, Sheila 218-220, 253
Williams, Dorian MFH 182, 219
*Wills (Dulverton) 182-184, 201, 248
Zuckerman, Lord (Solly) 147-148, 275

ABOUT THE AUTHOR

Marian Eason grew up on her family's Gloucestershire farm from the age of one and now lives on another family farm in Warwickshire. Called to the Bar in 1971, as an equestrian journalist she has researched numerous works including The Master of the Horse, racing books by Ivor Herbert and George Rainbird's An Illustrated Guide to Wine.

Her commissioned The Best Little Hunt in England was published in 2019. She has ridden horses competitively and followed hounds all her life.

Photo by Will Daunt